WILLIAM WORDSWORTH

Published titles

Morris Beja
JAMES JOYCE

John Mepham
VIRGINIA WOOLF

Cedric C. Brown
JOHN MILTON

Michael O'Neill
PERCY BYSSHE SHELLEY

Peter Davison
GEORGE ORWELL

Leonée Ormond
ALFRED TENNYSON

Richard Dutton
WILLIAM SHAKESPEARE

George Parfitt
JOHN DONNE

Jan Fergus
JANE AUSTEN

Gerald Roberts
GERARD MANLEY HOPKINS

James Gibson
THOMAS HARDY

Felicity Rosslyn
ALEXANDER POPE

Kenneth Graham
HENRY JAMES

Tony Sharpe
T. S. ELIOT

Paul Hammond
JOHN DRYDEN

Grahame Smith
CHARLES DICKENS

W. David Kay
BEN JONSON

Gary Waller
EDMUND SPENSER

Mary Lago
E. M. FORSTER

Cedric Watts
JOSEPH CONRAD

Alasdair D. F. Macrae
W. B. YEATS

John Williams
WILLIAM WORDSWORTH

Joseph McMinn
JONATHAN SWIFT

Tom Winnifrith and Edward Chitham
CHARLOTTE AND EMILY BRONTË

Kerry McSweeney
GEORGE ELIOT
(MARIAN EVANS)

John Worthen
D. H. LAWRENCE

William Wordsworth

A Literary Life

John Williams
Reader in Literary Studies
University of Greenwich

First published 1996 by
MACMILLAN PRESS LTD
Houndmills, Basingstoke, Hampshire RG21 6XS
and London
Companies and representatives
throughout the world

ISBN 0–333–57417–6 hardcover
ISBN 0–333–57418–4 paperback

A catalogue record for this book is available
from the British Library.

10   9   8   7   6   5   4   3   2   1
05   04   03   02   01   00   99   98   97   96

Printed and bound in Great Britain by
Antony Rowe Ltd
Chippenham, Wiltshire

Published in the United States of America 1996 by
ST. MARTIN'S PRESS, INC.,
Scholarly and Reference Division
175 Fifth Avenue, New York, N.Y. 10010

ISBN 0–312–15864–5

For
Anne, Mark and Rebecca

Contents

Note on Texts and Abbreviations

References contained in the text use the following format: abbreviated form; volume number where appropriate; sonnet number where appropriate; for *The Prelude* and *The Excursion* Book number where appropriate; page number; line number(s) where appropriate. Where the text already supplies information it will not normally be duplicated in the reference. Unless otherwise stated in the text or the reference given, the 1805 text of *The Prelude* is used.

ABBREVIATED FORMS

Borderers: *The Borderers*, William Wordsworth, ed. Robert Osborn (Ithaca and London, 1982).

DS: *Descriptive Sketches*, William Wordsworth, ed. Eric Birdsall (Ithaca and London, 1984).

EW: *An Evening Walk*, William Wordsworth, ed. James Averill (Ithaca and London, 1984).

EY: *The Letters of William and Dorothy Wordsworth, The Early Years 1787–1805*, ed. Ernest De Selincourt, second edition rev. Chester L. Shaver (Oxford, 1967).

HG: *Home at Grasmere*, William Wordsworth, ed. Beth Darlington (Ithaca and Hassocks, 1977).

LB: *Lyrical Ballads and Other Poems 1797–1800*, William Wordsworth, ed. James Butler and Karen Green (Ithaca and London, 1992).

LY II: *The Letters of William and Dorothy Wordsworth, The Later Years, Part II, 1829–1834*, ed. Alan G. Hill (Oxford, 1979).

MY I: *The Letters of William and Dorothy Wordsworth, The Middle Years, Part I, 1806–1811*, ed. Ernest De Selincourt, rev. Mary Moorman (Oxford, 1969).

MY II: *The Letters of William and Dorothy Wordsworth, The Later Years, Part II, 1812–1820*, ed. Ernest De Selincourt, rev. Mary Moorman and Alan G. Hill (Oxford, 1970).

PB: *Peter Bell*, William Wordsworth, ed. John E. Jordan (Ithaca and London, 1985).

Prelude: *The Prelude 1799, 1805, 1850*, ed. Jonathan Wordsworth, M. H. Abrams, and Stephen Gill (New York and London, 1979).

Prose: *The Prose Works of William Wordsworth*, 3 vols, ed. W. J. B. Owen and Jane Worthington Smyser (Oxford, 1974).

PW: *The Poetical Works of William Wordsworth*, 5 vols, ed. Ernest De Selincourt (Oxford, 1952).

RC: *The Ruined Cottage and The Pedlar*, William Wordsworth, ed. James Butler (Ithaca and Hassocks, 1979).

SP: *The Salisbury Plain Poems*, William Wordsworth, ed. Stephen Gill (Ithaca and Hassocks, 1975).

TP: *The Tuft of Primroses with Other Late Poems for The Recluse*, William Wordsworth, ed. Joseph H. Kishel (Ithaca and London, 1986).

W: *Benjamin the Waggoner*, William Wordsworth, ed. Paul F. Betz (Ithaca and Brighton, 1981).

WD: *The White Doe of Rylstone*, William Wordsworth, ed. Kristine Dugas (Ithaca and London, 1988).

1807: *Poems in Two Volumes and Other Poems 1800–1807*, William Wordsworth, ed. Jared Curtis (Ithaca, 1992).

1
Writing the Literary Life

Since his death in 1850, Wordsworth's life has been written many times. Modern scholarship has revealed the considerable extent to which Wordsworth rewrote and edited his own autobiography in *The Prelude* between 1799 and 1850, and what biographers have made of the raw material since has varied a good deal. The account this book offers portrays a man who seems to have spent at least the first forty or so years of his life working against the grain. He worked against the wishes and aspirations of those who, with both his parents dead, took on the task of supporting him through school and university. As a young man he identified with the political beliefs of those who were prepared to challenge and work against the political establishment of the day. As a poet he identified early on with contemporary trends, and began to write in ways specifically designed to challenge orthodox literary conventions, producing in consequence poetry guaranteed to make a reading public for his work hard to establish and retain.

A life of this kind set him under a constant obligation to justify – to himself as well as to others – why he was refusing to conform. Why should he alone persist in being awkward (in wishing to become a modern poet) when his brothers were doing their best to achieve what was expected of them? The result of this situation was to ensure that all Wordsworth's poetry – whatever else it was intended for – was caught up with a process of inscribing and reaffirming the course of the life he intended to lead. This is why time and again those who met him and those who read him were struck by the degree of self-absorption they encountered. Shelley was right:

> He had a mind which was somehow
>   At once circumference and centre
> Of all he might or feel or know;
> Nothing went ever out, although
>   Something did ever enter.[1]

1

Hardly a line he wrote (intentionally autobiographical or not) fails to contribute in some way to the structuring of a literary life he must first create and then defend against assault from those around him who would have it otherwise.

UNRESOLVED TENSIONS: 'THE PUBLIC WAY ... THAT SILENT ROAD'

> I love to walk
> Along the public way, when for the night
> Deserted, in its silence it assumes
> A character of deeper quietness
> Than pathless solitudes. At such a time
> I slowly mounted up a steep ascent
> Where the road's watry surface, to the ridge
> Of that sharp rising, glittered in the moon,
> And seemed before my eyes another stream
> Stealing with silent lapse to join the brook
> That murmered in the valley.
>
> (LB 277, 1–11)

These are the opening lines of 'The Discharged Soldier', an autobiographical fragment Wordsworth composed in 1798 when he was 28 years old. For the biographer these are 28 years of restless physical and mental travelling. They tell the story of a young man engaged in a private drama of self-discovery worked out concurrently with his discovery of the very public world of radical politics in both Britain and France. The story is made all the more intriguing by the fact that the biographer's quarry has the ability frequently to disappear from view. Despite copious documentation, his precise whereabouts are by no means always clear, while his frame of mind often remains obscure.

'The Discharged Soldier' (eventually revised for inclusion in Book IV of *The Prelude*) contains a number of clues as to why Wordsworth's life frequently becomes all but impenetrable at the points where the chronicler of events would most like to know what his or her subject was doing, thinking and feeling.

The poem begins with what seems a very positive statement from a man who enjoys being in the public eye. He describes himself as one who loves 'to walk/Along the public way'; but though the idea of the road carries with it the connotation of being before the public, the remaining part of the sentence turns us abruptly on to a very different thoroughfare:

> when for the night
> Deserted, in its silence it assumes
> A character of deeper quietness
> Than pathless solitudes.

As is so often the case elsewhere in his poetry, Wordsworth here counters a felt need to be visibly and actively part of the busy and public world of social and political affairs, with an equally strong instinct to retire into a secretive, hidden state of mind. The tension between the active life of a 'statesman' and a life of retirement is of course a theme regularly rehearsed in much eighteenth-century poetry. What is peculiarly Wordsworthian in 'The Discharged Soldier' are the consequences of the poet's syntactical presentation of the alternatives, and the implications of how profound the experience of the particular kind of solitude he seeks promises to be.

Wordsworth does not represent the two alternatives in two distinct, antithetical sentences; they are superimposed on one another within the grammatical framework of a single sentence. The 'public way' is both 'public' and at the same time 'Deserted in its silence'; and in the process we witness it assuming not just its predictable night-time quietness, but a quietness 'deeper' than that offered by 'pathless solitudes'. Wordsworth seems to wish to claim that retirement achieved while somehow still inhabiting a public domain provides a 'quietness' charged with meaning not available in the traditional trope of Virgilian retirement from the city to the country, from the busy seat of political power to the relative solitude of the rural estate:

> Be full, ye Courts, be great who will;
> Search for peace with all your skill:
> Open wide the lofty Door,
> Seek her on the marble Floor,
> In vain ye search, she is not there;
> In vain ye search the Domes of Care!
> Grass and flowers quiet treads,
> On the Meads, and Mountain-heads,
> Along with Pleasure, close ally'd,

Ever by each other's Side:
And often, by the murmering Rill,
Hears the Thrush, while all is still,
Within the Groves of Grongar Hill.[2]

Unlike John Dyer in 'Grongar Hill' (1726), turning his back on the 'lofty Door' and 'marble Floor' of the Court, Wordsworth avoids admitting any loss of influence in the public domain; indeed, his reflective diversion into the night has at the same time the effect of intensifying his purpose.

In a single sentence Wordsworth performs the disappearing act that has left successive biographers guessing. During the preceding years of hectic political crisis, he had not appeared on the 'public way' of radical political activity with anything like the degree of notoriety that many of those he associated with had: William Godwin, John Thelwall, George Dyer, Daniel Eaton, Joseph Johnson, Thomas Cooper, and in France, Antoine-Joseph Gorsas. In 1798 he was in fact planning to leave the country, having recently (with Coleridge) become the subject of a Government investigation. But here again, he could hardly be said to have had the satisfaction of meriting such attentions in the way one of his neighbours at this time, John Thelwall, undoubtedly had. So we may well be tempted to find in 'The Discharged Soldier' something in the nature of a face-saving fantasy, a claim that its author has achieved an alternative and superior prominence to that offered by the public way in the broad light of day:

Thus did I steal along that silent road,
My body from the stillness drinking in
A restoration like the calm of sleep
But sweeter far.

(11.21–4)

In Wordsworth's view this is manifestly no ordinary sleep; as the quietness is 'deeper' so the sleep is 'sweeter'. Deeper and sweeter than what? He does not say – it is not 'public' knowledge; and yet he has not left (he claims) the 'public way'.

Looking at what we do know of Wordsworth's life from the time when he left Cambridge in 1791 and became fully aware of and to some degree involved in the radical political life of his country, the option has been open to biographers either to see a man who singularly failed to register a presence in public life, one who walked in solitude at night while all about him were in plain view, or one who was indeed conspicuous, who had certainly earned the right to be as much a target of a Government spy as anyone else.

The circumstances surrounding Wordsworth's literary life in the 1790s are somewhat clearer and more easily stated than those involving his public life. Though he had written a great deal, he had published just three volumes of verse, and these had attracted only a very limited readership. In 1793 *An Evening Walk* and *Descriptive Sketches* appeared; in September 1798 *Lyrical Ballads*, a joint venture with Coleridge, was published. The reviews of *Lyrical Ballads* tended to cancel each other out, from the *British Critic*'s 'cordial approbation' and affirmation that 'They all have merit, and many among them a very high rank of merit', to the *Critical Review*'s verdict that 'The "experiment" has failed'.[3] Anything like a wide readership for Wordsworth was out of the question. By 1798 however, he had become firmly committed to the idea that his destiny was to be a poet, and with Coleridge's encouragement, he was investing that idea with grandiose aspirations. These years of his literary life hold no blind spots for the biographer in the way that his political life therefore does. Here he was most unambiguously, if not in the dark, at best only in the dimness of moonlight, and most certainly unremarked by the majority of the reading public.

Significantly, then, in 'The Discharged Soldier' of 1798 the 'public way' he describes appears to him as a double vision. The road of his political life runs into the night, and its very obscurity reveals another road described as an alternative way of life, active though mysterious, 'a stream':

> I slowly mounted up a steep ascent
> Where the road's watry surface, to the ridge
> Of that sharp rising, glittered in the moon,
> And seemed before my eyes another stream
> Stealing with silent lapse to join the brook
> That murmered in the valley.

A stream would certainly be an apt metaphor for his intended life as a poet; with Coleridge he had recently been planning an ambitious poetic project for which the title was 'The Brook'.[4] As yet there is an appropriately secretive air to this stream, 'stealing with silent lapse' to join what is as yet only a murmuring brook further off down the valley.

The poem goes on to relate Wordsworth's encounter with a soldier, discharged after being worn down by 'war, and battle, and the pestilence' (1.137). The man is a casualty of his country's aggressive foreign policy, and inevitably therefore his disturbing appearance, 'his cheeks sunken, and his mouth/Shewed ghastly in the moonlight' (11.50–1), stands as an implied indictment of England's political morality. In an earlier poem begun in 1793, 'Salisbury Plain', Wordsworth used the circumstances of the American War of 1776 to declare his hostility to the leaders of his nation, as they perpetuated a tradition of materialistically inspired aggression by declaring war on the newly formed French Republic:

> The nations, though at home in bonds they drink
> The dregs of wretchedness, for empire strain,
> And crushed by their own fetters helpless sink,
> Move their galled limbs in fear and eye each silent link.
>
> (SP 36, 447–50)

In 1798 there is no such didactic statement. Instead we read of the poet's efforts to ensure that the discharged soldier's immediate needs are attended to, and that some provision is made for his future welfare.

The public, political Wordsworth is muted in favour of the poet who seeks a solution through other means. It is a solution, we should note, not achieved by taking an alternative road, nor indeed by quitting the road he is on in favour of 'pathless solitudes', but by perceiving the same road differently. The political, 'public' context therefore remains; a poet must have a readership after all. But Wordsworth is here turning from the political didacticism of 'Salisbury Plain' to an art 'disposed to sympathy', and seeking:

> the deeper joy
> Which waits on distant prospect, cliff, or sea,
> The dark blue vault, and universe of stars.
>
> (11.18–20)

'The Discharged Soldier' would consequently appear to indicate the direction Wordsworth's life was taking at this point; a journey into the unknown, literally into foreign parts. No longer a young man – if not yet quite approaching middle age – he was on the point of travelling to Germany, driven out of England by financial necessity, forced to quit his temporary home at Alfoxden in Somerset sooner than intended as a result of the Government's suspicion of his activities; further motivated perhaps, as E. P. Thompson has suggested, by 'draft dodging' in the face of the war against Napoleon.[5] He was leaving behind him even the meagre readership he had achieved. In keeping with his poem, it all has the air of events taking place under cover of darkness, and with a typically Wordsworthian atmosphere of guilt and stealth. The literary life reveals itself here as a troubled search, not so much for poetry – the poetry was there in abundance – as for a readership; and it was a search destined to be bedevilled by Wordsworth's moonlit vision that paradoxically endorsed the view that his poetry worked best in secrecy and solitude; that it achieved its end (as he had done with the soldier) under cover of darkness. In this respect the relationship established between Wordsworth and the soldier in the poem is important.

An overtly political act of assistance will generally breed a sense of obligation; it will also imply the condemnation of others who are not willing or able to assist. Wordsworth's 'poetical' act of assistance in 'The Discharged Soldier' wins him only the qualified gratitude of the soldier, who retains his dignity and individuality to the full:

> He said, 'My trust is in the God of heaven,
> And in the eye of him that passes me.'
> (11.162–3)

Even as the soldier accepts the poet's assistance, he disengages himself from a relationship that would bind him too closely to his benefactor. The constituency of poetry is thus radically different from that of a politically oriented public life. It was with this contradictory vision of the vocation of a poet's career that Wordsworth was to struggle for the major part of his literary life, consciously antagonising his readership, while with equal anxiety he sought recognition in order to fulfil that vocation.

PLANNING A MODERN LITERARY LIFE

Wordsworth and his sister Dorothy set sail for Germany in September 1798, together with Coleridge and a young disciple, John Chester. The Wordsworths had no clear plans for the trip beyond doing some translation work that might bring in extra money once they returned to England. While Coleridge travelled first to Ratzeburg and from thence to Göttingen, Dorothy and William ended up in Goslar – more or less by accident – and found it virtually impossible to gain access into the close provincial world of middle-class society they found there. It was in the depressing circumstances of Goslar, made worse by the exceptionally cold winter of 1798–9, that Wordsworth began in earnest to write up his own literary life, what we now have as the 'Two Part' *Prelude* of 1799. This was the first version of what later became Books I and II of a five-book, and eventually by 1805, a thirteen-book poem.

In many respects *The Prelude* epitomises what was happening in English literature (and more generally in art) as the eighteenth-century cultural establishment fragmented, to be replaced by what is generally described as the Romantic Movement. Wordsworth's project, stumbled upon rather than carefully planned, was unique in the genre of poetry. Edmund Spenser had produced a chivalric epic in the sixteenth century, *The Faerie Queene*, in which by offering instruction to 'a gentleman or noble person in vertuous and gentle discipline', he both celebrated the virtues of life in Elizabethan England, and drew attention to areas of potential instability and danger.[6] In the aftermath of the English Civil War, John Milton had produced his religious epic, *Paradise Lost* (1667), which constituted both an account of the original fall of Man, and a reflection on the more recent collapse of a potentially resanctified political order.

From the mid-1790s, Wordsworth, with Coleridge's encouragement, had been planning *The Recluse*, a similar Miltonic epic around the consequences of a failed attempt in France and England to cleanse society from corruption. Though he was eventually to publish *The Excursion* in 1814, a substantial body of work which approximated to the Miltonic model, and though scholars have argued in recent years that *The Excursion*, with 'The Prelude' and *Home at Grasmere* (1800–6), effectively completed the *Recluse* project, the fact is that Wordsworth was diverted from his intention by an unavoidable compulsion to write poetry in an autobiographical, confessional mode. The autobiographical epic was new. Wordsworth considered it sufficiently unusual not to anticipate a readership for it beyond his family and a few close friends. For him it did not even merit a formal title; it could best be described rather than 'named' as a poem tracing the growth of his own mind, the private 'Prelude' to his major public work.

What this indicates, then, is the appearance, by chance rather than design, of a new focus for poetry, a disengagement from previous literary models which when analysed accords with many of the ways in which we are encouraged to identify Romanticism. Confessional poetry was of course not new, but in *The Prelude* we have egocentricity of a new order which, if not secularised, is certainly rendered unfamiliar by a pantheistic syncretism of Nature and God. Wordsworth's preparedness to write *The Prelude* as an essentially private project is indicative of a much broader literary tendency in the late eighteenth century. He was writing in a period when there was no longer a recognisable common reader for literature, and when the relative values of literary forms no longer seemed clearly understood. In this situation a crisis of confidence was developing when it came to proposing what constituted a fit subject for verse.

Prior to the 1790s, a significant factor in this changing situation had been the steady expansion of the reading public among the middle classes, specifically with the addition of women readers. With the appearance of writing in support of radical political ideas, readership had started to diversify in more complicated ways, with poetry, novels and pamphlets (notably Paine's 6d. edition of *Rights of Man Part II* in 1792) tapping a readership below the middle-class market. 'Paine's message', writes Richard Altick, 'made its way through a section of the public whose literacy, until now almost an unused talent, suddenly had been called into play'.[7]

It was a situation foreseen by Goldsmith back in 1770; for him it presaged the death of 'public poetry' as he had come to know it:

And thou, sweet Poetry! thou loveliest maid,
Still first to fly where sensual joys invade:
Unfit, in these degenerate times of shame,
To catch the heart, or strike for honest fame . . .
Thou guide, by which the nobler arts excel,
Thou nurse of every virtue, fare-thee-well![8]

This was a situation where the poet was obliged as never before (or so it seemed) to write his or her own literary life. It is not to be wondered at that in common with many contemporaries, Wordsworth repeatedly addressed the issue of the role of poets in society, and their progressive alienation; it is only natural that he tended to stress the validity of his own thoughts and feelings, claiming them as a 'natural' guide to composition. 'The endeavour of the author', wrote the reviewer of *Lyrical Ballads* in *The British Critic*, 'is to recall our poetry, from the fantastical excess of refinement, to simplicity and nature'; and he went on to agree with Wordsworth that 'the true notion of poetry must be sought among the poets, rather than the critics'.[9]

Though the picture remains an impressionistic one, with facts and figures difficult, if not impossible to verify, Wordsworth was born into the class of society which, since the beginning of the century, had been experiencing what amounted to a revolution in its literary life. In the course of the first half of the century, the appearance in increasing numbers of magazines and reviews reflected a steady increase in the number of publications of all kinds, along with the growth of a middle-class market eager not only to buy (or borrow) and read books, but also articles about books and the literary world. As the century progressed, working-class readers and writers, masculine and feminine, gradually began to emerge, generally as a result of patronage by middle-class intellectuals. Hannah More, for example, was responsible for bringing out Ann Yearsly's *Poems on Several Occasions* in 1785. Yearsly, a dairymaid and milk-seller, subsequently broke away from More's control, eventually setting up and managing her own circulating library.

The story of Wordsworth's career as a poet is intimately bound up with his assessment of this burgeoning readership and its taste in modern literature. Central to the debate these developments prompted was the question of how 'modern' literature should relate to contemporary issues. An eighteenth-century cultural model rooted in the classics had imposed an obligation on poets to display their society as the mirror of a sanitised classical world, designed for customers who were paying to be entertained and reassured, not brought up to date. This procedure had set poetry on a collision course with the realities of rural life in particular, given that city life already had a classically sanctioned reputation for being potentially morally unhealthy.

Few eighteenth-century poems illustrate the problem better than John Dyer's *The Fleece* (1757), a Virgilian celebration of England's wealth and power which focused on the wool trade. As Richard Feingold has pointed out, Dyer's 'vision of human work and human society' was one that 'was increasingly difficult to maintain'. *The Fleece* employs 'a rhetoric surging blindly past some discomfiting facts':

the tender eye
May view the maim'd, the blind, the lame, employ'd
And unreject'd age: ev'n childhood there
Its little fingers turning to the toil
Delighted: nimbly, with habitual speed,
They sever lock from lock . . .

Such 'delight', Dyer assures us, 'Kindles improvement in the op'ning mind'.[10]

The controversial territory into which Dyer leads us here has manifestly political implications, and the critical judgements of reviewers also frequently carried with them a political subtext which could easily break the surface of a debate explicitly pinned to cultural referents. Literary opinions and anxieties were rooted in the increasingly destabilising politics of social change.

By the time we come to see Wordsworth moving from an adolescent enthusiasm for poetry towards a serious commitment to writing, and to seeking out and educating a readership, poets like George Crabbe were already rebelling openly against a continuing attempt to depict rural life through the rose-tinted spectacles of sentimentalised classicism:

Yes, thus the Muses sing of happy swains
Because the Muses never knew their pains:
They boast their peasants' pipes; but peasants now
Resign their pipes and plod behind the plough.

In Book I of *The Village* (1783) Crabbe emphasises the drudgery, foul living conditions and poor health of rural labourers, male and female. The labourer and the poet are separated by a gap that is unambiguously a class divide, a class divide significantly pointed up by the issue of literacy:

By such examples taught, I paint the Cot,
As truth will paint it, and as Bards will not:
Nor you, ye Poor, of letter'd scorn complain,
To you the smoothest song is smooth in vain;
O'ercome by labour, and bow'd down by time,
Feel you the barren flattery of a rhyme?[11]

In 1786, aged 16, Wordsworth was still subscribing to the Virgilian rhetoric of Dyer's *Grongar Hill* and *The Fleece*; in 'Anacreon' the 'cot' still sufficed for a compound image of the labourer's dwelling as both home and infant's cradle:

> Here I see the wandering rill,
> The white flocks sleeping on the hill,
> While fancy paints, beneath the veil,
> The pathway winding through the dale,
> The cot, the seat of Peace and Love,
> Peeping through the tufted grove.
>
> (PW 2, 261–2, 41–6)

This was soon to change, however, and by the early 1790s he was beginning to depict the English countryside in a very different light. 'At the Isle of Wight 1793' describes the picturesque English land-scape threatened by the consequences of war with revolutionary France, 'The star of life appears to set in blood' (PW I, 307–8). Words-worth found himself figuratively and literally driven out of the 'tufted grove' as he journeyed from the Island up on to the barren wastes of Salisbury Plain:

> No shade was there, no meads of pleasant green,
> No brook to wet his lips or soothe his ear.
>
> (SP 22, 46–7)

What he and Coleridge resolved on from the mid-1790s, in contrast to the position taken by earlier poets such as James Beattie, Mark Akenside, Gray and Goldsmith, was a mission to establish a revit-alised poetic presence. This did not mean adapting their style to suit the current taste. Like William Cowper in 1785, the poet was being set a specific task. Cowper had been given a subject for poetry by Lady Austen to encourage him to write through his melancholia. Though Wordsworth and Coleridge set themselves a very different task in the late 1790s from that of Cowper's *The Task*, both *The Task* and *Lyrical Ballads* reveal an important way in which the relationship between poet and reader was shifting in concert with the changing times.

Cowper arguably moves from fulfilling an innocent demand by his aristocratic reader/patron to an attempt to influence her way of thinking:

> the age of virtuous politics is past,
> And we are deep in that of cold pretence.
> Patriots are grown too shrewd to be sincere,
> And we too wise to trust them.[12]

For Wordsworth and Coleridge, the search for a readership assumed from the first that creativity lay not only in producing poetry, but in fashioning a readership newly purged of the 'cold pretence' of the age. It was a readership that would have to be created from among an increasingly diffuse literate 'general public' who could not now be assumed to bring a suitable degree of critical discernment to their choice of texts. In this respect Coleridge discovered a kindred spirit in Rudolf von Langen, and he quoted his terse comment with approval in an essay for *The Friend* of 1809: 'how are we to guard against the herd of promiscuous Readers?'.[13] Poetry itself, therefore, stood in need of reform, and would become implicitly critical of its 'promiscuous' readership and its reactionary reviewers. Wordsworth's appeal to his 'gentle reader' in 'Simon Lee' (*Lyrical Ballads* 1798) carries with it essentially the same ironic criticism of modern 'gentility' that Dickens was to employ in the opening pages of *Little Dorrit* half a century later.

In 'Simon Lee', an old retainer who has worked himself to a standstill and now lives in appalling conditions is helped when, in a brief, undemanding act of assistance a tree stump is chopped down for him. The poet who performs this act represents both the writer and the reader of gentility; like Dickens's Monsieur Rigaud he might well have said, 'Have you ever thought of looking to me to do any kind of work? . . . No! You knew from the first moment when you saw me here, that I was a gentleman . . .'.[14] If the claim to gentility guaranteed anything in the modern world, it was a talent for loafing. Beyond the loafing propensity lay a far more profound malaise born of the cultural crisis that in Dickens is manifest in the stultifying 'dandyism' of *Bleak House*, and in the socially destructive boredom of Harthouse in *Hard Times*. For Wordsworth it hovers no less ominously over the anecdotes and characterisations of *Lyrical Ballads*. The dilettante, idle observer is everywhere.

Wordsworth's personal uncertainty and indecision is thus written into many of the poems, and in 'Tintern Abbey' (1798) it is located specifically at the point when he returned from France in 1793, a time of intense personal dislocation, and of social and political turmoil: 'I cannot paint/what then I was' (LB 115, 76–7).

The century-long debate over the relationship of authorship to readership had become inextricably enmeshed with social relationships defined in terms of political choice and action. Wordsworth's attempt in 'The Discharged Soldier' to create a single image of his intended literary career as a road which represented the familiar idea of the poet as set apart, while at the same time it retained the characteristics of an active political, public life, was a predictable enough consequence of his engagement with current thinking on contemporary literary culture. By the time he was preparing to leave England for Germany in 1798, it had led him to consider his art as in some ways radically free-floating from the political and religious establishments of the day; the truths he sought to communicate were discovered through intuition, seemingly by chance, not by cultural edict. These are all features which endorse a distinct, Romantic sensibility, and most of them inform the narrative and imagery to be found in 'The Discharged Soldier'.

With this in mind, one circumstance of Wordsworth's encounter with the soldier is particularly revealing. From the outset the poem insists that the scene depicted is 'Deserted in its silence' (1.3). Having read the whole poem the reader might subsequently conclude that in this Wordsworth has either been careless or dishonest. His sighting of the man and his grotesque appearance gains its full effect from our awareness that the soldier's solitariness, his 'desolation' (1.63), is witnessed in silence. Even the 'murmuring sounds' of his voice seem to be cancelled out as soon as mentioned, 'yet still his form/Kept the same fearful steadiness' (11.70–1). He utters 'A groan scarce audible' (1.79); but the passage then continues:

> Yet all the while
> The chained mastiff in his wooden house
> Was vexed, and from among the village trees
> Howled never ceasing.
>
> (11.79–82)

The howling mastiff must have been audible almost from the first. It is by such shocks, such reversals and contradictions that Wordsworth's poetry habitually works. The dog has effectively prohibited the soldier from seeking relief in the village close by, 'the village mastiff fretted me' (1.130). It is a metaphor for his rejection by the society that has used him to fight its wars; his reaction is predictably an extreme one, 'Felt at my very heart' (1.132). Neither poet nor soldier can appeal to the community for support; both are rejected and must turn back to seek help from 'an honest man and kind', 'a labourer', who lives on his own beyond the close circle of the village community. Wordsworth thus dramatises his sense of the poet's alienation through lines which appear to proceed in a careless, even absent-minded fashion. The meaning establishes itself by chance, after the lore of 'the poets, rather than the critics'.

The dog, so the soldier supposes, seems to be 'howling to the murmur of the stream' (1.134). We have seen why for Wordsworth the stream may be taken to signify the art of poetry he is determined to pursue; he is therefore identifying with the soldier in his loneliness. After a succession of bruising years seeking a way forward for his ailing country, he finds himself rejected in both his creative and his political endeavours. In keeping with the soldier's response to the barking of the dog, he has been driven out of his natural home. He has been left to sustain his literary life on his own, and must therefore write for himself the road upon which he means to travel.

No account of Wordsworth's literary life can therefore expect to escape having to engage with the process of personal myth-making which is written into his work at every point, and particularly into *The Prelude*. The task is not one of dismantling or removing the myth; rather it becomes a matter of disentangling the poetic persona Wordsworth is forever creating for himself as he writes, from the actual circumstances in which he lived and wrote. By attempting to do this we are able to appreciate to the full the way that a state of sustained tension between these two propositions fuelled Wordsworth's creative output. It is this that becomes, therefore, the subject of the literary life, a tension that denies our arrival at firm value judgements, where truth and illusion, reality and myth, cohabit as different sides of the same coin, perceptions of the same road, be it 'public' or 'deserted'.

The Prelude began to be composed at a point when Wordsworth was living in what amounted to a state of exile. Following a frustrated career in politics and failure to make any significant progress as a writer, he had arrived at a point where everything – including his physical isolation in Goslar – drove him to review his life to date, and to begin the process of formulating revised resolutions for the future. Goslar and the early *Prelude* undoubtedly marked a watershed in his life. It was at this point that with renewed determination he chose the literary life of a modern poet, and began to make it happen with a six-line rhetorical question:

> Was it for this
> That one, the fairest of all rivers, loved
> To blend his murmurs with my nurse's song,
> And from his alder shades and rocky falls,

And from his fords and shallows, sent a voice
That flowed along my dreams?

>   (*Prelude* 1799, 1, 1–6)

The distant, murmuring river of poetry which accompanied the experience related in 'The Discharged Soldier' becomes now the central feature of the opening lines of the 1799 *Prelude*. It is the dominant
voice of this new beginning, and for a while at least – far removed
from the public road – the mastiff is silenced.

WRITING THE EARLY CHAPTERS

Important as this moment was in the history of Wordsworth's literary coming of age, we should not lose sight of the fact that for
many years prior to this, his search for an identity had been accompanied by the conviction that he would somehow make sense of his
life through the act of writing. There is no shortage of evidence from
his letters that he cultivated the habit of living his life according to
literary precedents, first as an enthusiast for both the sublime and
the beautiful when he wrote to Dorothy describing his European
walking tour of 1790, and later as a disciple of the cult of sensibility
when writing to his friend William Mathews after his return from
Orleans and Paris in 1791–2 (EY 32–8; 111–13). While Wordsworth
then roamed restlessly across England in 1793, his sister Dorothy,
writing to Jane Pollard, described what she called 'his natural dis-
position' as identical to the solitary, melancholy hero of James
Beattie's poem *The Minstrel* (1771–4) (EY 100).

Dorothy's use of this text arose from her knowledge of it as one
of her brother's favourite poems, and we find Wordsworth himself
striking a derivative pose when he wrote to Mathews in February
1794:

> since I had the pleasure of seeing you, I have been do[ing] noth-
> ing and still continue to be doing nothing. What is to become of
> me I know not. . . .
>
>   (EY 112)

Mathews is to understand that his companion belongs in the literary
company of Rousseau, of Edwin (Beattie's Minstrel), of the hero of
Goethe's *The Sorrows of Young Werther* (1774), and Harley, the central

figure of Henry MacKenzie's sentimental novel, *The Man of Feeling* (1771). His mind hovers laconically above an unfeeling world, discoursing on its affairs in a tone of weariness and verging at times on arrogance:

> What rem[arks do] you make on the Portuguese? in what state is knowledge with them? and have the principles of free government any advocate there? or is Liberty a sound of which they have never heard? Are they so debased by superstition as we are told, or are they improving in anything? (EY 113)

Another facet of the letters of 1794 to Mathews is of course Wordsworth's declaration that he is 'of that odious class of men called democrats' (EY 119). This statement occurs as part of his response to Mathews's proposal to launch a journal for which Wordsworth suggested the title of *The Philanthropist*. Wordsworth's contribution to the discussion primarily consists of insisting that the journal embrace a radical political agenda in line with his own views. In his letter of June 1794 we learn that this is equivocal when it comes to 'the bare idea of a revolution', but uncompromising on the unacceptability of 'monarchical and aristocratic governments. . . . Hereditary distinctions and privileged orders of every species' (EY 124).

This is the political Wordsworth whose level of involvement and commitment it has proved so difficult to establish. Regardless of how seriously we take the extensive statements of political radicalism coupled with the *Philanthropist* scheme contained in these letters, what is beyond dispute is the way they are set within a highly self-conscious, mannered, literary context. In February he had airily informed Mathews that he was 'doing nothing'. In June, after outlining his political principles and discussing *The Philanthropist*, he explains that he is 'nearly quite at leisure', his time partly taken up with 'correcting and considerably adding to' *An Evening Walk* and *Descriptive Sketches*, and he goes on to ask Mathews to call on 'Johnson my publisher' to enquire how sales of 'these little things' are going (EY 119).

With the best will in the world, it is difficult not to read this as Wordsworth at his pretentious worst. Wordsworth the political radical and Wordsworth the poet were undoubtedly more than the literary creations of an affected epistolary style – they represent genuine facets of the man's personality, but they are here mediated through a palpably unnatural literary style. At 24, recently returned

from Revolutionary France with a lover and an illegitimate child on
his conscience, as well as a mission to terminate 'monarchical and
aristocratic governments', Wordsworth's literary equipment remains
rooted in the literary life he lived as a schoolboy at Hawkshead.
Paine's *Rights of Man* has, it is true, infiltrated the discourse of sensibility somewhat; but the letters to Mathews serve as a reminder
of how profoundly Wordsworth's ideas continued to be controlled
by his reading of William Cowper, James Beattie, Bishop Percy's
anthology of ballads, *Reliques of Ancient English Poetry* (1765), Joseph
and Thomas Warton, George Crabbe, Charlotte Smith, Robert Burns,
John Langhorne and William Shenstone.[15]

In his *Elegies* (dating from the early 1740s), Shenstone repeatedly
depicts the poet as the morose, alienated figure familiar to us from
Gray's 'Elegy in a Country Churchyard', Goldsmith's 'The Deserted
Village', and Wordsworth's own *An Evening Walk* and *Descriptive
Sketches*:

> Fain would I mourn my luckless fate alone,
> Forbid to please, yet fated to admire;
> Away, my friends! My sorrows are my own!
> Why should I breathe around my sick desire.[16]

Wordsworth adopted the personae of his predecessors for *An Evening
Walk*:

> Far from my dearest friend, 'tis mine to rove
> Thro' bare grey dell, high wood, and pastoral cove. . . .
>   (EW 29, 1–2)

The story of Wordsworth's literary life begins with his absorption of what constitutes a catholic array of poets which nevertheless
represent an emphasis on feeling and emotion guaranteed to create
the kind of sentimentality he eventually came to distrust, and in due
course attacked in parodic form in *Lyrical Ballads*.

He was the child of a generation of young readers liberated from
Augustan literary poise by being moved to tears at the suicidal fate
of Goethe's tragic hero in *Werther*. While a knowledge of Goethe
may be safely assumed – and indeed appears to be confirmed in a
letter to Coleridge written in 1799 (EY 255) – there is no record of
him having read Mackenzie's *Man of Feeling*. Mackenzie's hero is,
however, like Werther, clearly a model not just for a literary style,

but for an evolving concept of the poet as a man of feeling whose creativity could potentially threaten his very existence. When Harley speaks, his voice comes as a bizarre echo of the voice of the poet of radical political convictions who corresponded with William Mathews:

> There is a certain dignity in retiring from life at a time, when the infirmities of age have not sapped our faculties. This world ... was a scene in which I never much delighted. I was not formed for the bustle of the busy, nor the dissipation of the gay....[17]

Though his life between 1790 and 1794 had been very much a busy matter of 'bustle' and intense emotional experience, the literary persona Wordsworth cultivated in both his published and unpublished poetry prior to *Lyrical Ballads* was rooted in a modish world-weariness and melancholy. His childhood experiences had prepared him well for the discovery of kindred spirits in Beattie's Edwin and similar alienated, solitary poets he was to encounter, not least in the much-publicised tragic career of Thomas Chatterton, who took his own life at the age of 17 in 1770, the year William Wordsworth was born.

2

Early Years

With the death of John Wordsworth in 1783, the five Wordsworth children became the responsibility of their maternal uncle, Christopher Cookson. Their financial dependence on Cookson was absolute, and would remain so until the boys were in a position to make their own way in the world. Unlike his brothers, who seem to have accepted their fate without undue resentment, the pattern of William Wordsworth's early life became increasingly defined by his attempts to break free from the control that his uncle exercised over the direction of his life.

From Hawkshead School on through Cambridge, a reciprocal relationship began to evolve between his determination to win his independence, and his enthusiasm for literature. In the modern literature he read there were well-established links and associations formed between the artist (notably the poet) and what for him were peculiarly appropriate themes of melancholy and exile. The poet repeatedly appeared in the modish guise of the outcast; such was the case in Beattie's *Minstrel*, noted in the previous chapter as an important contemporary poem for Wordsworth. In the case of George Crabbe, the poet is both alienated from polite culture and potentially dissident; in the case of Thomas Chatterton, the poet becomes an archetypal tragic victim of society's insensitivity.

It is easy to appreciate why, given the circumstances of Wordsworth's childhood, the political connotations that such literary models could offer began to be articulated in his poetry of the 1790s. Wordsworth's quest for personal liberty, a growing inclination to write, and the appeal of radical politics intersected as his childhood gave way to a restless and eventful early adulthood, experienced in the shadow of Revolution in France, and scarcely less dramatic scenes of political and cultural turmoil at home.

COCKERMOUTH AND PENRITH, 1770–83

No biography is complete without an account of its subject's formative years. Compiling the known facts in the case of a repeatedly researched individual like Wordsworth is not a difficult task; going on to assess the significance of those facts for his development as a writer is a far less precise science. Assuming the link between experience of childhood and development as poet to be a worthwhile avenue of research, the first problem is that critics have been unable to arrive at a consensus as to whether or not the poet had a happy childhood.

The circumstances surrounding Wordsworth's early years make it perfectly feasible that he would at times have experienced considerable anxiety, indeed the information we have about family circumstances in general can be presented in such a way as to make it seem inevitable that Wordsworth must have consciously confronted a darker side to life from very early on. Yet the fact remains that we don't know – and will never know – how Wordsworth experienced his childhood at the time it was happening.

For Leslie F. Chard, writing in 1972, it is sufficient that Wordsworth should in restrospect 'stress the unfailing delight which the young boy felt in the presence of nature and in the company of his playmates'. Beyond this, he argues, all efforts at psychoanalytical criticism invariably distort what is in fact an essentially uncomplicated tale of a childhood of 'unfailing delight'. Chard's chief complaint is that too many critics have used the poetry in order to prove what they wish to believe about the life. The primary motivation here, he suggests, is the grinding of political axes, not the study of poetry. Chard argues from a particular view of what constitutes literary studies; we must start with the poetry (in this case *The Prelude*), and instead of discussing 'what . . . *should* have gone into the poem' discuss 'what *is* in it'.

The tendency to concentrate on what is absent from a text rather than on what is present has certainly become a hallmark of much recent criticism. Chard's frustration with critics who have in various ways spent time discussing 'absence' (including F. M. Todd, David Ferry and Geoffrey Hartman) draws from him what even a reader sympathetic to his case must surely begin to feel is a somewhat ingenuous reading both of *The Prelude*, and of the established historical narrative of the poet's childhood.[1]

In his earliest years Wordsworth lived in relatively affluent circumstances in the thriving market town of Cockermouth. The reason for this was that his father worked for the richest and most powerful political magnate in the north-west, Sir James Lowther. The Wordsworths inhabited – rent-free – the most impressive house and grounds in Cockermouth High Street. Given that Lowther is known to have been highly feared as a ruthless, tyrannical, unpredictable and neurotic politician, it is not unreasonable to assume that the family must inevitably have encountered some degree of ostracism in the town. What we cannot know, of course, is the extent to which this would have been a 'problem' for any of the children.[2]

Pressure of work on John Wordsworth (Lowther's 'Law Agent') meant that he was required to spend long periods of time away from home, and from 1775 on there is evidence that the children, Richard, William, Dorothy, John and Christopher, spent a good deal of time boarding with their maternal uncle Christopher at Penrith, and with John Wordsworth's brother Richard at Whitehaven.[3] There cannot therefore have been a great deal of community life for them beyond the immediate family, and with the early loss of both parents came an inevitable further fragmentation of that family unit. Ann Wordsworth died in 1778, the year William began his schooling at Hawkshead Grammar, and John died in 1783.

Ann's death had brought about the permanent removal of the brothers into the care of Christopher Cookson at Penrith, a far less congenial regime than that of Uncle Richard at Whitehaven, referred to with particular bitterness by Dorothy Wordsworth, who was sent to live with her mother's cousin, Elizabeth Threlkeld, in Halifax. 'Many a time', she wrote in 1787, 'Have William, John, Christopher and myself shed tears together, tears of the bitterest sorrow' as they suffered under 'the ill-nature of my Uncle' (EY 3). Against the depressing scenario offered by Dorothy (suffering in effect a double exile) it must be remembered that Richard, John and Christopher appear to have adapted far more readily to their changed circumstances than either Dorothy or William. William's continuing resentment towards Cookson is indicated by his refusal to attend his uncle's funeral in 1799.

It may well have been that Wordsworth spent his earliest years at Cockermouth playing happily in the garden, or raiding his father's rich and varied library, with no sense whatever of deprivation or insecurity. He subsequently appears, however, to have been the kind of person who found a more severely ordered regime than Cockermouth very difficult to take; and this does shed a helpful light on the spirit in which he responded to the cultural life at Hawkshead School after 1778, and how he was eventually to approach his decision to become a poet. Dorothy was evidently the one who most sympathised with him, and it is from her we catch the interpretation of events that reflects his state of mind:

We have been endeared to each other by early misfortune. We in the same moment lost a father, a mother, a home, we have been equally deprived of our patrimony by the cruel Hand of lordly Tyranny. (EY 88)

Dorothy's last statement is a reference to the fact that when John Wordsworth died, Lowther owed him over £4000. Characteristically he refused to honour the debt. As time passed, Lowther's refusal to pay the orphaned, beggared family of his Law Agent what he owed them gave rise to a more sweeping scorn Wordsworth cultivated for the aristocracy and the political establishment in general. Again, this was not at all the way in which his brothers responded, determined as they all were to pursue Lowther through the courts.

Much does indeed depend on how the information we have is used. Leslie Chard maintains that there was very little in Wordsworth's early life to encourage anything other than a politically conservative frame of mind: 'Wordsworth's early upbringing was politically conservative. In fact, his entire intellectual climate as a child was conventional.'[4] But it is equally possible to see the facts of the matter confirming the poet's childhood as a potentially bewildering experience (particularly for a child 'of a stiff, moody, and violent temper' as Wordsworth himself put it), where political loyalties were a central contributing factor to an atmosphere of uncertainty and resentment (Prose III, 372). We should not forget the fact that as a supporter of the Whig faction led by the Duke of Norfolk, Wordsworth's uncle Christopher was a sworn enemy of the Lowther political interest. Rarely if ever is this point offered as a reason why Cookson should have resented going to the trouble and expense of bringing up the children of one of Lowther's creatures. He did so in the first instance while his brother-in-law was still touring the countryside buying votes and generally perpetuating the empire of a man Cookson considered as evil as he was dangerous.

It is hard to imagine that the children did not from time to time have to listen to a rehearsal of their uncle's views on the situation. If this was indeed the case, Wordsworth's resentment of Lowther would have been in part fuelled by the man who, for other reasons, he felt was cruel and unsympathetic. Further to confuse the issue, Wordsworth must have felt a tug of family loyalty to his father, despite his growing knowledge of the nature of his job. No doubt he might too be seen as another victim of 'lordly Tyranny'. As time passed, and with the admonitions of his brothers, he may also have become aware of the fact that, despite the joyless and repressive regime of Penrith, his uncle Christopher was in his own way sincerely seeking to do his best for his sister's children. It was of course very much in Cookson's own interests to see the Lowther debt honoured.

Politics, we know, became a passion with Wordsworth as a young man, and his enthusiasm for political debate subsequently never waned. There is Sara Coleridge's oft-quoted memory of how in 1808 Wordsworth, Coleridge and Robert Southey would 'discuss the affairs of the nation, as if it all came home to their business and bosoms, as if it were their private concern'.[5] Given the circumstances of his upbringing it is not at all surprising that this should be so. The trauma of his parents' death was accompanied by his removal to an uncongenial environment heavily impregnated by political opinion. He must very soon have begun to take stock of the circumstances surrounding the Lowther debt, the attempts to retrieve the money through the courts, and his uncle's political convictions.

As a child of 8, newly arrived at Hawkshead School, he was obviously in no sophisticated sense 'political'; but it is very unlikely given his personal circumstances and the ambiance of the school (to be considered later) that a keen interest in political issues was long in developing. If he did not become a 'political' teenager in any precocious sense, he was most certainly a self-absorbed young man with a chip on his shoulder, enthusiastic about literature, and with reason to feel himself alienated from both wings of the traditional political spectrum, Whig and Tory. He was a young man who could not but be intensely aware of the consequences of political opinion in others. At Hawkshead it became possible for him to catch a glimpse of an alternative political agenda that lay beyond the Whig/Tory divide; this was the political world associated with both religious dissent and an enthusiasm for contemporary writing. Hawkshead was where the serious business of questioning the status quo undoubtedly did begin. Subsequently the coming of the French Revolution and eventual exposure to radical English politics in the 1790s offered the politically unaffiliated Wordsworth a new politics with which he could freely and eagerly identify.

The process is not difficult to understand: alongside a politics which repudiated both Lowther and Cookson with equal severity, lay the invitation to an alluring – if chancy – literary career which confirmed in terms of cultural alternatives the road to political rebellion; here was the basis of a literary life (the most attractive career he could aspire to) through which his rejection of Lowther and Cookson could be expressed. Bearing in mind his uncle's expectations of him, he would be enacting his rebellion as well as articulating it.

The kind of poet Wordsworth was going to become was the result of the subjection of his temperament to the specific pressures these formative years brought to bear on his cultural education, and we do not have to spend our time looking for what is missing or 'absent' from his poetry to discover evidence of Wordsworth's anger at social injustice, specifically when it refers to those who were in some way dispossessed, the outcast and the ostracised; we find him repeatedly exploring the theme of guilt, and manifestly haunted by fears of insecurity.

From what must inevitably be speculative reflection on these early Cockermouth and Penrith years, therefore, we can recognise something of the poet who was prepared for the appeal of radical political ideas, who was – by his own admission – inclined to introversion and rebelliousness, and who came to crave dependable friendship and critical approbation as a prerequisite for publication if not for writing. His sensitivity to adverse criticism and to accusations made about the content of his political agenda materially affected both the manner of his composition and the decisions he made when contemplating publication. While none of these things can be seen as replacing the need to read his poetry in order to understand what he wrote, they do provide an essential context for the literary life.

HAWKSHEAD AND CAMBRIDGE, 1778–91

From what we know of the management of the curriculum, of Wordsworth's fellow pupils and of the staff, Hawkshead Grammar School in the late eighteenth century appears to epitomise the way British society was beset by contending yet interrelated forces. Wordsworth's school exhibited evidence of both the liberal and conservative tendencies at work in cultural, religious and political life. Again, how we assess the implications for Wordsworth's development as a poet will depend upon how such evidence is marshalled and presented.

Hawkshead retained a traditional commitment to the classical curriculum. Equally important, and more innovative, was the teaching of mathematics and science. This was part of the process of preparing the more able scholars for progression to Cambridge University.

Hawkshead had close connections with St John's College. Wordsworth responded positively and ably to both branches of knowledge. There was nothing particularly unusual in such a curriculum, though the attention given to science would render Hawkshead somewhat more progressive than many similar institutions.

In Wordsworth's time (under four Headmasters, James Peake until 1781, Edward Christian to 1782, William Taylor to 1786, followed by Thomas Bowman), the regime was certainly relatively liberal; quite distinctively so when compared to what we know of Christ's Hospital at the time when Coleridge was there, or to Eton at the turn of the century.[6]

Together with the maintenance of traditional standards and expectations, therefore, Hawkshead offered a liberal ambience, reflected in particular in its encouragement of the reading of modern literature, and more especially in the emphasis given to the reading – and writing – of poetry. This reflects the particular bent of both William Taylor and Thomas Bowman. Library facilities at Hawkshead offered Wordsworth an enlarged version of his father's eclectic collection at Cockermouth. Bowman's 'Proposal for a new Library at Hawkshead' of 1789 gives a clear indication of the ambitious range of library provision that was being aimed at:

> I have long wished that our present Library might be extended; so as to take in all the English Classics, History, Geography, Topography, Chronology, Biography, Travels, Description of Manners, Customs and Ceremonies, Books of Taste, Literature, and Criticism, Natural Philosophy in all its Branches, Ethics, Natural History, Elementary treatises on popular Sciences, and approved works on all generally interesting subjects whatever.[7]

Compared with Coleridge's opportunities for reading under the tutelage of the Reverend James Bowyer at Christ's Hospital, Bowman's statement is remarkable.[8]

In such an atmosphere, where Langhorne, Beattie, Gray, Goldsmith, Burns, Crabbe, Charlotte Smith and many others were available to those who wished, it is not surprising to find that the encouragement to write existed as more than a statutory academic exercise. Wordsworth's first poems date from around 1784 when he was 14, and three years later he enjoyed the experience of having his sonnet 'On Seeing Mrs. Helen Maria Williams Weep at a Tale of Distress' accepted for publication by the *European Magazine*:

She wept. – Life's purple tide began to flow
In languid streams through every thrilling vein;
Dim were my swimming eyes – my pulse beat slow,
And my heart was swelled to dear delicious pain.
                                        (PW I, 269)

Wordsworth, predictably enough, adopted the popular contemporary language of sensibility; he was also experimenting with ballad
form while he worked at the rigorous classical disciplines of verse
represented in English by Pope and Dryden.

At a later stage of his life, many of the authors he read at this time
– Beattie, Burns, Crabbe and Langhorne, for example – certainly
came to be understood in terms of the political implications of their
poetry. What mattered to him in the 1780s was that the experience
he enjoyed was one of being allowed the freedom to range at will
through a dense and stimulating proliferation of modern poetry,
together with the encouragement to attain a grounding in classical
and scientific learning. The opportunities he took to go on random
and frequent expeditions into the Lakeland countryside – which he
so vividly recreated at a later time in *The Prelude* – suggest the extent
to which he relished his physical liberty alongside his growing
intellectual freedom.

Always present, we must remember, was the knowledge that such
freedom was conditional. Penrith was there to impose the ultimate
sanction, to call him in from the fells, to send him from Hawkshead
to Cambridge with firm instructions as to the nature of his studies
and their intended outcome. In response to this, Wordsworth's commitment to both intellectual and physical pursuits seems seldom to
have been less than reckless, and the underlying theme is the persistent celebration of the free spirit enshrined in both:

Our steeds remounted, and the summons given,
With whip and spur we by the chauntry flew
In uncouth race . . .
        . . . Through the walls we flew
And down the valley, and, a circuit made
In wantonness of heart, through rough and smooth
We scampered homeward.
                        (*Prelude* 1799, 72, 122–4; 135–8)

In his 1805 version of *The Prelude* Wordsworth linked this spirit of
a 'wantonness' harmonising with his natural surroundings, with his

growing awareness of the power of poetry. The 'passion' and the 'power' of poetry were envisaged as forces which removed it, and him, from the formal surroundings of learning, relocating it (as in 'The Discharged Soldier') on 'the public roads':

> ... Oft in the public roads,
> Yet unfrequented, while the morning light
> Was yellowing the hilltops, with that dear friend
> ... I went abroad, and for the better part
> Of two delightful hours we strolled along
> By the still borders of the misty lake
> Repeating favourite verses with one voice ...
>   (*Prelude* V, 182, 581–8)

Wordsworth's schoolboy poetry was of course heavily derivative; but in 'The Vale of Esthwaite', which he was working on at the time he left Hawkshead, the identification of writing with liberty is no less apparent, even if the statement is clogged with fashionable gothic imagery. The wild, terrifying spirit of freedom exhibited by nature is conceived of in literary terms as an angry, prophetic utterance:

> I lov'd to haunt the giddy steep
> That hung loose trembling o'er the deep,
> While ghosts of murtherers mounted fast
> And grimly glar'd upon the blast.
> While the dark whirlwind rob'd, unseen,
> With black arm rear'd the clouds between;
> In anger Heaven's terrific Sire
> Prophetic struck the mighty Lyre
> Of Nature ...
>
>   (PW I, 276)

In *The Prelude* of 1799 this moment recurs as one of invigorating, inspirational danger ascribed to an actual experience, and it suggests more boldly that Wordsworth himself is to be the bardic figure whose work it is to communicate the 'dark/Invisible workmanship that reconciles/Discordant elements':

> ... Oh, when I have hung
> Above the Raven's nest, by knots of grass

Or half-inch fissures of the slipp'ry rock
But ill-sustained, and almost, as it seemed,
Suspended by the blast which blew amain,
Shouldering the naked crag, oh, at that time
While on the perilous ridge I hung alone,
With what strange utterance did the loud dry wind
Blow through my ears; the sky seemed not a sky
Of earth, and with what motion moved the clouds!
(*Prelude* 1799, 2, 57–66)

If the enthusiasm of Bowman and Taylor for a catholic approach to reading in modern literature might suggest a whiff of Dissent in the crowded classrooms of Hawkshead Grammar School, it should be noted that alongside the dispatch of the more able pupils to St John's College, Cambridge to pursue, for the most part, eminently respectable academic careers, Hawkshead had equally strong links with the Dissenting Academies. The region had a long-established tradition of Dissenting education centred on Kendal, and Hawkshead had sent pupils on to the Warrington Academy, and to Caleb Rotherham's Kendal Academy until Rotherham's death and the Academy's closure in 1753. Pupils were subsequently sent to the Manchester Academy where an education of university standard was available; in Wordsworth's time they included Edward Holme, Edward Wakefield, Frederick and William Maude, Charles Morland, and Warren and Edmund Maude. In the immediate vicinity of Hawkshead, Baptists and Quakers existed alongside their Church of England neighbours without rancour.

Hawkshead was an important centre for Quakerism, and unlike the Quakers of the south who had for the most part pursued a policy of compromise with the Church of England establishment, many northern Quakers remained in active political opposition throughout the century, committed to their heroes, heroines and martyrs, among whom was the Hawkshead-born missionary, Lydia Lancaster. Richard Fergusson's account of the Quaker convert Aaron Atkinson, a packman who travelled and preached in the north and in Scotland, sounds like an early source for Wordsworth's 'Wanderer' figure, the philosophical pedlar who narrates *The Excursion* (1814). The Quakers had a Meeting House at Colthouse, where Wordsworth lodged for a time, and where on occasion he attended services. He would certainly have been told all about Lancaster, Atkinson and many others.[9]

The influence of Quaker rhetoric, of their dissident ideology accompanied by a penchant for narrative reinforcement, will have exercised a powerful formative influence on Wordsworth. For a child of his temperament, Hawkshead (situated beyond the pale of Lowther's political influence) seems for many reasons to have offered an ideal environment. Neither a Whig Harrow nor a Tory Eton, the school reflected rather the interplay of contemporary cultural, religious and educational forces, even as Anglican, Baptist and Quaker appeared to cohabit without undue difficulty in the surrounding district. Referring to an old verse supposedly popular in the area at this time, T. W. Thompson has reflected on the free spirit that linked Hawkshead and Kendal:

Hawkshead and Kendal are bound up together
Firstly by Wool and Lastly by Leather.
Both Live by their Trade in fair or foul Weather,
And pay scanty heed to Mighty Folks Blether.

'Who the "Mighty Folks" . . . were is anybody's guess', writes Thompson, 'Mine is that they were the leading Whig and Tory Politicians, for whose utterances a certain contempt may have been felt in both Hawkshead and Kendal.'[10]

Above all, Hawkshead School offered its pupils a degree of self-determination and self-expression by no means replicated elsewhere. William Taylor himself, while outwardly conforming to the standards of respectability required for his post, had Cambridge connections that suggest familiarity with potentially radical political views. While at Emmanuel College, Taylor had been a close friend of George Dyer. Dyer had left Cambridge in 1778, returning soon after as tutor to the family of Robert Robinson. Robinson was a Baptist minister who founded the Cambridge Constitutional Society and worked tirelessly for University reform. Dyer, as Nicholas Roe has written, was living and writing 'at the centre of dissenting and reformist activity in town and university'; and in due course, Taylor's Cambridge companion, now a confirmed republican, met Taylor's pupil, William Wordsworth, in London in the 1790s.[11]

Dyer's fate has been similar to that of his near contemporary, the poet William Crowe. Lovingly preserved tales of Dyer as an elderly eccentric have masked the identity of the younger committed dissident pamphleteer and poet. The work of Heather Glen and Nicholas Roe has helped considerably towards establishing him as a significant figure in radical literary circles at the time of the French

Revolution, and though there is no reason to suppose that William Taylor was converted to radical politics by Dyer while at Emmanuel College, the least that can be said is that he was keeping interesting company.[12]

It should further be noted that when the nineteenth-century local historian, Henry Swainson Cowper, came to narrate the eventual closure of the school, he linked it to his account of Hawkshead as a cradle of non-conformity (with specific reference to the Quakers). Obliquely, but unambiguously, the sad demise of the school is perceived as linked to its political orientation. Cowper looks back upon a non-conformist Hawkshead with little enthusiasm, implying that the school in the eighteenth century was in effect a non-conformist institution with a reputation for 'free teaching'. In due course, he suggests, the inevitable consequence for 'Hawkshead and other Grammar Schools founded on similar principles' was ignominious closure.[13]

Wordsworth's move from Hawkshead to Cambridge in 1787 took place in a renewed atmosphere of bitterness towards Cookson, who had required him to return unnecessarily to Hawkshead with his brothers John and Christopher in the autumn to await his October start at St John's. The move to Cambridge was important for many reasons, not least because Wordsworth was now faced for the first time with serious thoughts of preparing for a future career.

With the exception of William, finding careers for John Wordsworth's sons appears not to have created any undue difficulties. Richard, the eldest, began to study for the law in 1786; John, the least academically gifted, took service with the East India Company and went to sea; Christopher followed a successful career at Cambridge with ordination, eventually becoming Master of Trinity College. Ordination was the plan for Wordsworth also, but from the outset this seems unlikely to have appealed to him. He brought to Cambridge the spirit of free enquiry that had enriched his life at Hawkshead. At Cambridge he did indeed have the freedom to ignore the academic path chosen for him if he so wished; in the event he pursued it in a significantly modified and modernised form. The assumption was that he would succeed his uncle William Cookson (Christopher's brother) in his Fellowship at St John's; to this end there was already a supportive network of influence and interest in place for him from William Cookson through Wordsworth's father's cousin, John Robinson, MP for Harwich, to Edward Christian, formerly a Hawkshead master, now a rising lecturer at Cambridge in 1787.

It would be difficult to imagine a set-up less likely to appeal to
a young man of Wordsworth's temperament. What he grasped at
was the opportunity to plan for the moment at which he might finally free himself from the controlling hand of his uncle. Cambridge
was an institution that amply displayed the worst side of aristocratic profligacy, corruption and idleness. The Establishment that
up until then had been personified in Wordsworth's experience by
Lowther, was writ large across a university where the new student's
rank as a sizar (the lowest order of undergraduate) emphasised the
persistence of class distinctions within an institution he believed
should have functioned as a 'commonwealth'.[14]

Though still not yet manifestly a political rebel, Wordsworth's
determination to study after his own fashion at Cambridge signifies
a gradually emerging awareness of the social context from which
his own circumstances had arisen. His personal loss of liberty was
part of a much larger situation where natural justice and sincer-
ity were wanting. We find him refusing compulsory attendance at
chapel as a hollow ritual, refusing also to honour the deceased Master of St John's in the traditional way, because it required him to
write an epitaph for a man about whom he knew nothing.[15] It is not
unreasonable to assume that he was ready and able by now to compare the aristocratic grandeur of the Windermere estate of Richard
Watson, Bishop of Llandaff, with the religion and the social conscience of the Dissenters he had met around Hawkshead, and was
without doubt now beginning to discover in Cambridge.

A young man prepared to dig his heels in over such matters must
also be assumed to have been at the very least aware of the Dissenting lobby then making a name for itself at the University; in addition
to Dyer and Robinson there were Paley, Jebb, William Frend, Horne
Tooke and others. Undergraduates who were influenced by these
people were soon to become Wordsworth's companions: William
Mathews, James Losh and Francis Wrangham. Perhaps what was
most significant of all, Wordsworth continued to write poetry, and
in so doing he moved from a series of childhood compositions towards a seriously conceived apprenticeship aimed at finding his
own voice. At the centre of the various fragments and experiments
that belong to this 1787–90 period is the emergence of a substantial
poem in the picturesque style, *An Evening Walk*.

In the summer vacation of 1790, Wordsworth, continuing to ignore
the counsel of his elders, undertook an ambitious walking tour across
France and Switzerland into Italy with a fellow undergraduate,

Robert Jones. They were travelling through France in the early, heady days of the Revolution. Without fully entering into the politics of the event – considered, no doubt, to be primarily a French affair – the message was once more one of freedom, an ideal for him at this stage rather than a political credo, but no less significant for that. *The Prelude*, of course, offers us a reconstruction of the experience relevant to the time at which it was being written in 1804–5; what we have from 1790 is the journal letter he wrote to Dorothy dated 28 September.

There is very little if anything of revolution politics here beyond the assumption that the Revolution had been a laudable event, and that it was effectively over bar the celebrations:

It was the most interesting period to be in France, and we had many delightful scenes where the interest of the picture was owing solely to this cause. (EY 36)

As this and the following extract clearly indicate, we find here a young man tuning up to be a writer in the contemporary vogue for picturesque description, on the lookout for 'delightful scenes' and 'pictures':

I am a perfect Enthusiast in my admiration of Nature in all her various forms; and I have looked upon and as it were conversed with the objects which this country has presented to my View so long, and with such pleasure, that the idea of parting from them oppresses me with a sadness similar to what I have always felt in quitting a beloved friend. (EY 35)

The vocational seriousness with which Wordsworth was eventually to envisage his literary career had not yet emerged, but what must be remembered is that for Wordsworth, fast approaching the end of his time at Cambridge, the mere thought of seeking an alternative career to the one already decided upon for him by others, amounted to an act of rebellion that tacitly challenged not only his uncle's authority, but the authority of the established church which he was to join, and with it the authority of the political establishment.

An Evening Walk, derivative as it is, constitutes a genuine act of personal revolt. Wordsworth is seeking an alternative life to the one he was being channelled into, and he begins to construct and live that alternative life through his writing. Here, as in 'The Discharged

Soldier', the image of the road becomes a central metaphor for the poet seeking to build a future in the spirit of childhood freedoms:

> Return Delights! with whom my road begun,
> When life rear'd laughing up her morning sun;
> When Transport kiss'd away my april tear,
> 'Rocking as in a dream the tedious year;'
> When link'd with thoughtless Mirth I cours'd the plain,
> And hope itself was all I knew of pain.
>
> (EW 32, 27–32)

This is writing that signals the emergence of a seriously determined free spirit. It accords with his refusal to comply with the academic and social expectations of St John's, with his continued refusal to comply with the wishes of Christopher Cookson and other advisers of his generation, and with his restless pedestrian touring through England and France during the Cambridge vacations. In *An Evening Walk* he continued with the programme he had already set himself in an ornate poem written before leaving Hawkshead:

> Dear native regions, I foretell,
> From what I feel at this farewell,
> That, whereso'er my steps may tend,
> And whenso'er My course shall end,
> If in that hour a single tie
> Survive of local sympathy,
> My soul will cast the backward view,
> The longing look alone on you.
>
> (PW I, 2)

The potential readership for a 'loco-descriptive' poem out of the tradition of Goldsmith's 'The Deserted Village', Beattie's *Minstrel* and John Dyer's 'Grongar Hill', with their solitary, reflective poets weighing political folly in the balance, belonged to the new, expanding, middle-class market. This hardly signifies a radical, let alone a Jacobin ambition. It does, however, indicate Wordsworth aiming at this point for the popular market, and at a radically different kind of life from that already chosen for him.

The draft fragments of *An Evening Walk* show how the poem evolved in the first instance from his 'Vale of Esthwaite' project to a blank-verse piece, approximating to the style of James Thomson's

The Seasons (1726–30), then one of the most highly regarded descriptive poems of the century. From there Wordsworth progressed to
heroic couplets, removing the gothic element, and composing –
probably in 1788 – the central incident of a vagrant woman who
dies of exhaustion along with her two infant children. Such a sequence would be offering the reader nothing new; there are many
such passages scattered through contemporary poetry, including
The Seasons. The fact remains that Wordsworth's contribution is
notable both for its length and the tone of vigorous anger which
offsets an invitation to sentimentalism. Wordsworth was influenced
here by what had clearly been an attentive reading of John Scott's
Critical Essays on Some of the Poems of Several English Poets (1785).
James Averill has shown how important Scott's text was for establishing a number of 'modern' aesthetic principles that Wordsworth
was subsequently to develop and make very much his own in the
Preface to the 1800 edition of *Lyrical Ballads*. Scott demands 'preci-
sion' of the poet, and encourages the exploration of 'real existence'
rather than 'fictions'. In a footnote to the 1794 version of *An Evening
Walk*, Wordsworth identifies a factual basis for the female vagrant
incident by way of locating it in 'real existence' (EW 7–8; 148).

He also chose to make the woman a war widow. Originally he
borrowed a line from John Langhorne's 'The Country Justice'
(1774) to tell us where the husband had been killed: 'Minden's
charnel plain' is a reference back to the Seven Years' War of the
mid-century. Around 1793 this was exchanged for the politically
more contentious reference to the American War of Independence
and 'Bunker's charnel hill'. While loss of life in the Seven Years'
War might be deemed the consequence of a laudable patriotism,
the morality of fighting a war against American colonists had been
far more hotly debated. In either case this specific explanation of
the way the woman came to be wandering through the beautiful
countryside, casting the shadow of an undeservedly harrowing death
over our ability to enjoy the picturesque scene in the way we would
expect in this type of poem, injects a potential political agenda into
the piece sufficient to show that the life of the poet writing it is
destined to be both lyrical and angry:

> Oh! when the bitter showers her path assail,
> And roars between the hills the torrent gale,
> – No more her breath can thaw their fingers cold,
> Their frozen arms her neck no more can fold;

Scarce heard, their chattering lips her shoulder chill,
And her cold back their colder bosoms thrill;
All blind she wilders o'er the lightless heath,
Led by Fear's cold wet hand, and dogg'd by Death;
Death, as she turns her neck the kiss to seek,
Breaks off the dreadful kiss with angry shriek.

(EW 64, 279–88)

Though not in the event published until 1793, *An Evening Walk* confirms the seriousness with which Wordsworth was considering literary production as a means of securing his independence, and of building a life for himself in the future. It also shows him beginning to work through contemporary styles towards the production of something that had to be new if it was going to be appropriate to his own situation. Human presence in this poem, as it evolved through the many drafts and revisions, steadily pushes the picturesque genre towards an early Wordsworthian poem contemplating the mysterious and often unsettling relationship between humanity and the natural world, where death and disaster cohabit with beauty and peace; what M. H. Abrams has referred to as Wordsworth's investigation of 'the ineluctable contraries that make up our human existence'.[16]

It is from the drafts, notes, and fragments of these Cambridge years, along with the evidence of a disciplined programme of secondary reading, that we catch our first glimpse of a poet beginning to establish a habit of dogged application to his literary task, something which subsequently becomes a familiar trait; a serious and committed Wordsworth who differs sharply from the feckless youth his guardian frequently complained of at this time (EY 6).

Wordsworth's Cambridge career ended in January 1791 with a BA but no Fellowship. He spent the following months in London; where precisely is not certain. From there he went to Plas-yn-Llan, the home of Robert Jones in Denbighshire where the two of them continued to indulge their love of walking, though from the letters he wrote to his friend William Mathews at this time you would never have guessed it. In the autumn he returned to London, spending time also in Cambridge. He was not eligible for ordination until the age of 23; in the meantime further study at the University had been advised by his uncle William. Wordsworth was dodging and weaving his way towards a stay of execution, and he finally achieved it when his uncle Richard agreed to finance a second, apparently more seriously intentioned visit to France. The stated aim was to develop a more expert acquaintance with the language, with a view to taking service as a private tutor. With the example of George Dyer's appointment to the Robinson family in mind, we should reflect that Wordsworth's scheme by no means indicates a preparedness to hire himself out to the nobility; on the contrary, it might have signified a far more radical intent. Regardless of the thinking behind it, the proposal was sufficient to secure the permission – and the funds – he needed.

The looked-for escape, albeit temporary, had been achieved, and Wordsworth set sail for France from Brighton in November 1791. Whatever he may have hoped for from the trip, he can have had no idea how in the event it was going to turn out. He was looking to change his life from the course in which other hands had set it; France in 1792 certainly did that for him, but scarcely in the way he expected.

3

From France to Racedown: 1792–97

THE WANDERER

Settled into his first-floor apartment in the house of M. Gellet-Duvivier in Orléans, Wordsworth eventually wrote to his brother Richard, giving him to understand that the delay in correspondence had been occasioned initially by problems *en route*, and then by his desire, once arrived in Orléans (on 6 December 1791) to be able to give a full account of his 'arrangements' (meaning how much money he was spending). The letter is dated 19 December. 'I was detained at Brightelmstone from Tuesday till Saturday evening', he explains. While in Brighton he wrote a letter to William Mathews in which he further explained the delay as caused by 'adverse winds'. Richard was to understand that his somewhat feckless younger brother was living comfortably but unextravagantly, and that – despite news of the deepening revolutionary crisis in France – he was safe: 'We are all perfectly quiet here and likely to continue so' (EY 70).

As the following narrative will show, he could hardly have got it more wrong. It is doubtful whether, even as he wrote, he had the slightest intention of continuing to be 'quiet'; but he had no idea of the extent to which he was to be swept into a maelstrom of personal and political passions so intense that he would find himself returning throughout his creative life to the themes of guilt, punishment, retribution and reconciliation they initiated.

The first part of this chapter is primarily concerned to clarify the hectic order of events in Wordsworth's life while he lived in France, and in the years immediately following his return to England. What he wrote will be more closely considered in the second part, bearing in mind that the writing constitutes the way Wordsworth himself reconstructed a narrative of his life during these years. He begins with *Descriptive Sketches*, a poem that holds the France of 1792 at arm's length while he reminisces about the walking tour with Robert Jones in 1790. The full fury of his frustrated political anger and personal guilt are unleashed once he is back in England; he writes the *Letter to Llandaff*, and subsequently *Salisbury Plain*, following which he moves eventually into the start of a more settled and ordered domestic existence at Racedown on the Dorset–Somerset border (reunited with his sister Dorothy and developing an intimacy with Coleridge), and here, despite continued evidence of grinding rural poverty and social injustice, he is at last encouraged to believe that the next chapter of his life may be written in terms of reconciliation and reintegration with society, where previously all he could see was alienation.

The point at which Wordsworth knew for certain that his destination was France, rather than a return to study at Cambridge, must have been a particularly stimulating and exciting moment for the young poet; earlier in the year his time spent in London had undoubtedly thrown him into the frenetic world of radical politics and dissenting religion. Samuel Nicholson had taken him to hear the charismatic Joseph Fawcett preaching against Government corruption, and Nicholson would certainly have familiarised him with the aspirations of the Society for Constitutional Information, and probably introduced him to some of its members.[1]

He had successfully evaded the path laid down for him by his elders (continued study at Cambridge in oriental languages), while in the short term at least, the prospect of ordination had been deferred by the pursuit of a possible alternative career.

Yet despite all this, the only evidence we have to hand of Wordsworth's frame of mind can best be described as a calculatedly circumspect letter written to his diligent and careful brother; while to Mathews, where Wordsworth might have been tempted to be more spontaneous, he sent what must rank as one of his most affected, posturing letters. The last impression he wishes to give of himself as he watches the clouds at Brighton, waiting for the change in the wind that will take him to France, is of someone enthusiastically bound for the hub of revolutionary activity and gripped by a determination to become a successful writer. The closest we can get to an admission of the latter resolve in the letter to Mathews is his dismissive reference to 'My Uncle the clergyman' (William Cookson, Christopher's brother) who 'proposed to me a short time ago to begin a course of Oriental Literature, thinking that that was the best field for a person to distinguish himself in as a man of Letters' (EY 62). We can almost see the eyes rolling upward and the sigh of exasperation. Wordsworth knows that Mathews will share his contempt for his uncle's antiquated academic notion of the 'man of Letters'. In the spring, with Nicholson, Fawcett, and the dangerous, stimulating world of radical publishing before him, a career in 'Letters' had assumed a very different hue.

In Brighton, as he informed his brother, he had made use of his enforced stay to introduce himself to Charlotte Smith. Smith was a successful poet and novelist who had connections with a number of sympathisers with the Revolution in France, and had become part of the radical circle that centred upon William Godwin in England. She was able to supply Wordsworth with letters of introduction to Helen Maria Williams, then at Orléans, and to other political activists in France. Wordsworth intended to get involved – one way or another – in a full life of literature and politics in France, and Smith was evidently happy to do what she could for him.

Interestingly, in his letter to Richard, he clearly assumes that his brother will probably not have heard of Helen Maria Williams ('Miss Williams, an English lady who resided here lately'); or is it too much to suggest that this mode of description had been assumed in the hope that it might deflect his brother from the realisation that his 'Miss Williams' (EY 69) was *the* Helen Maria Williams, author of *Letters Written In France*, published the month Wordsworth had set sail? By December 1791, even Richard might well have heard of the woman who had declared the French Revolution 'sublime', who had written that in France, 'the love of liberty has pervaded all ranks of the people, who, if its blessings must be purchsed with blood, will not shrink from paying the price', and who described the Revolutionary song, 'Ça ira', as 'the beloved sound which animates every bosom with delight, and of which every ear is enamoured'.[2]

Wordsworth's reference to his meeting with Charlotte Smith offers us at least two possible narratives. The first has been indicated; she reinforces the image of Wordsworth preparing himself for an exciting voyage of discovery into Revolutionary France. The second is the narrative suggested by the style of the letter to Richard. Smith was a distant relation of the Wordsworths, and the letter – including its description of her 'politest manner' and 'civility' – is part of Wordsworth's politic assumption of the role of a dutiful young scholar who is always ready to honour his family.[3] There is more than a hint of this in the way he finishes his account of his meeting with her; he wants to be sure that the right people know about it: 'This with my best affection you will be so good as to mention to Captn. and Mrs. Wordsworth' (EY 68).

To whom did Charlotte Smith give her letters of introduction? By the time she met Wordsworth, she had lived a life that rivalled the plots of most novels in the sentimental genre in which she worked. She had coped for many years with an irresponsible husband and an unprincipled father-in-law; she had persevered as a writer against the prejudice of predominantly male criticism, had separated from her husband, and after many years of poverty had eventually emerged as a successful novelist and poet, known equally for her unorthodox opinions, and her sensitivity towards 'the "languages" of discrimination in society'.[4] Had Wordsworth appeared on her doorstep simply on the pretext that she was 'family', she would doubtless have been polite; had he played the part he assumed in his letter to Mathews, I rather suspect he would have left with a flea in his ear. To Mathews he is the Man of Feeling, Goethe's Werthe, and he describes himself as languidly drifting off to France hoping for 'considerable pleasure', 'some little improvement', but nothing of sufficient significance to alter the fact that 'I am doomed to be an idler thr[oughou]t my whole life' (EY 62).

Confronted with a successful writer in the modern taste, it is far more likely that Wordsworth eagerly seized the opportunity to discuss his own literary ambitions set against his unfortunate circumstances, not to mention the part played in them by a noble Lord; he could also feel free to discuss the current political situation, drawing on what he had made of his time in London; and then there was his imminent departure for France, where Smith, who had lived near Dieppe for a time after leaving her husband, could be expected to offer knowledgeable opinion and advice.

Taken all together, and not forgetting that we also have Dorothy's allusion (in a letter to Jane Pollard written in December 1791) to the 'productions of William's Muse' (EY 66) to remind us that his literary ambition was certainly no secret, we have not one, but a boatload of Wordsworths stepping ashore at Dieppe on 28 November, and arriving in Paris just two days later. Among these young men are the 21-year-old apprentice poet consciously preparing to take advantage of an 'artistic revolution' which had created a culture 'simply mad for poetry';[5] the sullen and rebellious young man who was fast learning a political language relevant to his dislike of the aristocracy and the established church; the dutiful nephew who was determined to spend his time in provincial France wisely and well; the man of sensibility, indifferently drifting from place to place in a mist of precocious world-weariness; and of course there is also a

Wordsworth as yet unhatched, the poet reconstructed by *The Prelude*, for whom all events were ultimately explicable in terms of the making of a 'poet', an intriguing and timely hybrid written up in 1804–5.

Wordsworth spent five days in Paris, and if, as seems most likely, he managed to fit into that brief time visits to the major sites of the Revolution to date (he mentions a visit to the National Assembly in his letter to Richard), this must have been due primarily to his use of Smith's letters of introduction. The member of the Assembly whose guidance he acknowledges may or may not have been Jaques Pierre Brissot, an influential member of the increasingly radical Jacobin Club; but the brief reference to the political situation in his letter (part of which was torn away at some point) indicates that whoever it was had certainly not lost the opportunity to deliver a lecture (or lectures) on the major issues then confronting and fragmenting radical opinion. There is certainly a suggestion that plans to return to Paris to pursue an active political life had been laid almost before he arrived at Orléans: 'I was at the national assembly, introduced by a member of whose acquaintance I shall profit on my return to Paris' (EY 71). At the time of writing to Richard he had also contacted Thomas Foxlow, an Englishman who had a cotton factory at Orléans, and who would no doubt also have felt obliged to summarise political events and prospects for the new arrival.

The political sympathies of Orléans were Royalist, and so-called émigrés, disaffected Royalists preparing if need be to leave France, were thick on the ground. The National Assembly and the King were at this time in dispute over how to deal with Royalists who had taken up residence abroad and were now therefore viewed as a threat to the Republic's stability. The King's actions were unpredictable (he had already attempted to escape from France, only to be brought back ignominiously) and the mood in Orléans must have been tense. For all that, Paris was clearly where the action was, and Wordsworth's sense that he was an observer rather than a participant in events must have been shared by many others in the town; it is not to be considered as peculiarly the fate of a foreigner. 'The truth is', he wrote to Mathews in May 1792, 'that in London you have perhaps a better opportunity of being informed of the general concerns of France, than in a petty provincial town in the heart of the king[dom] itself' (EY 77).

This is not to say that Wordsworth could find nothing to do. He not only kept himself busy writing poetry, he fell in love, and he also established a close friendship with Michael Beaupuy, a captain in the Revolutionary army whose regiment was stationed at nearly Blois. It was through Beaupuy that he came to develop an informed understanding of Revolutionary principles and aspirations. We know that by 3 February Wordsworth had left Orléans for Blois, and we know why, for by that time he had become the lover of Annette Vallon, who lived in Blois. Annette was 25 in 1791, a Roman Catholic whose politics in later years were to draw her into the Royalist resistance to the Revolution. The Vallons regularly visited the Dufour family; André-Augustin Dufour was a magistrate's clerk who lived in Orléans. Wordsworth and Annette probably therefore met in Orléans as he cultivated new acquaintances, sought to extend his vocabulary, and became increasingly aware of the complexities of the political drama unfolding around him. Within a few weeks of his arrival in Blois, Annette was carrying the Englishman's child.

The frustration that Wordsworth had voiced to Mathews about being stuck in a 'petty provincial town' is probably best read in part at least as a characteristic rhetorical flourish; there is a kind of pompousness which habitually invades his correspondance with Mathews, even when he had cause to discuss matters of urgent practicality, as was soon to be the case. Taken together, the experience of life in Orléans and Blois, and the relationship with Annette and Beaupuy, were more than sufficient to provide Wordsworth with a comprehensive education in the volatile process of Revolution in France. In both Orléans and Blois the case for conservatism was being strongly argued; in Blois the Revolution was being defended intellectually by Beaupuy, who also represented the country's preparedness to fight for its new freedoms; in Blois the exacting practical process of realising Revolutionary ideals in the community was being hammered out before Wordsworth's eyes and ears (with Beaupuy to translate and embellish) by the club Les Amis de la Constitution.

At Blois the young Englishman watched and listened as the liberal aristocracy rode the back of the tiger, and as the liberal Catholic wing (including the Vallon family) performed the same precarious balancing act. It was the recently elected constitutional Bishop of Blois, Grégoire, who, as a member of the National Assembly (dissolved in September 1791) had campaigned for the dethronement of the King. The manifest vulnerability of the Revolution was responsible all the while for an increasing radicalisation of its aims, the need to purify its ranks in order to stand united against its enemies. This encouraged a growing spirit of anti-clericalism along with a distrust of any whose attitude might be suspect, not least those with an aristocratic pedigree. It was a situation where Wordsworth could see a growing threat to the futures of men like Beaupuy and Grégoire, and most alarmingly, a threat to the safety of Annette and her family.

A second major revolutionary upheaval in Paris in August 1792 shifted the balance of power significantly to the left, and set a series of political struggles in motion that progressively marginalised Brissot, and supplanted the bourgeois initiative of 1789 with a populist movement headed by Robespierre. The fact that Wordsworth well understood this process becomes apparent from the account he saw fit to give Mathews in May of the fate of General Dillon, murdered by the Revolutionary troops he commanded after a calamitous engagement with the Austrians in April (EY 77–8). September 1792 saw food riots in Orléans, and mass executions in Paris as the fear of counter-revolution grew, accompanied by rumours that the prisons of Paris were becoming a recruiting ground for a counter-revolutionary army.

Wordsworth had been in France now for almost a year; in that time he had acquired a domestic crisis of major proportions, and stumbled into a political drama where he was destined to find himself repeatedly out of his depth. Dealing with the Annette problem and dealing with the Revolution were indissolubly linked tasks; but in both areas he was in reality powerless. Circumstances were remorselessly combining to force him to run away from Annette and from the Revolution. He was guilty on every count. As he made his way – on foot – to Paris in October, he was a much altered man, and poet, from the Wordsworth who had landed in Dieppe the previous November. And as before, the narrative attached to his progress towards the capital readily fragments.

He is the political activist, determined to play his part as a statesman in saving the Revolution from descending into anarchy. In the 'Chronological Table' provided by Thomas Hutchinson for his Oxford Edition of the *Poetical Works* in 1914, we are told that Wordsworth was 'on the point of offering himself as a leader of the Girondins', Brissot's relatively moderate faction now ranged against Robespierre's Jacobins. For Stephen Gill, the affair with Annette has a central part to play in shaping the narrative: 'Faced with Annette's pregnancy earlier in the year he reluctantly decided to take up William Cookson's offer of a curacy'.[6] In this incarnation Wordsworth may be seen as primarily motivated by the need to bow to the wishes of his guardian and his 'uncle the clergyman'; he will return to England, secure an income through ordination and bring Annette to safety. 'My Uncle the Clergyman will furnish me with a title', he wrote to Mathews. 'Had it been in my power I certainly should have wished to defer the moment' (EY 76).

In the same letter, however, he makes it clear that he 'need not be prevented from engaging in any literary plan'. He is therefore still also clinging to the hope of eventually becoming a poet. As a poet (rather than a politician or a husband) he is a young man addressing the issues of the day in a revised version of *An Evening Walk*, and a newly completed poem, *Descriptive Sketches*; he is now bent on continuing and extending these activities to emulate those of radical writers and journalists like Brissot, Gorsas and Paine, whose work he knows and admires.

In Mary Moorman's account, Wordsworth's decision to return from Paris in December 1792 is possibly the result of urgent entreaties from English contacts in Paris who feared for his safety, and certainly of financial necessity: 'There was nothing for it but to return home'.[7] Alternatively he may be considered as simply scared and confused to a point where he panics, and makes for home.

He is, to some degree, all of these people. His daughter, Anne-Caroline, was born at Orléans on 15 December, by which time Wordsworth was already back in England, attempting to take stock of the calamitous situation.

It was not until 1916 that Wordsworth's affair with Annette and the existence of Anne-Caroline became public knowledge. The immediate family could not be kept waiting for quite so long, however, and in consequence all offers of support from William Cookson to secure a curacy for Wordsworth were instantly withdrawn; he moved in with Richard at Staple Inn, relying for the time being on what his brother was prepared to advance him. What he did have were his two poems, *An Evening Walk* and *Descriptive Sketches*, and as he picked up the threads of his previous London acquaintances, he successfully negotiated their publication with the radical printer, Joseph Johnson.

The execution of Louis XVI on 21 January 1793, served to intensify the political debate in England in which Wordsworth now immersed himself, and his primary occupation in these early weeks of the year was to work on a radical pamphlet attacking the erstwhile liberal but now conservative Richard Watson, Bishop of Llandaff. It was an uncompromising profession of faith in the radical cause, and while he drew heavily on earlier, radical Whig sources, Wordsworth had no misgivings when it came to justifying the execution of the King against Watson's 'lamentation':

> You wish it to be supposed you are one of those who are unpersuaded of the guilt of Louis XVI. If you had attended to the history of the French revolution as minutely as its importance demands, so far from stopping to bewail his death, you would rather have regretted that the blind fondness of his people had placed a human being in that monstrous situation which rendered him unaccountable before a human tribunal.

He then recalls the speech of Grégoire, Bishop of Blois, denouncing the many state-sanctioned murders Louis had been responsible for. 'Think of this', he suggests to Watson:

> and you will not want consolation under any depression your spirits may feel at the contrast exhibited by Louis on the most splendid throne of the universe, and Louis alone in the tower of the Temple or on the scaffold. (Prose I 32, 56–72)

Guilt and retribution now pervade all Wordsworth's writing. In *Salisbury Plain* it is not the King of France who is found attempting to escape his just deserts, it is Wordsworth himself:

> as if his terror dogged his road
> He fled, and often backward cast his face.
> (SP 25, 127–8)

The 'violence' he has done in relation to Annette he can in some degree justify in terms of an abstract justification of Revolutionary violence. Watson it is, he tells us, who says, 'I fly with terror and abhorrence even from the altar of liberty'; Watson does not understand that 'Liberty . . . in order to reign in peace must establish herself by violence' (Prose I 33, 196–7; 103–4). But beneath the political narrative lurks a persistent biographical narrative, and this now leads him irrevocably to a renowned site of hideous retribution, the sacrificial altar of Stonehenge:

> Oh from that mountain-pile avert thy face
> Whate'er betide at this tremendous hour.

To hell's most cursed sprites the baleful place
Belongs . . .

                    (SP 23, 82–5)

Wordsworth's journey over Salisbury Plain and the first draft of
the 'Salisbury Plain' poem lay still some months ahead. While the
Letter to Llandaff was being written, his career as a poet revolved
around the fate of *An Evening Walk* and *Descriptive Sketches*. Joseph
Johnson was a sick man at this time, and his handling of Wordsworth's poems proved less than helpful to their prospects. *The Letter
to Llandaff* was altogether too much of a risk to publish, and its author
was left to reflect on less overtly dangerous literary schemes, among
them the possibility of a sentimental novel using a story he had heard
from Beaupuy concerning two star-crossed lovers, Vaudracour and
Julia. A very similar tale is told in the latter part of Helen Maria
Williams's *Letters, Written in France*.

There could now be no question of Wordsworth returning to
France; from February 1793 the two countries were at war, and
Wordsworth had nothing to offer Annette and her daughter had
he been able to spirit them over to England. A literary career was
not in the offing, despite evidence of some enthusiasm for the published work; a career in politics scarcely recommended itself to a
devotee of Republicanism and a defender of regicide in 1793. The
prospects were bleak.

Among renewed acquaintances at this time was William Calvert,
a contemporary at Hawkshead with both time and money on his
hands. One can imagine that it must have been to Richard's immense relief to hear of a scheme that would take his brother out
of London on a tour of the West Country with Calvert. Richard's
dearest wish was not unnaturally that his brother should find a job
so that he might start to contribute to the family's ailing finances;
the excursion with Calvert at least offered a much-needed period of
reflection well away from his seditious circle of friends, and the
influence of authors like Paine, not to mention the work of a new
and impressive radical philosopher, William Godwin. With money
advanced from Richard to set him on his way, Wordsworth left with
Calvert for the Isle of Wight in July.

Calvert presumably set out on this trip well aware that his old
schoolfriend had good reason to be depressed, and was in need of
considerable moral support. He can hardly have expected to find in

him the ideal travelling companion. There is no doubt that Wordsworth was brooding morbidly on the current political situation; it
is equally certain that he persisted doggedly in his writing of poetry,
his imagination feeding off his changing surroundings. The two
men saw the British fleet preparing to sail against the French while
they spent July on the Island, and a draft sonnet survives from that
moment, fraught as ever with images of conflict and violence:

> But hark from yon proud fleet in peal profound
> Thunders the sunset cannon; at the sound
> The star of life appears to set in blood,
> And ocean shudders in offended mood,
> Deepening with moral gloom his angry flood.
>
> > (PW I 307–8, 15–19)

They then set off across Salisbury Plain, managing to crash their
carriage in a ditch, and agreeing in consequence to part company.
Calvert took the horse and rode homeward, Wordsworth set off on
a solitary walk north-westward across the Plain. Of all the many
walks that Wordsworth was to make, this trek without doubt constitutes a major formative experience in his literary life. Arriving in
Bath, he walked on to Bristol, crossed the Severn and followed the
Wye valley past Tintern Abbey, making his way on into Wales to
Plas yn Llan, the home of his companion on the walking tour of
1790, Robert Jones. The landscape through which he initially trudged
as he came upon Stonehenge was very different from the cultivated
fields that surround the triangle of land now wedged between the
A303 and the A344.

Wordsworth, utterly bereft of all companionship, found himself
in an inhospitable, bleak landscape. Before him were the remains
of a civilisation whose nature he could only begin to guess at; the
stones had nothing to do with any point of cultural reference readily available to him, Druids were the stuff of Gothic nightmare, dilet-
tanti speculation, magic, prehistory:

> It is the sacrificial altar fed
> With living men. How deep it groans – the dead
> Thrilled in their yawning tombs their helms uprear.
>
> > (SP 27, 184–6)

In *Salisbury Plain* he sees the relevance of this place to his situation
all too clearly, however. His determination to be a poet along with

the domestic, personal and political upheavals of his youth and early manhood, were now brought together in the context of an experience of extreme marginalisation; like the stones, he simply did not belong. His own life (not to mention the political life of the Nation) had gone disastrously wrong. Like Stonehenge, he could look at it, but he could not begin to understand it.

The import of the poetry he consequently started to compose will be considered in the next section, but in his 'Salisbury Plain' narrative he was dealing with his nightmare existence by writing his way through it and out of it, even as he walked on, down from the Plain, towards Wales. Once arrived at Plas yn Llan, he was writing as he had never written before, and on a projected poem which in essence was to remain with him in one form or another for the rest of his life.

It was a poem that condemned an unjust society for the misery and despair it created, but it also pronounced its narrator guilty and in due course (in a later version of 1795) condemned him to death on the scaffold. Looking ahead to *The Prelude* Book X, it is possible to see something of the way his perception of his own story and that of a Revolution he clings to for support (while fearing the consequences) became elided:

> I scarcely had one night of quiet sleep,
> Such ghastly visions had I of despair,
> And tyranny, and implements of death,
> And long orations which in dreams I pleaded
> Before unjust tribunals, with a voice
> Labouring, a brain confounded, and a sense
> Of treachery and desertion in the place
> The holiest that I knew of – my own soul.
> (*Prelude*, 378, 373–80)

It still remains a matter of conjecture as to whether Wordsworth left Plas yn Llan to make his way briefly back to France. If he did, he witnessed the execution of the radical journalist Antoine-Joseph Gorsas, and no doubt also became convinced of the impossibility of bringing out Annette and their child. If he did not, it is no less interesting that much later in his life he should have come to believe that he had indeed been present at the death of a revolutionary writer he much admired, and had experienced at first hand the way the political situation in France was being radicalised beyond recognition to most of its fellow-travelling British supporters.[8]

Wherever he had managed to get to in the meantime, Wordsworth's odyssey of 1793 brought him to spend Christmas of that
year with the Whitehaven branch of the family, where another
modest sum of money awaited him from Richard. Contact was
renewed with the Calvert family at Keswick, and another Hawkshead companion, John Spedding, provided temporary lodgings at
Armthwaite. In January 1794 he travelled on to Halifax to be
reunited with Dorothy in the home of Elizabeth and William Rawson (Elizabeth was their mother's cousin). No one had been more
staunchly supportive of Wordsworth at this time than Dorothy. She
had lived since her father's death for most of the time as companion to her uncle William and his wife at Forncett Rectory in Norfolk
(William's 'my uncle the clergyman'), and identified with her brother
as an exile, and he clearly valued her unfailing sympathy. The
development of a close alliance between the two was now made
further possible by the continuing goodwill of William Calvert.

In April Dorothy and her brother were offered Calvert's farmhouse
near Keswick at Windy Brow in which to stay. It was manifestly a
liberating experience for Dorothy, enabling her to write a spirited
defence of her Bohemian lifestyle to her aunt at Penrith. Some old
scores are being settled here:

> In answer to the second of these suggestions, namely that I may
> be supposed to be in an exposed situation, I affirm that I consider
> the character and virtues of my brother as a sufficient protection,
> and besides I am convinced that there is no place in the world in
> which a good and virtuous young woman would be more likely
> to continue good and virtuous than under the roof of these hon-
> est, worthy, uncorrupted people so that any guardianship beyond
> theirs, I should think altogether unnecessary.
>
> I cannot pass unnoticed that part of your letter in which you
> speak of my 'rambling about the country on foot'. So far from
> considering this as a matter of condemnation, I rather thought it
> would have given my friends pleasure to hear that I had courage
> to make use of the strength with which nature has endowed
> me. . . . (EY 117)

Windy Brow afforded Wordsworth an opportunity to work hard
on the 'Salisbury Plain' text; the chance to write was what he coveted
above all else. They remained there through May, after which Wordsworth returned to Whitehaven, then went back to Keswick. Raisley
Calvert, William Calvert's younger brother, had become enthusiastic

about Wordsworth's ambition to be a poet, and Wordsworth in his turn clearly became attached to Raisley, who was seriously ill with consumption. In October he offered to accompany him to Lisbon where the invalid would escape the rigours of a northern winter. In the event he was too ill to travel, and died at Penrith in January 1795.

1794 had seen a sustained effort by the Government to minimise the threat of radical political ideas taking hold in Britain. From 1793 on through 1794 a series of trials in Scotland resulted in the successful prosecution and savage sentencing of Scottish radicals; leading members of the radical London Corresponding Society were arrested in the spring of 1794, and eventually brought to trial; their acquittals did not come until October, by which time many a potential reformer had backed off in the face of such determined action, coupled with evidence of popular support for the war against France. The suspension of Habeas Corpus between 1794 and 1801 made arrest without trial possible, and it was news of this development in particular that prompted Richard Wordsworth to send his brother a warning. He clearly had no doubts about the extent of William's radical views, nor of the likelihood of them becoming known to the public: 'I hope you will be cautious in writing or expressing your political opinions. By the suspension of the Habeas Corpus Acts the ministers have great powers' (EY 121). In November 1795 both the Treasonable Practices Bill and the Seditious Meetings Bill further tightened Government control of the situation.[9]

Wordsworth appears to have lost none of his sense of involvement with the world of political action, though the latter part of 1794 had clearly been dominated by his concern for Raisley Calvert. Raisley's generosity to him in his will did not mean instant relief from financial difficulty, though 'Mr. Raisley Calvert's generous intentions', as Richard put it, were a heartening development (EY 132). If we are to believe *The Prelude*, so also was the news of July 1794 that Robespierre had been executed, hopefully paving the way for a moderation of Revolutionary violence in France.

Early in 1795, Wordsworth clearly felt the itch to get back to London; for one thing he was very conscious of his moral obligation to start earning. In May 1794 he began to discuss the possibility of publishing 'a monthly miscellany' with Mathews and another partner. In June he suggests calling it *The Philanthropist, a Monthly Miscellany*, develops an extensive discussion of its composition, and confesses to having no money of his own to use in getting it up and running; he signed himself 'your fellow labourer and friend'. In October, with Wordsworth as far as ever from becoming a 'labourer', Richard included a thinly veiled rebuke to his brother for his inactivity in the same letter in which he responded to Raisley Calvert's decision to assist his brother financially (EY 118; 125; 132).

The professed aims of *The Philanthropist* indicate the extent to which Wordsworth had by now become an enthusiastic disciple of William Godwin, whose *Enquiry Concerning Political Justice* had been published in Februrary 1793. Wordsworth was initially to grasp eagerly at Godwin's eloquent vision of truth winning its way by the power of reason into the collective mind of the Nation, thereby ensuring the dawning of a new era of justice and freedom. What proved so compelling to many of those committed to achieving political change was the lucid, abstract simplicity of Godwin's conviction that rational argument on behalf of truth must prove invincible. It was the essentially abstract nature of Godwin's philosophy that subsequently bred the disillusionment that so many – among them Wordsworth – were to experience as oppression and social injustice seemed to continue unabated through the decade.

It was as an enthusiastic Godwinian that Wordsworth was to return to London, intending once more to try and establish himself as a writer. Mathews had found work as a Parliamentary reporter. While Wordsworth sat by Raisley's sick-bed in November and December, he was writing to Mathews that he felt unsuited to the demands that journalism would make on his abilities, though he insisted on his determination to be in London 'as soon as the case of my friend is determined' (EY 137).

He eventually arrived in Februrary 1795, and re-established contact with a widening circle of radical writers and political thinkers; but as we have seen, this was hardly the time to be reckoning to make a living out of radical authorship. Besides his acquaintance with leading lights in radical political opinion, William Godwin, Thomas Holcroft, Dyer and Losh, Wordsworth drifted into the companionship of contemporaries who tended more to liberal than to radical views: Francis Wrangham, Basil Montagu and the sons of John Pinney, a Bristol merchant, John and Azariah. The politics of the Pinney family belonged essentially to a pre-Revolution tradition of eighteenth-century British dissidence; they were 'Old Whig' or 'Commonwealthman' in origin, vociferous in opposition to the war with the American Colonies in the 1770s, and grounded in the arguments of seventeenth-century English Republicanism.[10]

We have seen enough of Hawkshead School's familiarity with Dissent to know that something of this tradition breathed in the class-rooms there for those with ears to hear. In France Wordsworth certainly did encounter the Commonwealthman writings of Harrington, Sidney and others of their generation as the bedrock of Beaupuy's libertarian ideology.[11] The Commonwealthman literary tradition lived on in the libraries of London Corresponding Society members, and members of the Society for Constitutional Information. These texts informed the rhetoric of radical pamphleteers and poets, and they were to take their place among the 'biographical papers' Wordsworth proposed for *The Philanthropist*: 'those distinguished for their exertions in the cause of liberty, as Turgot, as Milton, Sydney, Machiavel, Beccaria etc. etc. etc.' (EY 125–6).

While he admired and sought out the company of the London radicals, notably William Godwin, it was with men like Basil Montagu, Francis Wrangham and the Pinneys that Wordsworth clearly found the companionship he badly needed, after a difficult period that had reached a grim and depressing climax with Raisley Calvert's death. Calvert had come to admire and believe in the young poet's talent; Wordsworth now evidently had a similar effect on his friends in London. This should serve as a reminder that while we are attempting to keep in touch with the many and various details of his life during these years, to know Wordsworth at the time was without doubt to be left in no doubt of his overriding ambition to be a poet. Montagu, who in many respects looks like a lame-duck replacement for Calvert in Wordsworth's affections, seems to have been profoundly impressed. The Pinneys appear to have recognised the need for Wordsworth to be given a chance to settle well away from London if he was to concentrate on his writing. They were able to offer him, with Dorothy, Racedown Lodge, an isolated house on the Dorset–Somerset border which the family infrequently used as a hunting lodge.

At Racedown, with his sister, with Basil Montagu's son whom they had agreed to educate, and with occasional visits from members of the London circle and other friends, Wordsworth was to take stock of his poetical and political progress; he was to move further into his commitment to poetry even as he began to make certain fundamental adjustments to his reading of his life in relation to the political events and personal relationships he had experienced. Following what amounted to a serious nervous breakdown not long after his arrival, he began to work his way towards a period of intense and prolific composition. This in turn led to his appearance in print as the joint (but still 'anonymous') author with Coleridge of *Lyrical Ballads* in 1798. He had become a revolutionary poet, rather than a radical politician.

In August 1795 Wordsworth was at Bristol awaiting the arrival of Dorothy. He met Joseph Cottle, the radical printer, who offered him ten guineas for a current work; he met Robert Southey and Coleridge. He was known for his political sympathies in these circles, and he was recognised as a poet. On 26 September Wordsworth, Dorothy and the young Basil Montagu arrived at Racedown.

It was possible now for him to envisage the reality of living a literary life. He had published works to his name; what was almost more to the point was that he had extensive notebook drafts of poetry waiting to be prepared for the press. He had acquired the reputation among a small but significant literary circle for being decidedly progressive in outlook; he therefore had encouragement, and he had somewhere to live. The narrative of 'Salisbury Plain' provided him with a framework for his way forward, and it channelled his course away from a political career that had scarcely broken the surface of his social life, towards a literary career that publication – however minimally – had made a reality. It is time therefore to review the literary achievement of these restless years.

THE POET

Written in France during 1792, *Descriptive Sketches* was dedicated to Robert Jones as a reminiscence of the walking tour the two men had made in 1790, 'two travellers plodding slowly along the road, side by side, each with his little knapsack of necessaries upon his shoulders' (DS 32). Inevitably Wordsworth's state of mind in 1792 was going to impinge on the memory of how he had seen the countryside and the Revolution two years before. He probably began to work on the poem very soon after arriving in France, but if, as Mark Reed suggests, the major period of composition took place after mid-May 1792, Wordsworth would have had the full benefit of Michel Beaupuy's enthusiastic homilies, and would have seen him depart to rejoin his regiment; he would also by this time have been forced to separate from Annette, following the Vallon family's anger at how the affair had gone.[12]

There was no overt intention on Wordsworth's part to use this

poem as a vehicle for a comparative analysis of his state of mind
in 1790 and 1792; his purpose was defined by a far more traditional loco-descriptive ambition, controlled in the main by his intention to produce a marketable product on his return to England. But
Goldsmith's 'The Deserted Village' had long since shown how conjuring up a remembered landscape could act as an effective vehicle
for social comment. *Descriptive Sketches* pointed Wordsworth in a
similar direction, creating in the process a poem that rehearses
the format of what in due course became the sophisticated basis of
'Tintern Abbey', a poem that turns on the juxtaposition of the Wordsworth of 1793, and of 1798.

The poetry of *Descriptive Sketches* is executed as an act of
memory; it is a series of revisitings within which is embedded a
sense of the power of the past to confirm the restless and painful
fluidity of the present:

> – The mind condemn'd, without reprieve, to go
> O'er life's long deserts with its charge of woe,
> With sad congratulation joins the train,
> Where beasts and men together o'er the plain
> Move on, – a mighty caravan of pain . . .
> 　　　　　　　　　(DS 56, 191–5)

For all Wordsworth's absorption of modern ideas about poetic diction learnt from John Scott, the language here remains that of stilted,
late-eighteenth-century sensibility. The poet/narrator seems to be
defined by the morbid genre Wordsworth has adopted, rather than
by his own experience of life.

As the poet matured, so the language evolved away from this
model, confirming the complex significance of memory as a central
feature of Wordsworth's creative instincts:

> 　　　　　that serene and blessed mood,
> In which the affections gently lead us on,
> Unitil, the breath of this corporeal frame,
> And even the motion of our human blood
> Almost suspended, we are laid asleep
> In body, and become a living soul.
> 　　　　　　　　　(LB 114, 42–7)

'Tintern Abbey' of 1798 emphasises the strength to be drawn from
the remembered landscape, rather than from the meaning of other

poems on similar subjects, while in the 'Elegiac Stanzas Suggested
by a Picture of Peele Castle' of 1805, Wordsworth's memory of the
impression the castle had made on him previously leads him to
reflect that the loss of his brother John (drowned in 1805) has in
some way acted as a stabilising experience, even though 'a power
is gone':

> So once it would have been, – 'tis so no more,
> I have submitted to a new control:
> A power is gone, which nothing can restore;
> A deep distress hath humanised my soul.
>   (*1807* 130, 33–6)

In both these later examples the poetry is driven by a determination to confront the manner in which an actual experience has
wrought a change on the writer's personality. In 1792 the poet has
neither the confidence nor the skills he subsequently attained, and
falls back on modish eastern imagery to describe the desert where
life is 'a mighty caravan of pain'; we are jostled by borrowed oriental images, and by an insistence on physical movement notably
absent from the other passages.

In a state of what at the time would certainly have been very real
fear, anxiety and personal guilt, the trauma of separation (from
Annette and Beaupuy) and impending loss, Wordsworth reaches
for the rhetoric of eighteenth-century sensibility to cast it into poetic
form:

> Farewell! those forms that, in thy noon-tide shade,
> Rest, near their little plots of wheaten glade;
> Those steadfast eyes, that beating breasts inspire
> To throw the 'sultry ray' of young Desire;
> Those lips, whose tides of fragrance come and go,
> Accordant to the cheek's unquiet glow;
> Those shadowy breasts in love's soft light arrayed,
> And rising, by the moon of passion sway'd.
>   (DS 52, 148–55)

Language such as this was to be radically purged of its derivative
delicacy in the course of the next five years; the poet of Alfoxden
and *Lyrical Ballads* gradually materialised as Wordsworth grimly

wrote his way closer to the articulation of his own story of personal guilt and political alienation through the 'Salisbury Plain' texts.

One consequence of this was that his commitment to poetry in the years from France to Racedown led him from a genteel eighteenth-century concept of a creative life lived in retirement, to one of creativity banished to the wilderness. At Racedown he could look back on what must have seemed many years of his life spent composing poetry in the context of solitary and furtive ramblings. Against this was set his conflicting drive to establish for himself a public life as a radical journalist, an ambition which of course bore no relation to the public life that others had been hoping he would achieve. All these things stood in need of urgent resolution when Racedown became possible, and Racedown was where he found himself able to set about reconstructing his shell-shocked poetic persona.

The poet he begins both to create and to discover in *Descriptive Sketches* was a solitary being who, in the latter part of the poem, turns away from personal, confessional utterance 'by the moon of passion sway'd', towards a public, political rhetoric which reaches potentially far beyond the generalisations that traditionally informed the loco-descriptive poems of his eighteenth-century forebears.

Liberty gained by Revolutionary France is described as threatened by reactionary powers – which would include, of course, Britain – who were determined to make war on a cause he believed sanctioned by Nature:

> rejoice, though Pride's perverted ire
> Rouze Hell's own aid, and wrap the hills on fire.
> Lo! from th'innocuous flames, a lovely birth!
> With its own virtues springs another earth:
> Nature, as in her prime, her virgin reign
> Begins, and Love and Truth compose her train;
> With pulseless hand, and fix'd unwearied gaze,
> Unbreathing Justice her still beam surveys ...
>   Oh give, great God, to Freedom's waves to ride
> Sublime o'er Conquest, Avarice and Pride,
> To break, the vales where Death with Famine scow'rs,
> And dark Oppression builds her thick-ribbed tow'rs
>   (DS 116, 780–95)

In 'The Discharged Soldier' the conflict between seeking a public for the poet, and his commitment to a reflective life drawing on wisdom born of solitude, is brought together in the single image of the poet. The poet's life offers a unified embodiment of this contradictory state, and expresses it in the one utterance describing his nocturnal encounter with the soldier. In *Descriptive Sketches* the poetry acts to emphasise the *distinction* between a public and a private retired persona. The final lines turn us firmly away from the public rhetoric, and portray the apprentice poet of 1790 and 1792 as a personality divided between two discourses, not yet in possession of a technique capable of depicting the contradictory priorities in a creatively unified relationship:

> To night, my friend, within this humble cot
> Be the dead load of mortal ills forgot,
> Renewing, when the rosy summits glow
> At morn, our various journey, sad and slow.
>   (DS 118, 810–13)

Though *Descriptive Sketches* is indicative of how much remained to be done for Wordsworth to achieve his full identity as a poet, it illustrates the extent to which he was already a poet whose commitment to Nature was defined in the context of his powerful instinct for political commitment.

The excursion across France of 1790 which the poem memorialises was, it should be remembered, effectively an act of rebellion. It was undertaken at a time when serious preparation for final exams should have been his priority; it was pursued against the advice of those who saw it as, to say the least, risky in the light of the political situation. The journey itself had been to a considerable degree inspired by William Coxe's travelogue, *Sketches of the Natural, Civil, and Political State of Swisserland* and its French translation by Ramond de Carbonnières. It was a popular book which extolled the liberty of the Swiss and thus provided a broader political context to Wordsworth's own private act of defiance.[13] As the circumstances of 1790 blend, as inevitably they do, with those of 1792, the poet is discovered as a figure who defies authority in what seems a public arena, while simultaneously describing his retreat into a world of picturesque solitude. It is the motif considered in Chapter 1, a theme that recurs repeatedly throughout his work; the motif of the public highway at night, invaded by the ghostly presence of the soldier complementing the poet's marginalisation.

We have in both poems a representation of the quintessentially Romantic *angst*: the poet seeks a public (this one urgently so in

1793), while wilfully plunging himself into exile. In Wordsworth's case he quits France to engage in a private battle with his guilt-laden conscience on Salisbury Plain; at the same time he publicly denounces 'Th'Oppressor's dungeon' not to a London audience or congregation, but to the emptiness of 'the huge plain', and without a publisher in sight; following which he goes to ground at Plas yn Llan, a period of obscurity which still confounds the most ardent of scholars (SP 38, 542; 22, 62).

Central to the structure of 'Salisbury Plain' is the female vagrant. In *An Evening Walk*, as we have already seen, she exists as a senti-mental stereotype who begins to assume a more focused political role, specifically through her anger. In 'Salisbury Plain' the aban-doned, bereaved woman naturally assumed additional personal significance for Wordsworth, weaving an important biographical, confessional element into his writing. For the apprentice poet, how-ever, there remained the need for literary models, and for Words-worth at this time, the primary model became without doubt James Beattie's *The Minstrel* (1771–4).

In *The Minstrel* Beattie is defining (and in the process beginning to redefine) the role of the poet. Everard H. King has argued that 'the informing principle' of the poem is 'the nature, function and scope of poetic autobiography', and with Beattie's fledgling poet, Edwin, as a role model – 'Song was his favourite and first pursuit'[14] – Wordsworth clearly does begin to transfer from *The Minstrel* to his 'Salisbury Plain' text themes that were to remain central to his work: the essentially isolated and alienated situation of the modern writer, the shift from a sense of cultural location in a progressive present to a notion of medievalism as spiritually volatile compared with the materialism of contemporary eighteenth-century society, and the risk that intense creativity might prove to be a step towards madness, 'Some deem'd him wondrous wise, and some believed him mad'.[15]

The 'poet' becomes a 'Minstrel' using the Spenserian stanza of Edmund Spenser's sixteenth-century mock medieval *The Faerie Queene*, and Edwin is warned off the practice of poetry unaccom-panied by political wisdom when a hermit directs him back out of the wilderness towards the more social existence of a 'comprehens-ive mind':

'Tis he alone, whose comprehensive mind,
From situation, temper, soil and clime
Explor'd a nation's various powers can bind,

And various orders, in one Form sublime
Of policy, that midst the wrecks of time,
Secure shall lift its head on high, nor fear
Th'assault of foreign or domestic crime,
While public faith, and public love sincere,
And industry and law maintain their sway severe.[16]

The contending demands of a social (political) life over against that
of the poet is a central theme of Beattie, and is developed in relation
to the poet's intense experiences of nature in a way that Wordsworth
evidently recognised as peculiarly pertinent to his own development. He held tightly to this narrative even as he appears to have
held on tightly to the text of *The Minstrel* throughout this period,
adopting the Spenserian stanza form for 'Salisbury Plain'.[17]

In 'Salisbury Plain' the way to the female vagrant directs the narrator along a lonely track that leads him away from a world where in
the past love and affection were to be found thriving in a pastoral
society, a place where poets might confidently feel they belonged.
The poem begins with an evocation of primitive society:

The hungry savage, 'mid deep forests, rouzed
By storms, lies down at night on unknown plains
And lifts his head in fear . . .

(SP 21, 3–5)

But the savage was fortunate because he knew no better, and was
therefore 'strong to suffer'. It is a far worse state to experience such
a cruel existence in the aftermath of a time when 'Refinement's genial influence' has flourished; to have been driven out of a 'genial'
world in consequence of a general decline in morality, the growth
of materialism, and corruption among the Nation's leaders:

the state
Of those who on the couch of Affluence rest
By laughing Fortune's sparkling cup elate,
While we of comfort reft by pain depressed,
No other pillow known than Penury's iron breast.

(SP 21, 21–8)

Wordsworth contrives an echo of Milton's Adam and Eve driven out
of Eden into a barren landscape, as the male traveller 'Measured each

painful step' on to Salisbury Plain.[18] He thus establishes a resolutely anti-pastoral setting for the poem in defiance of the dominant poetic conventions of the day, and of the conventional image of the poet; and he does this despite the fact that his critique of society is in many respects no different from that already expressed by Goldsmith, Langhorne, Beattie and Cowper.

The poem is 'new' to the extent that the figure of the poet is dramatically expelled from physical contact with a pastoral world, and thus loses any chance of contact with the kind of good people who might still be found there. There is no solemn hermit available on Wordsworth's Salisbury Plain as there was for Edwin on 'Scotia's mountains'; his story contains as yet no human or natural source of redemption, only evidence of ruin and despair. As the female vagrant's story unfolds, the narrator's own guilty fears are eclipsed by an indictment of the British political establishment and the heartless society it has bred.

Not far beneath this political surface, however, as the tale unfolds, we sense the workings of Wordsworth's autobiographical attempt to write himself closer to his own role as a poet, and to discover how that poet should relate to society in the wake of his experiences to date: Lowther, Cookson, Hawkshead and Cambridge, Beaupuy, Annette, his vocation to write, the pressure on him to find a career. As in the 'Discharged Soldier' fragment, he seeks to penetrate the issue by investigating his response to an encounter with a victim of social and political injustice. In 'Salisbury Plain' he uses a female vagrant, in the process lifting her out of an older tradition of poetry and modernising her function as he politicises her cultural significance.

It is of considerable importance for our understanding of the way in which Wordsworth's political views evolved that, as in *An Evening Walk*, her role is politicised in relation to the late 1770s and the American War. In Stephen Gill's Cornell edition of the 'Salisbury Plain' poems the fact that Wordsworth is reading the war with Revolutionary France in terms of the politics of war with the revolutionary American colonies some twenty years before is not made clear.[19] It ought to be because the issues involved in the two conflicts were very different, and that helps to explain to a significant degree why the radical politics of the 1790s were to present such difficulties to Wordsworth and many other would-be progressives.

Those lobbying for peace with the American colonies in the 1770s could reinforce their economic and political arguments with the moral one that held it was wrong to oppress and wage war on those who were effectively your kindred. The female vagrant of 'Salisbury Plain', her father, her husband and her children, are the victims of such a war. Initially they are the victims of the greed of the local landowner who turns the girl and her father off their smallholding. The woman's husband joins the army in order to be able to keep his family in a time of economic hardship. The evil of soldiering has been forced on these people, the state is guilty of making war; the blood of its victims is on its head. In Godwinian terms the soldier cannot be blamed for the evil into which he is coerced, living 'a cursed existence with the brood/That lap, their very nourishment, their brother's blood' (SP 31, 314–15).

The new radical populism of France, now threatening the British Constitution, demanded a radicalised reading of the notion of brotherhood. In 'Salisbury Plain' the idea of 'brotherhood' retained a semi-literal meaning, recalling the fact that the young soldier's enemies might well be his countrymen who had emigrated in search of a new life in a fairer society. As Wordsworth heaped personal tragedy upon personal tragedy in 'Salisbury Plain' – revising the poem to do so once he had arrived at Racedown – so the political ideology behind the narratives becomes less secure. As his commitment to the abstract idealism of Godwin became increasingly strained, so the poet who was being created by the poem became potentially more and more isolated, and more and more 'guilty'.

Racedown had come as a necessary retreat from life in London; a breathing space all had felt was needed. Initially Wordsworth appeared to use it as he had the chance of withdrawal to Windy Brow in 1794. Extensive revisions to 'Salisbury Plain' were put in hand, and publication was confidently discussed with Cottle early in 1796; but by the time the manuscript (which had circulated from Azariah Pinney to Cottle to Coleridge to Charles Lamb) was eventually returned unpublished to Wordsworth in June of that year when he was back in London on a visit, there is every indication that he no longer saw it as the means by which the public he was looking for would be found. For one thing, he clearly no longer had any confidence in the Godwinian politics that had inspired the poem and helped sustain his anger.

Over against what he now dismissed as Godwin's 'barbarous writing' (EY 170), he had the experience of Racedown as the provider of a relatively stable domestic *ménage* in stark contrast to the restless, fearful and traumatic days spent in France, and his subsequent wanderings across the English countryside. Now he shared his life and work with Dorothy in an increasingly interdependent relationship. The domestic circle was enhanced by the presence of young Basil Montagu, who engaged their time and patience in practical matters of education. From November 1796 to June 1797, Mary Hutchinson, a long-standing friend of the family and Wordsworth's future wife, came to stay at Racedown by way of a holiday after nursing her sister Peggy. Mary had been at Ann Birkitt's school in Penrith as an infant with Wordsworth, and they had met again as teenagers in the summer of 1787 in Penrith, when an early intimacy was probably established. At Racedown the possible future scenario of Dorothy, Mary and William living in a more intimate relationship presented itself, and the experience laid the foundations for what was to be the future ordering of the Grasmere household.

Within a day of Mary's departure, Coleridge arrived. Already an acquaintance, he now swiftly became one of the family, and his enthusiasm for Wordsworth's gifts as a poet began to play a major role in the way Wordsworth now steadily realigned his life around a revised concept of the relationship between his literary life and his social responsibilities.

Wordsworth had without doubt reached a point of emotional and psychological crisis with the completion of the 1795 revisions of what he retitled *Adventures on Salisbury Plain*. Weaving in additional Godwinian narratives to complement the initial female vagrant story had failed to exorcise the demons that haunted his own story; the guilt and confusion he himself felt in the aftermath of his experiences since leaving Cambridge overwhelm the latter stages of the 1795 text, and the sailor/protagonist is finally found guilty of murder and confronts the consequences of his actions on those he loved. Wordsworth writes here from the heart of a personal nightmare. No Godwinian theory of 'necessity' can mitigate his sense of personal responsibility:

> For him alternate throbbed his pulse and stopp'd;
> And when at table placed the bread he took
> To break it, from his faltering hands it dropp'd,
> While on those hands he cast a rueful look.
> His ears were never silent, sleep forsook
> His nerveless eyelids stiffened even as lead;
> All through the night the floor beneath him shook

And chamber trembled to his shuddering bed;
And oft he groan'd aloud, 'O God that I were dead'.

(SP 153, 784–92)

Godwin decreed the sailor not guilty; but Godwinian abstract
reasoning about the guilt of Nations driving the oppressed into
crime, and the power of the 'herculean mace/Of reason' (SP 38,
544–5) to dispel this curse, failed to convince. The sailor, like Wordsworth himself setting out from London with Calvert, had 'fled, a
vagrant since, the murderer's fate to shun' (SP 125, 99).

In the isolation of Racedown, set among the rolling Dorset hills,
Wordsworth began painfully to deal with the problem by dealing
with Godwin. Abstract, radical enlightenment political theory was
replaced by the recognition of the importance of the emotional impact
of domestic relationships kindled among the beauties of nature:

'Twas Summer and the sun was mounted high.
Along the south the uplands feebly glared
Through a pale steam, and all the northern downs
In clearer air ascending, shewed far off
Their surfaces with shadows dappled o'er
Of deep embattled clouds. Far as the sight
Could reach those many shadows lay in spots
Determined and unmoved, with steady beams
Of clear and pleasant sunshine interposed –
Pleasant to him who on the soft cool moss
Extends his careless limbs beside the root
Of some huge oak whose aged branches make
A twilight of their own, a dewy shade
Where the wren warbles while the dreaming man,
Half-conscious of that soothing melody,
With side-long eye looks out upon the scene,
By those impending branches made more soft,
More soft and distant.

(RC 43, 1–18)

This passage, written early in 1798 as an introduction to a new narrative Wordsworth began in the late spring of 1797, contrasts dramatically with the unredeemed bleakness of the 'Salisbury Plain' texts.
It presages his evocation of a pantheistic healing power instinct in
Nature, the source of a resolution for the tragic subject of the new
story, 'The Ruined Cottage'.

What most certainly had not disappeared from the landscape around Racedown was plentiful evidence of the hardships suffered by its inhabitants in time of war. The political issues remained to be dealt with, and they remained Wordsworth's major subject for poetry. The lyrical introduction to 'The Ruined Cottage' was added only after the story of Margaret, struggling to cope with the natural 'sorrow and distress' of poor harvests compounded by 'the plague of war' which had taken her husband from her, had been written (RC 53, 138; 136).

The female vagrant motif persists in Wordsworth's work, therefore, and with it his sense of the political issues involved; at the same time he steadily modified his former, rationalist reading of those issues. This is very clear from a fragment composed at the same time that 'The Ruined Cottage' was being written. It describes a baker's cart stopping at the door of a cottage because the horse has been accustomed to do so. As the inhabitants, including 'Five little ones', come out of 'their wretched hut', the baker cracks his whip, 'and you were left, as if / You were not born to live, or there had been / No bread in all the land'. It is a disturbing piece of writing, not least for the undertone of sadism that accompanies the image of dearth. We sense that a profoundly unnatural occurrence is being rendered all the more so because the horse is an agent of what is natural, and has spontaneously paused.

The poet is then addressed by a woman who says simply, 'that wagon does not care for us'. She means a great deal more, as the remaining lines explain:

> her look and voice
> Made up their meaning, and bespoke a mind
> Which being long neglected, and denied
> The common food of hope, was now become
> Sick and extravagant. . . .

This is without doubt a description of radical political fervour as a sickness, a sickness for which a heartless and cruel establishment is responsible, but a sickness nevertheless. The suffering, deprived individual is:

> driven to that state
> In which all past experience melts away,
> And the rebellious heart to its own will
> Fashions the laws of nature.

The driver's whip has made the horse bend 'to its own will'. The relationship of man to nature has been perverted; it is Godwinianly perverted, in that man's belief in his ability to achieve ultimate control of his destiny through his own perfected rationality of mind has denied a greater power to sustain and cherish humanity. This greater power is to be found in Nature; it is alive in the visionary summer landscape which eventually prefaced 'The Ruined Cottage', 'Pleasant to him who on the soft cool moss/ Extends his careless limbs . . .'. The fevered, furtive, radical response to the social injustice of the baker's cart that stops only to move on, will thrive if their is a denial of 'all past experience' (RC 463).

In other words, the modern radical belief in man's unaided ability to right all wrongs through the power of his own reason flies in the face of the lessons of history, which teach that violence inevitably follows such arrogance, and that violence begets violence and will create only greater misery.[20]

In a determined bid to gain a public for his work, and to develop his restorative vision, Wordsworth began a new and ambitious project in 1796. This was his tragedy, *The Borderers*. He had no doubt been encouraged to explore the dramatic genre by Coleridge, who had been invited by Sheridan to produce a tragedy of his own. Here, it seemed, with Coleridge's help, was an opportunity to earn money, to come before the public, and to write what in effect was to be the next chapter of his own autobiography:

> Let us suppose a young Man of great intellectual powers, yet without any solid principles of genuine benevolence. His master passions are pride and the love of distinction. He has deeply imbibed a spirit of enterprize in a tumultuous age. He goes into the world and is betrayed into a great crime. (*Borderers* 62, 1–5)

This is how Wordsworth began the essay which accompanied the first version of *The Borderers*. It refers to the central figure of the play, Rivers (who is renamed Oswald in the revised 1842 version); it refers in part to Wordsworth, who is also represented by the character of Mortimer, 'an amiable young man' whom Rivers seeks to corrupt and destroy. The outcome of the play is bleak, Rivers has his way, and Mortimer's final speech is reminiscent of the Salisbury Plain wanderer, doomed to suffer, 'A thing by pain and thought compelled to live,/ Yet loathing life' (*Borderers* 294 11.273–4). Yet Wordsworth's own riposte is now clear; the analysis of the evil Rivers is a critique of Godwin himself, arrogant in his self-contained world of so-called moral fixities, bereft of true feeling for others:

> He presses truth and falsehood into the same service. He looks at society through an optical glass of a peculiar tint: something of the forms of objects he takes from objects, but their colour is exclusively what he gives them, it is one, and it is his own. Having indulged a habit, dangerous in a man who has fallen, of dallying with moral calculations, he becomes an empiric. He disguises from himself his own malignity by assuming the character of a speculator in morals and one who has the hardihood to realize his speculations. (*Borderers* 65, 76–84)

Mortimer is beguiled by this arrogant and speciously rational thinker into causing the death of the aged, blind Baron Herbert, the frail representative of political stability in the medieval world of political instability in which Wordsworth sets the play.[21] In probably the best-known moment of the drama, he is restrained from murdering Herbert by seeing the likeness of the old man's daughter in his face, and by catching a glimpse of a star through a crevice in the roof of the cell in which he lies. Mortimer, in other words, has been prevented from seeing Herbert in isolation, or solely as Rivers has presented him; he is the father of the woman he loves, and the healing effect of realising this familial relationship is sealed by an intimation of the wonders of nature, 'and by the living God, I could not do it –' (*Borderers* 168, 291).

But eventually Rivers'/Godwin's determination to 'fashion the laws of nature ... to [their] own will' ('The Baker's Cart'), or to look at 'society' as an 'object ... through an optical glass of a peculiar tint' ensuring that its 'colour is exclusively what he gives them' (*Borderers*), brings Mortimer to the state Wordsworth himself had been in when ready to extol regicide in his *Letter to Llandaff*.

In a scene which closely parallels Hamlet's discovery of Claudius at prayer, Mortimer decides to destroy Herbert not by the sword, but by abandoning him to the heath. Interestingly Herbert at this point describes himself as 'Like a Mendicant/Whom no one comes to meet' (*Borderers* 198 11.92–3), creating an encounter reminiscent of that which had taken place in Wordsworth's youth between himself and the discharged soldier. But Mortimer is here the unredeemed Wordsworth, and leaves Herbert to starve. The point is that sentence has been passed, and now there are no excuses; Mortimer and

Wordsworth can part company, Mortimer bearing Wordsworth's guilt upon his back.

Hazlitt recalled that when in London in 1795, Wordsworth had advised a young student to 'throw away his books of chemistry and read Godwin on necessity'.[22] Two years later we find Wordsworth concluding his Introduction to *The Borderers* with what he intends to be the final nail in the coffin of an evil and dangerous doctrine:

> We insensibly suppose that a criminal action assumes the same form to the agent as to ourselves. We forget that his feelings and his reason are equally busy in contracting its dimensions and pleading for its necessity. (*Borderers* 68, 183–6)

In recognising Wordsworth/Mortimer as guilty, and in delineating the causes of guilt through the sophistry of Godwin/Rivers/Wordsworth, Wordsworth was attempting to free himself in order to take the next decisive step forward in his literary career. It began with the fragments we have already begun to consider, and continued in the coming months with his move to Alfoxden and the development of his relationship with Coleridge. It blossomed in the production of *Lyrical Ballads* and the plan for a major, epic work of public poetry.

4

Alfoxden

By the time Wordsworth made the move from Racedown to Alfoxden he had found a public; but it was a public defined in a very particular and limited sense. The nature of the readership he had secured for his work was to have a profound and lasting effect on the way he subsequently developed as a poet. It consisted of a small coterie of primarily literary but also political friends and acquaintances that linked London with Bristol and his native Cumberland. Two members of this group could be said to have achieved public reputations in the wider sense; they were Robert Southey and Samuel Taylor Coleridge. Coleridge's *Poems on Various Subjects* had sold out in its year of publication, 1796; and it was Coleridge who was clearly becoming the most seriously impressed with what he had seen of Wordsworth's poetry.

What followed now appears to have been the discovery on the part of both men that each had qualities they could admire in the other to the point of wishing to prolong and deepen their friendship. From an acquaintance, therefore, there rapidly developed a much stronger bond rooted in the business of defining and living a literary life appropriate to their times.

In early spring 1797, Wordsworth was in Bristol for ten days, during which time he visited a number of his friends. Basil Montagu had been visiting his son and was being put on a coach back to London; among others, Wordsworth then called on James Losh and Joseph Cottle; he also met John Wedgwood, who was taking a particular interest in Coleridge's literary career. Before returning to Racedown, Wordsworth sought out Coleridge in his recently acquired cottage in Nether Stowey, at the foot of the Quantock hills in Somerset.

Coleridge, struggling among other things with a difficult marriage, was describing himself at this time (to Cottle) as living in the depths of despair.[1] What seems to have happened at Nether Stowey was the eruption of an animated, inspiring discussion of all things literary, and not a few things political. In the wake of this session, Coleridge wrote to Cottle on the subject of composing an epic poem. No doubt in their conversation, the two men had worked through various

69

versions of the purpose of the literary life, and here lay the foundation of what would provide Wordsworth with his long-term vocational vision.

They parted on this occasion with a mutually renewed sense of
purpose, Coleridge probably more so than Wordsworth. It was
Coleridge who subsequently sought Wordsworth out, arriving at
Racedown in early June 1797, eagerly determined to renew the process of mutual encouragement. He then hastily arranged for William
and Dorothy to pay a return visit to Nether Stowey. They arrived
early in July and were joined in the tiny cottage by Charles Lamb.
The party overflowed into the garden of Coleridge's neighbour and
benefactor, Thomas Poole.

This was Wordsworth's 'public', hand-picked, eager to be impressed, peculiarly sensitive to the circumstances that brought
them all together. On the one hand, they were very conscious of the
burning social and political issues of the day, yet they were equally
absorbed in their private, enchanted world of poetry and ideas.
W. H. Auden was to reflect on a not dissimilar situation; here perhaps is Poole's garden, become a fragile sanctuary revisited in the
1930s:

The creepered wall stands up to hide
The gathering multitudes outside
  Whose glances hunger worsens;
Concealing from their wretchedness
Our metaphysical distress,
  Our kindness to ten persons.[2]

The coterie of 1797–8 may very well be considered as a group
of people thankfully transported from the rigours of daily life into
an idyllic world of close companionship, filling the shady spots
of Poole's summer garden with words, ideas, or reflective, unem-
barrassed silences; or wandering off together across the wooded
slopes of the Quantock hills. Coleridge captured the magic of it in
his poem 'This Lime Tree Bower my Prison':

                    Now, my friends emerge
Beneath the wide wide Heaven – and view again
The many-steepled tract magnificent
Of hilly fields and meadows, and the sea,
With some fair bark, perhaps, whose sails light up
The slip of smooth clear blue betwixt two isles

Of purple shadow! Yes! they wander on
In gladness all. . . .³

Needless to say, this is not a wholly accurate picture of the way
it was. The view in this poem is seen from the lime tree bower in
Poole's garden, and that is because Coleridge is in part memorialising
an act of carelessness on the part of his wife that kept him at home
when the rest of the party had gone off walking on the hills.⁴ The
emotional force of the poem owes much to our awareness that its
author has been denied the immediate restorative effects of what
was literally, of necessity, an imagined landscape. In the end it is
the imagination, fed by nature, that promises to rescue the stranded
poet:

'Tis well to be bereft of promised good,
That we may lift the soul, and contemplate
With lively joy the joys we cannot share.
(11.65–7)

By the same token we may well consider that the group as a whole
was engaged in conjuring up a world of philosophical retirement in
the midst of an awareness of its absence, or at best its illusory and
capricious nature.

Wordsworth brought to Poole's garden not only his own keen
experience of the fragility of human happiness in a hostile world,
but also his constant readiness to offer practical assistance to fellow-
sufferers. To the list we know of – William Mathews, Raisley Calvert,
Basil Montagu – there was now a major addition. Coleridge, 'poor
Coleridge': brilliant, creative, charismatic, yet teetering on the brink
of black depression, mismatched with Sara, thanks to a hasty and ill-
thought-out scheme to set up an earthly paradise in North America
along with Robert Southey.⁵ Coleridge embodied precisely the kind
of cause William and Dorothy felt well qualified to understand, and
they were eagerly prepared to devote their energies to his welfare.

With this in mind, a further *frisson* to the Nether Stowey experience for the Wordsworths would have been the condition of Charles
Lamb. Lamb was still deeply shocked by the recent murder of his
mother by his sister in a bout of insanity. He had sat with the others
listening to Wordsworth reading his newly finished poem, 'Lines
Left Upon a Seat in a Yew Tree'. He subsequently confessed to its

timely therapeutic power, and wrote to Coleridge asking for a copy
of it. There was certainly plenty here to take the Wordsworths out
of themselves, and when it became apparent that with Poole's help
they need not return to Racedown, but might instead rent nearby
Alfoxden House, they did so at once.[6]

As Dorothy described it to Mary Hutchinson, Racedown was
beautiful:

> There is everything here; sea, woods wild as fancy ever painted,
> brooks clear and pebbly as in Cumberland, villages so romantic;
> and William and I, in a wander by ourselves, found out a seques-
> tered waterfall in a dell formed by steep hills covered by full-
> grown timber trees. (EY 189)

But it could also be bleak and cruel, as William chose to describe it
to William Mathews:

> We do not see a soul. Now and then we meet a miserable peasant
> in the road or an accidental traveller. The country people here are
> wretchedly poor; ignorant and overwhelmed with every vice that
> usually attends ignorance in that class, viz – lying and picking
> and stealing etc. etc. (EY 154)

It was at Racedown that Wordsworth finally gave way to the pressures of a life where little seemed to have gone right. Even the
fruits of Raisley Calvert's legacy were now threatened by the need
to repay what he had been loaned to finance his trip to France.[7]

Wordsworth's depression had in turn put Dorothy under intense
pressure. The winter of 1796 had been a cruelly cold one, and hedged
about by money worries and by constant anxiety for the brother she
had effectively championed against the authority figures of the family circle (her behaviour since Windy Brow had established her as
a fellow Bohemian), she became very ill. Racedown had represented
a tremendous step forward in the lives that both brother and sister
felt they wanted to live; but it had equally been a time of anxiety
and uncertainty.

While much of that anxiety did not disappear with their removal
to Alfoxden in July, the summer of that year finds Wordsworth entering on what was to be a remarkable year for composition, a period
generally understood to be one of inspired creativity when his work
took on a new, distinctive quality, and the future direction of his

literary life became firmly embedded in his mind. We can begin to appreciate what was happening if we look in particular at the changes that took place in the way Wordsworth depicted nature at this time, and also at the way he began to vary his narrative formulae from the 'Salisbury Plain' texts towards the composition of poems like *Peter Bell*, 'The Thorn' and 'The Idiot Boy'.

Photographic landscape description had never been Wordsworth's primary concern. The influence of the introverted, confessional qualities of the new writing of his time led him to make use of landscape as a means of charting the changing states of his mind. The visible reality of nature is therefore charged with an intangible quality of restlessness; that which is seemingly fixed, dependable, knowable, becomes potentially unpredictable, as fickle as the mind under pressure, likely to swing from elation to depression. The dominant landscape of the Racedown poetry manifestly reflects a depressive state of mind; it is hostile, barren, bleak, a place haunted by despair and threatened by madness. It should be stressed that this is a mental landscape. Only secondly is it Salisbury Plain, or the view from Racedown at its bleakest, loneliest worst:

> I cross'd the dreary moor
> In the clear moonlight; when I reached the hut
> I enter'd in, but all was still and dark –
> Only within the ruin I beheld
> At a small distance, on the dusky ground,
> A broken pane which glitter'd in the moon
> And seemed akin to life. There is a mood,
> A settled temper of the heart, when grief,
> Become an instinct, fastening on all things
> That promise food, doth like a sucking babe
> Create it where it is not. From this time
> I found my sickly heart had tied itself
> Even to this speck of glass.
> (RC 468, 1–13)

This extract from a longer fragment, headed 'Incipient Madness' by Wordsworth, is redolent of the Racedown mood and landscape. There is a desolation in the prosaic 'when I reached the hut', there is a disturbing undercurrent of sadism in the linked images of the broken pane of glass and the sucking babe; that which is alive, young and vulnerable is juxtaposed to that which only seemed akin to life.

Unlikely as it may seem, this poetry, along with the 'Baker's Cart' lines, constituted the first stages of the new project that was destined eventually to steer Wordsworth off the 'dreary moor' towards the landscape depicted at the end of the previous chapter, 'Pleasant to him who on the soft cool moss/ Extends his careless limbs beside the root/ Of some huge oak' (RC 43, 10–12). The new narrative, 'The Ruined Cottage', had progressed to a significant length at the time of Coleridge's visit to Racedown. Before long it was being considered as the basis for the great poem of the age which Coleridge and Wordsworth convinced themselves it was Wordsworth's job to write.

The narrative pattern of former years was still firmly stamped on the surface of the story. The central character, Margaret, repeated the familiar journey from domestic happiness to abandonment and penury and eventually death:

> Yet still
> She loved this wretched spot, nor would for worlds
> Have parted hence; and still that length of road
> And this rude bench one torturing hope endeared,
> Fast rooted at her heart, and here, my friend,
> In sickness she remained, and here she died,
> Last human tenant of these ruined walls.
>
> (RC 72, 522–8)

The difference between this and the 'Salisbury Plain' narratives lay primarily in the emergence of a new kind of narrator, whose job it was to explain and resolve the tragedy as best he could. Previously the storyteller's state of mind reflected that of the female vagrant; both were victims. In 'The Ruined Cottage' Wordsworth registers a significant shift in his sense of himself by giving the narration to a wise and philosophic wanderer, a pedlar, whose appearance effectively moves Wordsworth's construction of his own literary life on into a new chapter.

The circumstances of Margaret were no less bleak than those of the Salisbury Plain outcasts; the narrator, however, is able to dissociate himself from the haunted, guilt-ridden victims of the story. This was an exorcism already partly realised in the separation of himself from Mortimer in *The Borderers*; it now further evolved through the Pedlar, who was being written into 'The Ruined Cottage' manuscript as the Alfoxden period gets under way. It was this evolving text that Wordsworth – with Coleridge at his elbow – came to view as the basis for the epic poem he was destined to produce. Wordsworth's personal reclamation from despair was potentially a public as well as a private matter. A way had to be found to project his experience into the public arena, the aim being nothing less than the reclamation of a nation shaken by political unrest, war and hardship.

In March 1798 Wordsworth wrote to James Tobin that he had composed 1300 lines of poetry 'in which I contrive to convey most of the knowledge of which I am possessed' (EY 212). This project he called *The Recluse*, 'a poem which I hope to make of considerable utility' (EY 214). Nine hundred lines of *The Recluse* were supplied by the revised 'Ruined Cottage' of March 1798. The remainder was supplied by 'The Old Cumberland Beggar' and 'Old Man Travelling' written up in the course of 1797–8, lines entitled 'A Night Piece', and the 'Discharged Soldier', lines with which we are already familiar.

If we turn now to Kenneth R. Johnston's commentary on these foundation *Recluse* poems, the way in which Wordsworth's relentless autobiographical drive was being bent towards a formal, public poetic intention at this time becomes clear:

> They are all blank verse narratives with strong meditative overtones, and can easily be imagined as a connected set of 'pictures' or 'views' of Man, Nature, and Society. Moreover, they all follow the rudimentary plot which Wordsworth, left to his own devices at this time, could hardly vary: walking along a road, he meets somebody who tells him his or her life-story. Since these life-stories have little plot themselves, other than the wearing facts of life's constant losses (of love, family, welfare, faith, hope, and sanity), the true plot of the first *Recluse* poems, as of many of the lyrical ballads Wordsworth composed subsequently in 1798, becomes the effort of an external narrator to respond adequately to a tale he's been told and now retells.[8]

The external narrator has been told a tale; essentially it is Wordsworth's own story, a very real part of which was taken up with 'walking along a road', meeting somebody, exchanging views. The 'adequate' response is one that will to some degree reassure the listener that life's 'constant losses' are justified. The *Recluse* poems begin to work towards a narrative of redemption, and here we have the theme that marked the poetry composed during Wordsworth's brief time at Alfoxden: the *Recluse* poetry, *Lyrical Ballads*, and *Peter Bell*.

The poem that had so moved Charles Lamb, 'Lines Left upon a Seat in a Yew Tree', encapsulates the change that Wordsworth was now documenting. The narrative in this case is based on the story of a Lakeland clergyman, William Braithwaite of Satterhow:

> He was one who own'd
> No common soul. In youth, by genius nurs'd,
> And big with lofty views, he to the world
> Went forth, pure in his heart, against the taint
> Of dissolute tongues, 'gainst jealousy, and hate,
> And scorn, against all enemies prepared,
> All but neglect: and so, his spirit damped
> At once, with rash disdain he turned away,
> And with the food of pride sustained his soul
> In solitude.
>
>   (LB 48–9, 12–21)

The genesis of the poem is unclear. Parts of it may date back to the Hawkshead years (1786–7); but it was composed in the main between February and July 1797 at Racedown.

Braithwaite is beyond redemption; he sinks into a mood of morbid regret at his failure to attain public recognition. There, but for the grace of Coleridge, Dorothy, and a small coterie of supportive readers, goes Wordsworth. In the final paragraph of the poem the poet of *Lyrical Ballads* is able to separate himself from a man who felt the world owed him widespread adulation, a man who is left with only envy 'to think that others felt/ What he must never feel':

> O, be wiser though!
> Instructed that true knowledge leads to love,
> True dignity abides with him alone
> Who, in the silent hour of inward thought,
> Can still suspect, and still revere himself,
> In lowliness of heart.
>
>   (11.39–40; 55–60)

This is the autobiography of an artist whose self-respect has survived neglect, and who is now turning the experience into a positive credo.

The danger, however, is that the artist who has stressed the virtues of a life of 'retirement', albeit without bitterness, will find it hard to make the move into a more public role should the opportunity arise. The wisdom of the Pedlar in 'the Ruined Cottage' is presented as a summation of the natural law; that is to say, it is available in democratic fashion to all who take time to reflect on nature. In reality, Wordsworth is writing for a coterie he knows will reflect on nature in the required manner, and *against* a wider reading public he considers as yet unenlightened.

The peopling of these poems is equally problematic. The central figures of Wordsworth's poetry frequently display an aura of potential dissidence, running against the political grain of an establishment which has good reason to fear the anger of the dispossessed and starving; but at the same time they can be determinedly lowly. The poetry of 1798 introduces us to people who for a variety of reasons have been driven to the margins of society where they seem destined to remain. They exist in their twilight world as subject matter for the informed and sensitive poet who is on hand to retrieve them for his readership. Wordsworth becomes the go-between capable of putting such people once more in touch with a desensitised society. Writing for a sympathetic coterie, itself at one remove from that society, Wordsworth was able to create and sustain that idea of his work. Exile becomes emphatically the right place to be; but there then follows a consequent ambiguity about the position of the poet sage whose task it is to go public; building the bridge from coterie to 'common reader' was a task that in Wordsworth's case was destined to remain unfinished until *The Recluse* (the poem intended as his major public work) had been abandoned.

Wordsworth's initial mouthpiece for *The Recluse*, the Pedlar, is no ordinary mendicant; this fact in itself highlights the problematic nature of what he was attempting. The Pedlar is heir to a sophisticated dissenting intellectual tradition that includes Erasmus Darwin, Joseph Priestley, James Hutton, radical French thinking and Unitarian theology as well as those tales of intrepid Quakers and hedge priests told to the Hawkshead schoolboy.[9] An essential ingredient for this conception had been supplied by Coleridge: pantheism. This offered a theological corollary to political democracy in the conviction that God existed organically throughout creation; there was but one life, and in the permeation of all things by that one life lay an implicit challenge to privilege. Where this equalitarian conviction was particularly important for Wordsworth was that it questioned the autonomy of reason. Godwinian reform in its most radical formulation was founded in rational analysis , the fruits of which were to be made manifest in society through appropriately reformed institutions and rewritten laws.

In marked contrast, Pantheism recognised subtle mystical forces at work, frequently beyond the limited scope of Man's intellect; such forces resisted rationalisation. The value of feelings, of emotions, of sorrow or pity in the face of tragedy, was brought to the fore in contrast to anger at the impotence of individuals to set injustice right through direct political action. Stoical patience, a trust in the underlying, ultimately levelling powers of nature to fulfil its proper ends, was thus encouraged.

Wordsworth would have us believe that the Pedlar intuits such truths from his close proximity to nature:

> He was only then
> Contented, when with bliss ineffable
> He felt the sentiment of being, spread
> O'er all that moves, & all that seemeth still
> O'er all which lost beyond the reach of thought
> And human knowledge to the human eye
> Invisible, yet liveth to the heart
> O'er all that leaps & runs, & shouts, & sings
> Or beats the gladsome air, o'er all that glides
> Beneath the wave, yea in the wave itself
> And mighty depth of waters. Wonder not
> If such his transports were for in all things
> He saw one life & felt that it was joy
> One song they sang and it was audible
> Most audible then when the fleshly ear,
> O'ercome by grosser prelude of that strain,
> Forgot its functions, & slept undisturbed.
> These things he had sustained in solitude
> Even till his bodily strength began to yield
> Beneath their weight.
>
> (RC 355, 1–20)

The Pedlar is the philosopher Wordsworth aspires to become. Indeed, sitting in Poole's garden with Lamb hanging on his every word, sensing Coleridge's need for him, he could perhaps be pardoned for beginning to persuade himself that he was indeed entering on a new chapter of his life as a recluse poet, strangely able to reach out and touch the world with his 'one life' conviction while remaining a disembodied voice. As the passage above illustrates, he was certainly exploring ways of describing this phenomenon:

One song they sang and it was audible
Most audible then when the fleshly ear,
O'ercome by grosser prelude of that strain,
Forgot its functions, and slept undisturbed.

The 'grosser prelude' to the one life is to be found in all the longer pieces preceding this; in *An Evening Walk* and *Descriptive Sketches*, in the Salisbury Plain poems and *The Borderers* Wordsworth journeys wearily towards this sublime moment of realisation (one eye on his much-needed readership), to discover in the process that sleep, a loss of control by the 'fleshly ear' is a condition of such a 'transport'.

It is the same paradox stated at the outset in 'The Discharged Soldier'. The public road; but the public road at night. And those lines were of course written at this time, and like the 'one life' passage on the Pedlar, they found their way eventually into *The Prelude*.

It is important to remember that the narrative structure of 'The Ruined Cottage' maintains a distinction between the philosopher of the pantheistic one life, and the pupil/poet. This is consistent with the model provided by Beattie's *Minstrel*, where the young poet is subjected to the tutelage of an elderly, bardic hermit. The effect of this is to place at one remove the ideal of a humble, philosophic existence; it is an inspiration, a source of resolution for the young aspirant who retains the option of life in a less severely anchorite mode, and the possibility still of an active political role.

What is most evident from his draft lines on the Pedlar is the way Wordsworth is firmly establishing a position in opposition to Godwin, and affirming a positive belief in a mystical explanation for life in a seemingly unfair world. The medium for grasping this is nature via poetry. It was the establishment of this as a basis for thought – a natural progression from the earlier work – that effectively freed Wordsworth to produce his other two major achievements of this year: the poetry of *Lyrical Ballads*, and the narrative poem, *Peter Bell*. In both cases the autobiographical element is evident throughout, but the poems float more freely from the controlling, obviously personal narrative element of *An Evening Walk*, *Descriptive Sketches*, 'Salisbury Plain', and *The Borderers*.

The final poem for *Lyrical Ballads* was to be 'Tintern Abbey', in which the Wordsworth of 1798 looked back to the Wordsworth

of 1793, walking off Salisbury Plain and on up into Wales by way
of the Wye valley. For *Peter Bell*, begun in April 1798, Wordsworth
returned to the same period, recalling his encounter with an itiner-
ant seller of pots at Builth Wells:

> The countenance, gait and figure of Peter, were taken from a wild
> rover with whom I walked from Builth, on the river Wye, down-
> wards nearly as far as the town of Hay. He told me strange stor-
> ies. . . . (PB 3–4)

Between *Peter Bell* and 'Tintern Abbey', composed in July of the
same year after his departure from Alfoxden, we can see Wordsworth repeatedly attempting to gauge how he had changed in the
course of the past five years.

Peter Bell provides a particularly valuable insight into how his
approach to the task could vary. The Prologue describes the poet
attempting to make his escape from the real world by floating off
through the clouds in a little boat shaped like the crescent moon
(PB 44, 7). The style is frivolous (in marked contrast to 'Tintern
Abbey'), 'The world for my remarks and me/ Will not a whit the
better be' (PB 48, 43–4). The poet is brought back to earth by the
need to keep his promise to tell some children the story of Peter
Bell:

> 'Oh here he is!' cried little Bess;
> She saw me at the garden door.
> 'Oh here he is!' cried Mistress Swan,
> And all at once around me ran
> Full nine of them or more.
> (PB 58, 141–5)[10]

Everything suggests a lack of seriousness. From 1798 this becomes a characteristic Wordsworthian posture from which he seeks
to deliver a profoundly serious statement. Meeting Wordsworth for
the first time in May 1798, William Hazlitt noted his 'convulsive
inclination to laughter about the mouth',[11] and in *Peter Bell* we can
see how much of that humour was channelled into self-parody. The
Prologue parodies the serious, public poet Wordsworth would be,
leaving him with a handful of children and a few long-suffering
adults to entertain with a 'tale':

And I, as well as I was able
On two poor legs to my stone table
Limped on with some vexation.
                    (PB 56, 138–40)

Several of the *Lyrical Ballads*, notably 'Simon Lee', 'Anecdote for Fathers', and 'We Are Seven' (noted as a cause for mirth among the coterie) are built on self-parody and rely on a degree of appropriate knowingness on the part of the reader. After the gritty seriousness of 'The Ruined Cottage' and 'The Pedlar', *Peter Bell* explodes into a parodic (but equally serious) exercise on the same theme.

The character of Peter Bell is a satanic, unredeemed version of the Pedlar. With its roots in an encounter of 1793, the poem remains biographically consistent with the way in which Wordsworth saw himself in 1798. Peter has a long and painful journey to make from selfish inhumanity towards love. He is indeed a parodic sketch of the Wordsworth described in 'Tintern Abbey', fleeing through the Wye valley, unaware of the power of nature about him. Like the Pedlar, he has spent his life amid nature. The Pedlar 'wandered far, much did he see of men/ Their manners, their enjoyments and pursuits/ Their passions and their feelings, chiefly those/ Essential and eternal in the heart' (RC 359, 190–3). Of Peter likewise we learn 'Sure never man like him did roam', but by contrast:

As well might Peter in the Fleet
Have been fast bound, a begging debtor;
He travelled here, he travelled there,
But Peter never was a hair
In heart or head the better.
                    (PB 62–4, 205–10)

Peter thus personifies the unredeemed aspect of nature itself; he encapsulates all the senseless and unfeeling brutality of the natural world:

A savage wildness round him hung
As of a dweller out of doors;
In his whole figure and his mien
A savage character was seen
Of mountains and of dreary moors.

To all the unshaped half human thoughts
Which solitary Nature feeds
'Mid summer's storms or winter's ice,
Had Peter joined whatever vice
The cruel city breeds.

                    (PB 68, 266–75)

This is clearly not the same as the young Wordsworth remembered
in 'Tintern Abbey'; but having said that, in certain important ways
there remains common ground. Peter's 'savage wildness' and 'savage character' are present to some degree in the man 'Flying from
something that he dreads . . . in the hour/ Of thoughtless youth'
(LB 118, 72, 90–1).

When Peter discovers a short-cut to his destination it is difficult
not to see the narrative as an autobiographically explicit account of
Wordsworth's belief that Godwinian philosophy had signposted a
false short-cut to the goal of a perfect society. Recognising the familiar, pervasive imagery of the road, we read how Peter is tempted
away from it, and becomes more and more angry as the newly
chosen path fails to live up to its promise. Support for indulging in
a reading of this kind comes from Hazlitt, who recalled Wordsworth's manner of reading *Peter Bell*: 'Whatever might be thought
of the poem, "his face was a book where men might read strange
matters," and he announced the fate of his hero in prophetic tones'
(PB 5). This was a characteristically 'serious' poem, which is to say,
the 'prophetic tones' rub shoulders with a 'convulsive inclination to
laughter' where fear, nervousness and delight are all intertwined.

At first it seems as though Peter's intended short-cut has proved
successful in an unforeseen way. He discovers an ass standing by
the river on its own; a useful beast easily stolen. But the ass refuses
to move, and eventually collapses by the river bank. In the process
of beating the animal Peter receives a shock:

Yet in a fit of dastard rage
He stooped the ass's neck to seize
And in the clear deep stream below
He spies an ugly sight, I trow,
Among the shadows of the trees.

Is it the shadow of the moon?
Is it the shadow of a cloud?
Is it a gallows there pourtrayed?

Is Peter of himself afraid?
Is it a coffin or a shroud?
(PB 88, 526–35)

It is in fact the drowned body of the ass's owner, whom Peter eventually proceeds to fish out:

He pulls, he pulls, and pulls again,
And he whom the poor ass had lost,
The man who had been four days dead,
Head-foremost from the river's bed
Uprises like a ghost.
(PB 98, 651–55)

Both Peter and *Peter Bell* are designed to represent the extreme opposite from the Pedlar and 'The Ruined Cottage' (the infant *Recluse*). Peter, like the Pedlar, encounters hardship, deprivation and death. Unlike the Pedlar, however, he is locked into a world of wholly self-centred wickedness:

He was a carl as wild and rude
As ever hue and cry pursued,
As ever ran a felon's race.
(PB 66, 243–5)

Despite his proximity to nature it is a life during which 'Nature ne'er could touch his heart' (PB 66, 261). In the back of Wordsworth's mind will have been his own anger and despair of earlier years. In *The Prelude* he was later to describe how his judgement in the early 1790s suffered from a lack of sensitivity to nature and an over-wrought enthusiasm for rationalist political thinking. In the poetry of late Racedown and Alfoxden he begins assiduously to carve out an autobiography appropriate to that reading. He is, among other things, still dealing with the memory of Annette. Nothing can erase the guilt, but a convincing explanation of how it came about might help to salve the wound. Wordsworth at his most despicable is therefore reflected in the Peter Bell who is cruelly unfaithful to 'A sweet and playful Highland Girl' (PB 130, 1138).

The turning-point comes with the discovery of the drowned man. This incident originated in an experience he later described in *The Prelude*, when as a schoolboy he witnessed the recovery of the body of a drowned man from Esthwaite Water:

At length, the dead man, 'mid that beauteous scene
Of trees and hills and water, bolt upright
Rose with his ghastly face, a spectre shape
Of terror even....

(*Prelude* V 176, 470–3)

There is no mistaking the way that, as *Peter Bell*, 'The Ruined Cottage'
and 'The Pedlar' intertwine, they are themselves being merged with
memories which link childhood to the momentous, guilt-laden years
of the early 1790s to produce an autobiographical sequence designed
to show that Wordsworth had, by 1797–8, begun to live a poetic life
that recognised a responsibility to society.

For Peter Bell, the realisation that he is staring at a dead man in
the river is a shock sufficient to render him senseless. Before this,
Peter had tried to capture the ass; its love for its dead owner enabled
it to withstand the beating it had received. When Peter revives, he
does what the ass is waiting for and retrieves the body, even as
Wordsworth is retrieving the memory of the Esthwaite incident:

The man who had been four days dead
Head-foremost from the river's bed
Uprises like a ghost.

(PB 98, 653–5)

Like the horse in 'The Baker's Cart', the ass is a creature of the
natural world. The horse is forced to move on unnaturally by the
driver's whip. The situation here is turned around. Peter now does
the ass's will; he struggles on to the creature's back and meekly
allows himself to be taken to the home of his master.

At the cottage we find, in effect, the Margaret of *Peter Bell*. Her
sorrow is here redeemed, because Peter is redeemed. His care now
is only for someone in need other than himself:

He raised her up and while he held
Her body propped against his knee
She waked, and when the woman spied
The poor ass standing by her side
She moaned most bitterly.

'Oh God be praised! my heart's at ease,
For he is dead, I know it well!'

Of tears she poured a bitter flood
And in the best way that he could
His tale did Peter tell.

(PB 142, 1261–70)

Wordsworth's every effort at this point in his career is related to his need to reconcile the heartbroken, bitter moan of the devastated widow with the woman who can say in the same breath, 'God be praised! My heart's at ease'. Peter's salvation lies in these tragic circumstances, and good has come out of despair and death where nature (in the form of the ass) has been allowed to dictate.

If *Peter Bell* constitutes a retrospective chapter in the poet's life, dwelling on the darker side of his life, then *Lyrical Ballads* may be considered a celebration of the self-knowledge Wordsworth felt he had gained. The Ballads represent an important step forward in the writing of his literary life. He produced what were for the most part anecdotal poems for his immediate circle of friends, while he took stock of the long-term task of developing the autobiographical theme for his epic 'public' poem.

The new life at Alfoxden continued to have its worries; to the permanent financial crisis could now be added the fact that the new tenants were arousing the political suspicions of a loyalist neighbourhood. The country (and in particular this part of it) daily expected a French invasion, as Coleridge's poem 'Fears In Solitude' reminds us; and as Henry Tilney informs Catherine Moreland in *Northanger Abbey*, England was a country 'where every man is surrounded by a neighbourhood of voluntary spies, and where roads and newspapers lay everything open . . .'.[12] Given the inclusion of the known radical, John Thelwall, in the Stowey/Alfoxden coterie, the foreign appearance (swarthy, with an unfamiliar accent) of the Wordsworths, combined with their restlessness to trigger off reports that led to the dispatch of James Walsh, a Government spy, to investigate the activities of Alfoxden's inmates and their associates.

Much later in his *Biographia Literaria* (1817) Coleridge recalled the experience as a light-hearted interlude: the spy who half-heard the poets' discussion of the philosopher Spinoza reported what he had taken to be an insulting reference to his own 'Spy-Nozy' activities. At the time it would have been far more difficult to laugh off; Thelwall had already been there, and could confirm that their liberty, perhaps even their lives, might depend upon what Walsh chose to report back to London.[13]

For all this, it was a time of great happiness, no doubt enhanced by the sense that such a life must needs be lived for the moment. Wordsworth's restless physical activity continued unabated, but now it was a shared experience, erupting in spontaneous expeditions with Coleridge across the Quantocks and into Devon, across Exmoor, through the Valley of the Rocks, and seemingly perpetually back and forth to Stowey. While *Peter Bell* was being written, a clutch of shorter lyrics and narrative poems appeared, all in their way celebrating Wordsworth's sense of deliverance from despair. While all was not yet resolved, at least the way forward might be glimpsed and the present enjoyed rather than stoically suffered.

Between them, Wordsworth and Coleridge soon found they had the makings of a distinctive volume of modern poetry. Coleridge outlined their intentions some 17 years later in his *Biographia Literaria*. In Coleridge's poems 'the incidents and agents were to be, in part at least, supernatural; and the excellence aimed at was to consist in the interesting of the affections by the dramatic truth of such emotions, as would naturally accompany such situations, supposing them real'. By way of contrast, Wordsworth's 'subjects were to be chosen from ordinary life ... where there is a meditative and feeling mind to seek after them'.[14] Quite apart from obvious differences in subject-matter, Wordsworth's poems tended to adopt an increasingly radical commitment to a simplicity of style. The project gathered momentum as the coterie's agenda came to include discussion of the poems.

Coleridge's 'The Ancient Mariner', 'This Lime Tree Bower', 'Frost at Midnight' and 'Fears in Solitude' inspired Wordsworth's lyric vein, and the radical discourse of neighbours (Poole and Cottle), and of less frequent visitors (Thelwall and Hazlitt) sharpened the commitment to a radical theory of poetic style.

The first poem in the volume was Coleridge's 'Ancient Mariner'; Wordsworth's first poem was 'Lines Left upon a Seat in a Yew Tree'. The latter, as we have already seen, is a confirmation of the fact that the guilt-ridden, friendless Wordsworth of France and its aftermath has been exorcised. Suitably, therefore, he followed this with an extract from the 'Salisbury Plain' text for which the female vagrant is the sole narrator, replacing the sailor/Wordsworth. It is the woman's account we hear of how an uncaring, materialistic society progressively destroys her family and brings her to the borders of insanity. The politics of the poem remain as trenchantly critical of the political nation as they were in 1793–4, but in public Wordsworth does not associate himself with any of the guilty or victimised parties.

Representations of the abandoned woman and child continue to haunt the pages of *Lyrical Ballads*, but they are now identified far more as skeletons in society's cupboards rather than any that might belong to the poet.

In 'The Thorn' a jilted woman is described by an observer who is manifestly not the poet, and who continually attempts to distance himself from the narrative, stressing the second-hand status of the grim story he tells. She may not have given birth to her lover's child, she may not have murdered it and buried the body by the thorn. We shall never know the truth because her story has been hung about with rumour and fantasy:

> I've heard the scarlet moss is red
> With drops of that poor infant's blood;
> But kill a new-born infant thus!
> I do not think she could.
>
> (LB 84, 221–4)

In such circumstances the prospect of relief for the suffering woman is made virtually imposssible.

The implicit message here is that the popular, sentimental ballads of the day trivialise serious issues, a point which is central also to 'The Idiot Boy'. 'The Thorn' and 'The Idiot Boy' both have a parodic strain in common with the superficially frivolous tone of *Peter Bell*. The style of 'The Complaint of the Forsaken Indian Woman' is by contrast elegiac and beautifully modulated. Here the tragedy of the dying woman, abandoned by her tribe and parted from her child, focuses on a collective tribal act in the interests of survival rather than on an act of individual callousness:

> Too soon, my friends, you went away;
> For I had many things to say.
>
> (LB 113, 49–50)

The emotional experiences that had scarred Wordsworth's life by no means disappear from the poetry completely, however, and in 'The Mad Mother' they seem to surface explicitly:

> Dread not their taunts, my little life!
> I am thy father's wedded wife:
> And underneath the spreading tree

We two will live in honesty.
If his sweet boy he could forsake,
With me he never would have stay'd:
From him no harm my babe can take,
But he, poor man! is wretched made,
And every day we two will pray
For him that's gone and far away.

                    (LB 90, 71–80)

Retribution is a recurring theme throughout *Lyrical Ballads*, but it is articulated quite differently from the dramatic, self-absorbed manner in which it rolls through the Salisbury Plain texts and on into *The Borderers*. The most politically radical expression of it is found in 'Goody Blake and Harry Gill'. This poem also reflects an ongoing debate of 1797–8 between Wordsworth and Coleridge on the relative importance of 'action and situation' as opposed to 'meaning' in a work of art (as Wordsworth put it in the Preface he wrote two years later for a subsequent edition of *Lyrical Ballads*).[15] Listening to *Peter Bell* and other poems being read, Hazlitt noted the way Wordsworth imparted meaning of the utmost gravity to poetry whose action, situation and execution certainly approached the banal if they did not actually arrive there. 'Goody Blake and Harry Gill' is a case in point.

The poem is based on a tale told by Erasmus Darwin in his *Zoonomia* (1794–6), an encyclopedic handbook of medical information that was without doubt the most widely consulted hypochondriac's handbook of its day. In the second volume, Darwin illustrates the way in which the mind, once convinced of a bodily ailment, can override nature to make real what would otherwise be non-existent symptoms. Wordsworth reduces Darwin's anecdote to a tale simple in style and matter. Yet for him the very plainness of the lyric (its 'action and situation') is a necessary defamiliarisation of what is expected of 'the Poet', and serves to emphasise the seriousness of the point, the 'meaning'. The point is essentially political.

Goody Blake, destitute and cold, thieves from her mean landlord to stay warm. The issue is the same as that pursued over many a portentous stanza in the 'Salisbury Plain' poems: the responsibility for crime belongs in a situation such as this not with the perpetrator of the theft (or murder, as in the case of both 'Salisbury Plain' and 'The Thorn'), but with the individual, or the society, inhumane enough to drive the perpetrator to such a pitch of desperation.

Reviewing *Lyrical Ballads* for the *Monthly Review*, Charles Burney was quick to see beyond the simplicity of the style to the disturbing implications of the politics:

> if all the poor are to help themselves, and supply their wants from the possessions of their neighbours, what imaginary wants and real anarchy would it not create.[16]

Goody Blake curses Harry Gill for his meanness:

> 'God! who art never out of hearing,
> O may he never more be warm!'
> (LB 61, 99–100)

And he, like the subject of Darwin's anecdote, shivers with cold to his dying day.

The curse is both comic and serious; it is poised between a joke and an apocalyptic prophecy, and has Wordsworth's 'convulsive inclination to laughter about the mouth' that no doubt gave way to a guffaw when he read the anecdote in *Zoonomia* following the one he used for the poem. Having swallowed some sealing wax by mistake, a parson is told by a friend (as a joke) that it would seal up his bowels. Despite 'cathartics' and 'a great many evacuations', the idea took hold of his imagination so that he sickened, and eventually died.

The Jacobin political tendency that Burney had noted is apparent throughout the collection. The injustice suffered by individuals links 'The Female Vagrant' and 'Goody Blake and Harry Gill' in particular with 'Simon Lee' and 'The Last of the Flock'. 'Lines written at a small distance from my house' is a graphic account of a Bohemian in-crowd (mixing with the likes of John Thelwall) simply asking to be considered subversive:

> No joyless forms shall regulate
> Our living Calendar:
> We from to-day, my friend, will date
> The opening of the year.
>
> Love, now an universal birth,
> From heart to heart is stealing,
> From earth to man, from man to earth,
> – It is the hour of feeling.

One moment now may give us more
Than fifty years of reason;
Our minds shall drink at every pore
The spirit of the season.
                    (LB 63–4, 17–28)

There is, beyond a general reading of these lines as a commitment
to Romantic 'feeling', a far sharper set of referents that relate to the
reconstitution of the calendar by the French Revolutionaries in September 1792 (a 'living Calendar' to replace a dead past of 'reason'),
'We from to-day, my friend, will date/ The opening of the year';
there is a clear echo of the international aspirations of the Rights
of Man, 'Love, now an universal birth'; and there is a comprehensive rejection of the past and its apologists (Watson and Burke) in
favour of the present 'moment' that 'may give us more/ Than fifty
years of reason'. 'The spirit of the season' is revolution, the tone is
one of hedonistic intoxication, precisely what loyalist propaganda
charged the Jacobins with, and exactly how James Gilray and others
depicted them; a loose-living, immoral rabble:

Then come, my sister! come, I pray,
With speed put on your woodland dress,
And bring no book; for this one day
We'll give to idleness.
                    (LB 64, 37–41)

A subversive view of received wisdom on education and authority
are the subject in particular of 'We Are Seven', 'Anecdote for Fathers'
and 'The Idiot Boy'. 'We Are Seven' and 'Anecdote' specifically
attack the assumption that a rational view born of adult experience
in society is superior to a child's spontaneous, uninformed and
individual response. In 'The Idiot Boy' the serenity of the isolated
idiot child's irrational world compares very favourably to the adult
world of communal muddle and panic. Behind these specific in-
stances lies a more general, radical reappraisal of wisdom. It is in
fact in keeping with the literary life that Wordsworth was constructing for himself that he should argue that an important condition for the attainment of wisdom is retirement. This was hardly a
new idea for the eighteenth century, but earlier celebrations of retirement maintain a strong notion of continuing social relationships
between the rich and powerful who have estates to which they may
on occasion 'retire'.

Wordsworth's retirement suggests far more an act of defiance in the face of a literary and a political establishment of which he is emphatically not a part. In his retirement he learns the wisdom of the socially marginalised, of the fool, and of the child. This is in stark contrast to the Augustan ideal proposed by Samuel Johnson. The astronomer in *Rasselas* (1759) lacks a social life, and his unremitting solitude results in madness. At the end of the chapter dealing with his plight Johnson argues that schemes of social 'reformation' are frequently hatched in solitude (without the leaven of common sense achieved in open debate) and must therefore be suspect:

> Such, says Imlac, are the effects of visionary schemes: when we first form them we know them to be absurd, but familiarise them by degrees, and in time lose sight of their folly.[17]

'Expostulation and Reply' and 'The Tables Turned' are poems that develop the theme of wisdom in a way that emphasises the poet's place within his own circle of friends, and his indifference to the world beyond. They arose from a debate with Hazlitt, and remain locked within a particular moment of private discourse. The readership Wordsworth has now, but lacked then, can only eavesdrop. The spontaneity of the child is recommended to the adult in defiance of the wisdom of past ages, and in particular defiance of the scholarship of the Enlightenment:

> One impulse from a vernal wood
> May teach you more of man;
> Of moral evil and of good,
> Than all the sages can.
>   (LB 109, 21–4)

And this is best learnt alone (meaning in effect in the company of a few chosen friends), and in a state of 'wise passiveness', the latter being what Wordsworth, a frustrated radical activist, probably most needed to hear:

> Nor less I deem that there are powers,
> Which of themselves our minds impress,
> That we can feed this mind of ours,
> In a wise passiveness.
>   (LB 108, 21–4)

Quite apart from the fact that *Peter Bell* became too long to include in *Lyrical Ballads*, the drafts show that Wordsworth had begun to have difficulties with it, and it was not until 1819 that he finally published it. 'The Thorn' and 'The Idiot Boy' are there to do for the *Ballads* what *Peter Bell* would also have done, explore a characteristic lack of communication between individuals which in *Peter Bell* is resolved through Peter's new-found sensitivity to nature. Like 'The Thorn', 'The Idiot Boy' takes many stanzas to tell a simple tale. Lack of communication here results not so much from the idle and shallow mind exhibited by the narrator of 'The Thorn', as from a misplaced commitment to 'action'. Action, not 'wise passiveness' fills the poem. Betty Foy panics when Susan Gale is taken ill. She sends her son, the idiot boy, for the doctor. Had she looked twice she would have seen that Susan was not seriously ill, and needed only rest in order to recover. But the child is sent, is lost, is in fact perfectly safe on his pony who (like the ass in *Peter Bell*) is utterly trustworthy, as the child knows; he is at ease in his 'simple' passive way with nature and allows himself to be taken unhurriedly on his journey at nature's pace. Thus it should have been with the horse in 'The Baker's Cart', thus it eventually is between Peter Bell and the ass:

Who's yon, that, near the waterfall,
Which thunders down with headlong force,
Beneath the moon, yet shining fair,
As careless as if nothing were,
Sits upright on a feeding horse?

Unto his horse, that's feeding free,
He seems, I think, the rein to give;
Of moon or stars he takes no heed;
Of such we in romances read,
– 'Tis Johnny! Johnny! as I live.
                    (LB 101, 357–66)

'The Thorn', 'The Idiot Boy' and *Peter Bell* are all narrative explorations of Wordsworth's theme of assessing active and passive roles, of weighing the poet Wordsworth against the politician Wordsworth. The actively angry witness of social and political injustice is set alongside the sage in reflective 'retirement'. Together these poems begin to formulate Wordsworth's assessment of his current situation.

The *Ballads* establish their meanings as much by their interaction as by their single presences. 'The Idiot Boy' needs 'The Female Vagrant'; they both belong with 'Simon Lee'. Even as Wordsworth is attempting to establish a coherent chronology for his life, so his poems begin increasingly to represent the composition of one book where poems as different in their initial appearance as 'The Idiot Boy' and 'Simon Lee' are complementary.

The first edition of *Lyrical Ballads* concluded with 'Lines written a few miles above Tintern Abbey'. It is understandably one of the most written about of Wordsworth's poems. In the context of this discussion it serves to bring together a number of the themes already considered in relation to the *Ballads*.

'Tintern Abbey' is an autobiography in summary. In it Wordsworth lays claim to a new maturity as a poet. Visiting the Wye valley with Dorothy in July 1798 he remembers back five years to 1793, when the poet of 'Salisbury Plain' (having lost his companion) was making his way into Wales. From a distance of five years Wordsworth judges himself not then to have been fully in control; it was a time both of fear, 'a man/Flying from something that he dreads', and of 'dizzy raptures' (LB 118 11.70–1, 86). Five years later, he is in control; it is the fact that he is now able to record the difference that enables him to claim (as he was also doing through the persona the Pedlar) that he had grasped a knowledge of the 'one life' in terms of a tranquillity of mind not available to him before:

> that serene and blessed mood,
> In which the affections gently lead us on,
> Until, the breath of this corporeal frame,
> And even the motion of our human blood
> Almost suspended, we are laid asleep
> In body, and become a living soul:
> While with an eye made quiet by the power
> Of harmony, and the deep power of joy,
> We see into the life of things.
> (LB 117, 42–50)

This is the wise passivity of a mature poet; the maturity lies partly in the recognition that there is loss here also. As a young man he enjoyed a sense of closeness to the physical world without which we are diminished. Sadness is a necessary part of the process, therefore. It results in the wavering mood of the following passage:

And now, with gleams of half-extinguish'd thought,
With many recognitions dim and faint,
And somewhat of a sad perplexity,
The picture of the mind revives again:
While here I stand, not only with the sense
Of present pleasure, but with pleasing thoughts
That in this moment there is life and food
For future years.

(LB 118, 59–66)

Wordsworth's *Lyrical Ballads* were to a significant degree a state-ment of his continued commitment to radical political thinking, though 'Tintern Abbey' makes clear the fact that he was conscious in a number of ways of having become a different person (polit-ically as in every other way) from the angry traveller who passed through the Wye valley in 1793. 'Simon Lee', 'The Last of the Flock', 'The Female Vagrant' and 'Goody Blake and Harry Gill' all indic-ate the extent of his continuing disaffection from society, and his cynical view of the political establishment. His initial response had combined a Godwinian commitment to rationalism with an ambi-tion to enter the active political arena in order to assist in putting things right. But circumstances forced him to recognise that this would not be possible. Against the Godwinian life, he now wrote the life of a person no less committed to political justice, but one who was first and foremost a writer, needing time and space to work, needing solitude (while craving company). He inscribed the life of the Pedlar across his own as more honourable, powerful and influential than that of the politician.

Faith in rationalism was replaced by a determined recognition of the spiritual and numinous in day-to-day human experience. Rationalism had fuelled the Godwinian conviction that a corrupt society might be redeemed by an appropriate programme of political reform. Wordsworth had replaced this belief with poetry commit-ted to the study of corrupt or misguided individuals within soci-ety whose redemption (achieved in terms of individual spiritual enlightenment) promised the eventual redemption of society. The poetry is concerned with the victims of political injustice as indi-viduals, real people, rather than as ciphers for a list of abstract evils to be banished by law from society.

Simon Lee represents a general problem within society which relates to class difference; but the problem only becomes known from personal contact with Simon Lee himself, the man who cries too much in gratitude, forcing the reader to think again about his case. The same is true of the shepherd in 'The Last of the Flock'. It is the feelings and powerful emotions of these individuals which take us beyond words, beyond reason, and carry the case into the heart:

> No peace, no comfort could I find,
> No ease, within doors or without,
> And crazily, and wearily,
> I went my work about.
> ('Last of the Flock' LB 87, 75–8)

We probe beyond the narrator's tale here, as we do with 'Simon Lee' and 'The Thorn', in the process discovering that it is from the heart that change must first come. Thus the *Lyrical Ballads* release the theme of emotion and its crucial role for us:

> For I have learned
> To look on nature, not as in the hour
> Of thoughtless youth, but hearing oftentimes
> The still, sad music of humanity,
> Not harsh nor grating, though of ample power
> To chasten and subdue. And I have felt
> A presence that disturbs me with the joy
> Of elevated thoughts; a sense sublime
> Of something far more deeply interfused,
> Whose dwelling is the light of setting suns,
> And the round ocean, and the living air,
> And the blue sky, and in the mind of man,
> A motion and a spirit, that impels
> All thinking things, all objects of all thought,
> And rolls through all things.
> ('Tintern Abbey' LB 118–19, 89–103)

The latter part of 'Tintern Abbey' constitutes a tribute to the role Dorothy had played in helping Wordsworth cultivate his mature relationship with nature and society, with his fellow man, and with poetry. He indicates how important it was for him to feel that he not only had Dorothy's companionship, but a secure place within a supportive circle of friends. The pain, fear, agony and anger of recent years could now be subsumed in nature. In addition to Dorothy, he

now had friends to encourage him, friends who in turn needed
him.

In the final lines of 'Tintern Abbey', though , we return to Dorothy,
and the nagging concern that the Wye valley memorialises a poetic
gift that Wordsworth can now no longer claim as his own. We are
to understand that Dorothy, as a woman, retains a spontaneity in
her response to nature that her brother, as a mature male given now
to reflection ('elevated thoughts'), has lost since his earlier expedition
to Tintern. He now implies that for him to become a complete poet
(a genuinely 'modern' poet), Dorothy must be on hand to exercise
a perceptive insight he himself no longer enjoys.[18]

There were plainly unresolved contradictions here; there was a
far from healthy aspect to Wordsworth's journey towards his maturity as a poet. The coterie context is the first thing, the presumed need
for Dorothy is the second, contained within the first. In one respect,
Wordsworth was beginning to think of himself as nearing his literary
goal. *Lyrical Ballads* rejoiced in the existence of a readership. Yet as
preparations were made with Cottle to go to press, the fact remained
that the wider reading public, the ultimate destination for the poetry,
might well be expected to be hostile. If the politics were not to prove
a problem, the fact that these were poems which all too frequently
deconstructed received notions of poetic decorum almost inevitably
would be:

My gentle Reader, I perceive
How patiently you've waited.
And now I fear that you expect
Some tale will be related.
        ('Simon Lee' LB 70, 61–4)

Such a thing was all very well among friends, but how would the
paying 'gentle Reader' beyond Nether Stowey and Alfoxden feel
about having their sentimental tale of Simon Lee taken away from
them and replaced with a moral conundrum? It was never going to
be easy to pursue a literary life that flourished initially in the rich
soil of a small, select, sympathetic audience, and did so in defiance
of Augustan literary and political decorum, even while it craved the
ear of the nation. The first edition of *Lyrical Ballads* retains the cosy
glow of coterie work. The poems flaunt their lack of respect for traditional social values and literary conventions, and in consequence

they lay claim to the right to exercise a freedom in choice of form and subject-matter which is quintessentially Romantic.

Finding themselves deprived of Alfoxden as a place to live, the Wordsworths' next move was not (*Lyrical Ballads* in hand) towards the barricades, but into palpable exile. In September 1798 four friends, Wordsworth, Dorothy, Coleridge and John Chester, set sail for the Netherlands and Germany.

5

The Making of a Modern Poet: 1798–1805

After what was in effect their eviction from Alfoxden, the Wordsworths arrived in Bristol early in July 1798, lodging temporarily with Joseph Cottle. There followed two desultory 'tours'; four days in the Wye valley followed early in August by a tramp through South Wales culminating in a visit to John Thelwall. Returning to Bristol they duly set out on a leisurely progress via Blenheim and Oxford, to arrive in London at the end of the month, 'a very pleasant journey per foot, per wagon, per coach, per post-chaise' (EY 226–7). In September they travelled to Yarmouth, bound for Hamburg with Coleridge and John Chester. On 3 October William and Dorothy set out on the journey south from Hamburg to Braunschweig, and then on to Goslar where they took lodgings. They stayed there until February 1799, returning to Hamburg by a circuitous route, exploring Saxony, and meeting up once more with Coleridge. They eventually returned to England in late April or early May.

From Yarmouth they travelled on to Sockburn-on-Tees on the borders of Yorkshire and County Durham, the home of Mary Hutchinson, Wordsworth's future wife. Sockburn became their base while Wordsworth investigated the possibilities of a more permanent home in the Lake District. In December 1799 Wordsworth and Dorothy took possession of Dove Cottage (then known as Town End, the name of the hamlet where it stood on the road from Ambleside to Grasmere) at a rent of £8.00 a year. They were to remain there until May 1813.

The Wordsworths had left England at a time when fear of a French invasion was at its height. The Bristol area was understandably rife with rumours of the imminent arrival of Bonaparte and the French fleet. The Somerset coast was known to be a favourite target, and in February 1797 an invasion force of 1200 troops originally intended for Bristol made its way ashore not so many miles away at Fishguard. With the arrival of a Government spy sent to check out what to the locals seemed the very suspicious lifestyle of the new tenants of Alfoxden, Wordsworth and Coleridge were drawn out of their coterie world of new poetry and radical ideas to be thrust into the very real world of espionage, counter-espionage, spies, informers, long prison sentences, transportation and the hangman's noose; John Thelwall was on hand as a reminder that this was a game played for high stakes in which no quarter was being given.

William and Dorothy were left with no choice but to leave Alfoxden; but why Germany? And even more intriguing, given Dorothy's claim that such an expedition had for some time been considered as offering intellectual and financial inducements, why go to the uninspiring provincial backwater of Goslar? Biographers over many years have offered explanations ranging from an acceptance of Dorothy's account in her letter to Mrs William Rawson (EY 220–1), through the very feasible chaos theory which sees Goslar as one more chance landfall after Orléans, Blois, Windy Brow, Racedown and Alfoxden, to E. P. Thompson's notion that it was a calculated retreat by Wordsworth and Coleridge designed to avoid their call-up.[1] Draft-dodging might explain Germany; it does not explain Goslar. The answer to that one is almost certainly the hit-and-miss pursuit of cheap living: 'provisions very cheap, and lodgings very cheap' (EY 233).

Wordsworth's literary life was destined to be significantly affected by his readiness to leave England on the eve of the publication of a book of poems assured of a much wider circulation than any volume he had previously produced; and it is with the consequences of Goslar and Germany for Wordsworth's development as a poet that this biography is primarily concerned.

To set this aspect of the Goslar period in perspective, it is necessary first to be reminded that Wordsworth had long exhibited as much reluctance to enter the public domain as a poet, as he had cherished the ambition to live as a poet. The reasons for this are not hard to deduce. From his childhood onward, Wordsworth's character had been to a significant degree formed from having lived his life as an outsider. At Hawkshead he had been the outsider of the Penrith family unit that came into being with the death of his parents. That strained relationship was to a large extent responsible for setting him up as an outsider at Cambridge, an experience he was to reaffirm (avoiding reference to the Cooksons) in the course of the next few years; university life, he wrote in *The Prelude*, offered him rewards:

which then
I did not love, nor do I love them now:

Such glory was but little sought by me,
And little won.

(Prelude III, 94, 69–72)

The cumulative effects of his travels abroad and the unpaid Lowther debt confirmed his alienation from both his Uncle Christopher's patronage and from his country's political establishment. The latter was now also to find its way into his autobiography, reconstructed around several strategic omissions:

I began
To think with fervour upon management
Of nations – what it is and ought to be,
And how their worth depended on their laws,
And on the constitution of the state.

(Prelude X, 396, 684–8)

No specific mention of Lowther here, nor of Annette. Bohemian living (frowned upon by a family anxious about financial security) and radical political sympathies produced writing that assumed – indeed required – a public hostile to its alienated progenitor. The poet had been rescued from this creative vortex not by any reconciliation with the public, but by the support of a sympathetic coterie. With *Lyrical Ballads* in Cottle's hands Wordsworth had arrived in a characteristically oblique fashion at a point where public exposure was imminent. It was both what he had long been planning for, and least desired.

The publication of *Lyrical Ballads* was a messy business, Cottle deciding to transfer the business to a London publisher. The book came out on 4 October 1798, though the volume was already being circulated and discussed while Wordsworth was in London in September. Though not published in vast numbers, it was not long in becoming known as an anthology containing experimental verse. The reviews that followed did nothing to dampen the interest of potential readers.

Had Wordsworth remained in England he would have been eased out of his coterie into a forum containing a gradually expanding readership voicing many shades of literary and political opinion. The young man on the public road at night would have been forced to deal in some way with a gradual increase in traffic as dawn broke.

But this was not the case; the next phase of his literary career continued in a renewed atmosphere of isolation.

Indifferent to the expense, Coleridge and Chester parted from the Wordsworths in Hamburg to seek the intellectual stimulation of life among the German literati of Ratzeburg and subsequently Göttingen. Wordsworth, walled up in Goslar, drove his literary life forward on two fronts. He began writing more lyrics with a view to extending *Lyrical Ballads* in a direction that he, and literally he alone, felt was appropriate; and he proceeded to construct a literary life for himself in an autobiographical poem (the infant *Prelude* intended for coterie readership only) that legitimised the modern poet who was further refining the modernity of the *Lyrical Ballads*. The form and function of modern poetry were established in the light of one poet's childhood experiences; the public were to have as little influence on the matter as Christopher Cookson had ever had influence on Wordsworth's choice of career. 'Nature', not society, was the arbiter:

> Thus did my days pass on, and now at length
> From Nature and her overflowing soul
> I had received so much that all my thoughts
> Were steeped in feeling.
> (Prelude 1799, 25, 445–8)

It is easy enough for us to appreciate that in his private autobiography, Wordsworth was able to construct 'Nature' in the light of a reconstructed narrative of his life. While one Wordsworth had arrived on the doorstep of public accountability, another Wordsworth was evolving independently, one who would eventually have to confront his already published self. This situation would in turn fashion the further development of the poet. The Goslar period may sound like a grim interlude in many ways, but in other respects it constituted a heady experience of unhindered creativity, both in terms of what was written, and of what was resolved about what should be written and why.

In Hamburg, Wordsworth had gone with Coleridge to visit Friedrich Klopstock, the 74-year-old poet famous for his epic religious work, *Messias*. He was also studying the work of younger German poets, in particular Gottfried Burger, with whose ballads he might have been expected to empathise. His response, however, betrays a constant impatience; what he finds may be popular, but it never in his estimation measures up to the idea of modernity he

was steadily developing in his own mind. Writing to Coleridge, his
response to Burger quickly becomes a rehearsal of his own poetic
aims:

> I wish him sometimes at least to make me forget himself in his
> creations. It seems to me, that in poems descriptive of human
> nature, however short they may be, character is absolutely neces-
> sary, etc.: incidents are among the lowest allurements in poetry.
> (EY 234)

Wordsworth's distrust of 'incident' at the expense of what he
here calls 'character' had become a central tenet of his poetic belief.
Incidents were the stuff of the literary decorations and fripperies
he had early learnt to find suspect from his reading of John Scott's
Critical Essays while still at Cambridge. 'Character' signifies Wordsworth's quest for a more permanent and serious meaning to poetry,
a genuine insight into 'human nature'. He complains to Coleridge
that instead of 'character' in Burger's poems, 'I see everywhere the
character of Burger himself'. By the time he came to write the Preface
for the new edition of *Lyrical Ballads* of 1800, he was able to elaborate considerably on this train of thought.

With reference to two poems, 'Old Man Travelling' (1796–7) and
'The Two Thieves' (1799–1800), he explains that they contain 'characters of which the elements are simple, belonging rather to nature
than to manners, such as exist now and will probably always exist
. . .' (Prose I, 128). The theory of modernity that the Goslar experience
had enabled him to fashion, in the process attaching it uniquely to
his own life experience, is here encapsulated in three phrases. Firstly,
'the elements are simple'. Secondly, it belongs 'rather to nature than
to manners' (alternatives that more appropriately pin down the distinction he was pursuing earlier between 'character' and 'incident').
Thirdly, what is thus delineated 'will probably always exist'. We
have therefore simplicity, nature and permanence. The lyrics written
in Goslar, where there was nothing to do but write the poetry that
was within him rather than around him, embodied the merits of this
programme:

> A slumber did my spirit seal,
>   I had no human fears:
> She seem'd a thing that could not feel
>   The touch of earthly years.

No motion has she now, no force;
  She neither hears nor sees;
Roll'd round in earth's diurnal course
  With rocks and stones and trees!
                    (LB 164)

Goslar was a 'slumber'; the only movement to be found was embedded in nature itself, and Wordsworth set about explaining to himself that the key to this knowledge lay in his own Lakeland childhood, spent among the permanent forms of nature. In the *Lyrical Ballads* Preface of 1800 he was able to summarise his convictions by explaining that his ballads were distinct from other 'popular poetry of the day' because 'the feeling therein developed gives importance to the action and situation and not the action and situation to the feeling' (Prose I 128, 161–3). The indeterminate circumstances of 'A slumber did my spirit seal' are a characteristic feature of Wordsworth's modernity; we work against the poems if we try to unravel them at the expense of responding to 'the feeling therein developed'.

Goslar became the crucible of Wordsworth's modernity. It was an excited and inspired poet who assured Coleridge that but for the 'uneasiness and heat' engendered by his intense creativity, 'I should have written five times as much as I have done. . . . When I do not read I am absolutely consumed by thinking and feeling and bodily exertions of voice or of limbs, the consequence of those feelings' (EY 236).

The bitterly cold winter months spent living in Goslar find Wordsworth continuing to reassemble his life as a poet in terms of positive creativity. In the same way that latterly at Racedown and Alfoxden he steadily revised the negative, guilt-ridden mood of the 'Salisbury Plain' texts, we can see him taking the punishing winter weather in Germany, and turning it to a triumph of creative achievement by association with memories of his schooldays:

And in the frosty season, when the sun
Was set, and visible for many a mile
The cottage windows through the twilight blazed,
I heeded not the summons. Clear and loud
The village clock tolled six; I wheeled about
Proud and exulting, like an untired horse
That cares not for its home. All shod with steel
We hissed along the polished ice in games

Confederate, imitative of the chace
And woodland pleasures, the resounding horn,
The pack loud bellowing, and the hunted hare.

(*Prelude* 1799, 5, 150–60)

The poet who has retreated to Goslar from London literary circles
on the eve of publication of *Lyrical Ballads* recalls both the experience of being part of a group of children, and also abruptly leaving
them to be on his own. In their games the children anticipate entry
into the crowded, physically active, not to say aggressive world of
adulthood, 'The pack loud bellowing, and the hunted hare'. What
Wordsworth remembers, though, is characteristic not just of how
he behaved on these occasions, but of his behaviour in general:

Not seldom from the uproar I retired
Into a silent bay, or sportively
Glanced sideway, leaving the tumultuous throng,
To cut across the shadow of a star
That gleamed upon the ice. . . .

(11.170–4)

From being a part of public events, he retires, 'sportively/ Glanced
sideway, leaving the tumultuous throng'; he is the congenital outsider, relishing his solitude, an experience that requires absolute
cessation of movement, an end to 'the pack loud bellowing'; it opens
up for him a glimpse of the infinite. For Wordsworth this represents a moment of contact not with the ephemeral motion of the
hunt, but with the unending movement of the entire earth. Notice
how this experience transforms winter into summer at the end of
this passage:

then at once
Have I, reclining back upon my heels
Stopped short – yet still the solitary cliffs
Wheeled by me, even as if the earth had rolled
With visible motion her diurnal round.
Behind me did they stretch in solemn train,
Feebler and feebler, and I stood and watched
Till all was tranquil as a summer sea.

(11.178–85)

Setting the skating episode alongside the new lyric, 'A slumber did my spirit seal', illustrates clearly what was happening as Wordsworth sought to extend *Lyrical Ballads*. The private reminiscence is reconstructed around the need to establish a moment (or moments) in his life when a feeling that 'the earth had rolled/ With visible motion her diurnal round' had actually been known to him. From this experience, worked through in a complex poetic form incorporating, as J. H. Alexander has argued, epic blank verse, lyric, conversational and Juvenilian satirical influences, Wordsworth quarries the dramatically simplified modern lyric poem, focusing on 'the feeling therein developed': 'Rolled round in earth's diurnal course/ With rocks and stones and trees'.[2]

In consequence, the lyric is as much a part of the poet's autobiographical project as the emergent *Prelude*; indeed the pursuit of a radically reviewed notion of the interrelatedness of things is essential to Wordsworth's sense of his modernity. In the west country, Coleridge's enthusiasm for pantheism had supplied a specific framework within which to work. Projected now on to his creative life in Goslar, Wordsworth's developing sense of his life and poetry as an interlocking narrative was to lead him in due course to be almost as concerned about the ordering of his poetry as with the writing of it. His life, in its entirety, is to be ordered, sifted and variously written up to become his poetry. Traditional distinctions – between what is and what is not a fit subject for poetry, between prose and poetry even – are overturned.

The modern poet, evolving in this way and in isolation, is also writing into the story a 'modern' readership, while leaving behind an unregenerated public, among whom will be 'The pack loud bellowing ... the tumultuous throng' who had hunted the Wordsworths out of Alfoxden.

Goslar provided Wordsworth with opportunities to neutralise negative influences, and explore what had been positive in his experience. This task involved continuing the work of Alfoxden to redeem the guilt of 'Salisbury Plain' (the text was revisited briefly yet again at this time). He did this in part by recasting the deserted female figure of previous work in the role of a liberated pantheistic spirit of poetic inspiration, reconciling nature and art:

The floating clouds their state shall lend
To her, for her the willow bend,
Nor shall she fail to see

Even in the motions of the storm
A beauty that shall mould her form
By silent sympathy.
    (LB 'Three years she grew', 221, 19–24)

The female vagrant had already been edited into *Lyrical Ballads* (1798) from the 'Salisbury Plain' manuscripts to give her a significantly revised appearance; here she is being even more drastically reconstituted.

There remained, of course, a continuing fear of darkness and disillusionment. 'Strange fits of passion I have known' investigates how a devastating emotional experience may be triggered off by an apparently simple, even trivial occurrence. As the poet rides to his loved one's cottage, he watches the moon while in a state of reverie. But the moment that the moon drops out of sight behind the cottage roof he has a premonition of the woman's death.

It is indeed a strange fit of passion, a 'wayward thought' (LB 162 1.25), reminding us that the power of natural objects upon our minds may scatter the rational self to the four winds in a moment. The power of nature and the power of emotion are two major facets of Wordsworth's modernity, our lives may be as easily shattered as enriched by them; the autobiographical episode which tells of stealing a boat on Ullswater illustrates just this. Dorothy transcribed both the skating incident and the boat-stealing passage in the joint letter to Coleridge of 14/21 December. What had been the guilty conscience of the poet of 'Salisbury Plain' is made easier to cope with on Ullswater by invoking a more profound experience of sublime awe and fear, brought to the fore (as in 'Strange fits of passion') by a relatively insignificant event.

As he rows from the shore, 'a huge cliff,/ As if with voluntary power instinct,/ Upreared its head', and as he rows on it seems, 'like a living thing', to stride after him. He claims to remember a sense of disorientation, an experience which eradicates from his mind 'familiar shapes/ of hourly objects, images of trees,/ Of sea or sky'; he has already recalled how the cliff 'Rose up between me and the stars'. The boundaries of perception are dramatically and shockingly extended; until this moment he had a firm sense of the parameters of his world:

I fixed a steady view
Upon the top of that same craggy ridge,
The bound of the horizon.

The line of the roof in 'Strange Fits of Passion' is used in a similar way to the 'craggy ridge' here. The moon drops behind the roof, the mountain rears up from behind the ridge. The shock is immense. We are left with the remembered perception of powers and forces which, like those perceived in the skating passage, are of a larger, more portentous order than humanity, 'they do not live / Like living men'. But although guilt and fear are present, the function of the narrative is to transform the emotions attached to the localised incident into a grain of serious knowledge regarding the absolute. It is, in effect, the prising open of an escape-route from the immediate causes of his guilt (the motif of the abandoned woman continues to register in the lyrics he writes) into a realm where he as a poet may put his personal experience to use in a higher cause.

In the passage he subsequently added to the boat-stealing narrative, he confirmed the positive, benign role of the 'beings of the hills ... that do not live / Like living men':

> thus, from my first dawn
> Of childhood, did ye love to intertwine
> The passions that build up our human soul
> Not with the mean and vulgar works of man,
> But with high objects, with eternal things,
> With life and Nature, purifying thus
> The elements of feeling and of thought....
> (*Prelude* 1799 I, 3–4, 81–138)

In resolving to write his way into the contemplation of 'eternal things', he relegates the 'works of man' to the realms of the 'mean and vulgar'; but the process of writing poetry which seeks to purify 'feeling and thought' is in danger of setting him permanently at odds with a 'mean and vulgar' readership.

The first review of *Lyrical Ballads* to appear was by Robert Southey, writing for the *Critical Review* in October 1798. In many ways it was the most acute of the early readings, and pointed up the nature of the gap Wordsworth's lyrics were likely to open between reader and writer. 'No tale', Southey wrote of 'The Idiot Boy':

> less deserved the labour that appears to have been bestowed upon this. It resembles a Flemish picture in the worthlessness of its design and the excellence of its execution.[3]

In Wordsworth's terms, Southey is missing the importance of 'character', the 'feeling' explored through the poem's personae, over against 'incident', the 'action and situation' promoted by the poem's design. Excellence there was, evident skill in the 'execution', and other reviewers tended to agree. Here was undoubtedly an able writer. But as Southey had perceived (no doubt as much from his proximity to the Stowey/Alfoxden coterie as from his reading of the ballads), here was a poet set on a questionable modern experiment in form and subject-matter likely to test the patience of his 'mean and vulgar' readership to the limit.

There were no reviewers looking over Wordsworth's shoulder in Goslar, however, only the memory of a somewhat grotesquely bewigged Klopstock clinging to a threadbare epic tradition, and sundry poems by Burger, Goethe, Wieland and Lessing to hand, none of them answering to Wordsworth's creative thirst. He could proceed unchecked. The lyrics he wrote were imbued with the simplicity of execution he sought; they were meditative distillations from his autobiographical blank verse, or in one notable case, from his actual circumstances huddled round the stove with Dorothy in Goslar on 'one of the coldest days of the century'. He watches a fly:

> Stock-still there he stands like a traveller bemaz'd;
> The best of his skill he has tried;
> His feelers methinks I can see him put forth
> To the East and the West, and the South and the North,
> But he finds neither guide-post nor guide.
> (LB 'Written in Germany' 226, 21–5)

The usual account of Wordsworth at this time (culled from the correspondence and duly embroidered by biographers) might prepare us to see the poet as the fly. Indeed the man who fled from Alfoxden might well have seemed to have ended up in Goslar precisely because his literary life had as yet no 'guide-post nor guide'. The poem, however, insists that the poet is not like the fly; not any longer, anyway. Here we have Wordsworth positively oozing good humour and creativity at every pore in the style of modern 'simplicity' that was destined to earn him such notoriety:

> while I
> Can draw warmth from the cheek of my Love;
> As blest and as glad in this desolate gloom,

As if green summer grass were the floor of my room,
And woodbines were hanging above.

(11.31–5)

The final lines of the skating passage come to mind with the onset
of summer in winter, but only with respect to the 'feeling therein
developed'.

It was in Goslar that Wordsworth sketched out one of his most profoundly simple lyrics, 'The Childless Father'. The poem opens with
an invocation to the hunt, reminding us yet again of the skating
passage. In this instance 'the chace' is contrasted with the measured
sadness of an old man whose daughter has died six months previously. He goes in due course to join 'the noise and the fray', but 'with
a tear on his cheek'.

The poem dwells on the intersection of the activity of public life
and the dignified maintenance of reflective solitude:

Now fast up the dell came the noise and the fray,
The horse and the horn, and the hark! hark away!
Old Timothy took up his staff, and he shut
With a leisurely motion the door of his hut.

(LB 227, 13–16)

There is in that 'leisurely motion' a mastery of grief and an insistence
upon an independent response to the mass activity of the hunt. He
joins, but on his own terms. Once more a part of public life, Timothy
also lays claim to his individuality. The wretchedness of bereavement in isolation is turned to strength in public. Like the other lyric
pieces, this is poetry underpinned by pervasive autobiographical referents. It is a poetry of deeply contending forces, simply and bleakly
realised; action and situation refer us to equally insistent public and
private yearnings, to the dilemma of the modern poet in search of
a readership while destined to be alienated, to the fate of a fly who
has the unseasonable wish (it knows not how) to travel far and wide,
set against the poet finding the fulfilment of his love in his garret
(though is 'the cheek of my love' also a sin in the eyes of the world?).

The positive experience of writing in Goslar is even responsible
for an unusually elaborate joke in Wordsworth's correspondence.
In the letter of 27 February to Coleridge, he reflects on the primitive
circumstances of their lodgings:

We intend to import into England a new invention for washing. Among other advantages which our patent will set forth we shall not fail to insist upon the immense saving which must result from our discovery which will render only one washing basin necessary for the largest family in the kingdom. We dare not trust this communication to a letter, but you shall be a partner, Chester likewise. (EY 257)

As Wordsworth and Dorothy set off on their homeward journey, we face the intriguing prospect (as we did when Wordswoth left for France in 1792) of reflecting on how many Wordsworths can be identified heading for England in the spring of 1799. When Coleridge met them at Göttingen, he described both brother and sister in a letter to Poole as depressed, 'melancholy and hypped'.[4] Coleridge was here describing the consequences of the uncertainty that surrounded all their future plans. Given Coleridge's own anxieties on this score, we must allow for the possibility that he was dramatising what was certainly for him an emotional issue. The Wordsworths had long since decided to settle in the north, and William had no qualms about adopting – to a degree at least – the life of a recluse, indeed he had spent the last few years of his life writing himself into just such a role.

The difference between the two men in this respect was clearly discerned by Dorothy in her letter to Coleridge of 14–21 December 1798. In her preamble to the skating passage she refers to 'the North of England . . . whither we wish to decoy you':

A race with William upon his native lakes would leave to the heart and imagination something more Dear and valuable than the gay sights of Ladies and countesses whirling along the lake of Ratzeburg. (EY 238–9)

Coleridge (with continued domestic turmoil awaiting him at home) had been counting on picking up the threads of life in the West Country coterie pretty much where he had left off. The thought that he might leave his familiar haunts around Bristol for the north had little if any appeal. He may well have been the most 'hypped' of the three.

While one Wordsworth sets off for home depressed and uncertain, still reeling from the effects of the Goslar winter, another – for all Coleridge's account – is leaving Goslar with a sense of having set his literary life on a positive and productive track, and is encouraged in consequence to set about putting his domestic and financial affairs in order, even while he takes a firm grasp of his literary career in the public domain.

Starting with a letter to his brother Richard from Sockburn, Wordsworth fired off eleven letters (that we know of) between 13 May and 2 September 1799 to his brother, to Josiah Wedgwood, Joseph Cottle and to Thomas Poole on settling his financial affairs, sorting out the muddle over the publication of *Lyrical Ballads* while gauging their success with the public. Richard was to understand that he was no longer dealing with a wastrel: 'I hope soon to be in a condition when I shall have no more occasion to trouble you. I have received 30 Guineas from Cottle, as part payment for my book' (EY 269). Wordsworth's intention was to take control of *Lyrical Ballads* in every respect; this had to mean easing Coleridge out.

Back in England he was now forced to take account of the critical reception of his work. With Southey's review in front of him his first response was frustration and disappointment. The effect of adverse criticism (despite encouraging words from Cottle on sales and the tenor of another notice in *The Monthly Review*) was to throw him into despair. Marjorie Levinson has identified a Wordsworth who can sound like 'a man so assured of his entitlement that he can trust his originality to be received as intelligible and valuable'.[5] This was the Wordsworth of Goslar who now had to confront the fact that he was not understood, and was likely to be designated a misfit in the literary life of his nation. He was a poet whose conception in isolation decreed a continued existence in isolation.

In his own defence, Wordsworth cultivated an attitude of scorn for a public literary life. Yet again he slid away from the 'pack loud bellowing' towards the solitary world of his own mind's making. 'My aversion from publication increases every day', he wrote to Cottle. Publication, he claims, was only ever a means of making money ('for pudding'). Southey knew this, he complained; 'If he could not conscientiously have spoken differently of the volume, he ought to have declined the task of reviewing it' (EY 267–8).

Most intriguingly of all, when floating the idea of dropping Coleridge's 'Ancient Mariner' from a 'second edition' of *Lyrical Ballads*, he characterises the Goslar lyrics (along with others in the making) as 'some little things which would be more likely to suit the common taste' (EY 306–11). How real in 1799 is Wordsworth the poet and cynic, a man prepared to pander to the lowest denominator in public taste if it means paying off his debts and guaranteeing 'pudding'?

Adjusting to a public role in politics or poetry was a problem Wordsworth never overcame; it surfaces at Sockburn at this time with particular urgency, having been embedded in various ways in his life from his earliest years. He was driven back to *The Prelude* and to the work of constructing a life story for himself that offered protection from the bruising experience that the public exposure of his modernity was proving to be. True to character, it rendered him equally stubborn in his determination to proceed with his literary life in the way he thought best. He might cultivate a cynicism which helped him deal with the 'common taste'; he would never be able to take a cynical view of his own writing.

In addition to Goslar lyrics, the second volume of *Lyrical Ballads* he now planned included poems composed at Grasmere in the course of 1800. In the Preface he set about writing for the expanded collection, he brought together the major features of his modernity already considered.

At the outset he stresses the modernity of his 'experiment'. Marrying 'the real language of men in a state of vivid sensation' to 'metrical arrangement' promises poetry which may 'interest mankind permanently' (unlike the 'popular poetry of the day'). Given the fact that 'I have pleased a greater number, than I ventured to hope I should please', a more detailed explanation of what is intended is owed to the reading public as a duty of the poet (Prose I, 118–22).

Characteristically, the tone of these opening paragraphs conveys the impression that Wordsworth has had to be prompted by others to undertake the task. What also emerges is an emphasis on the seriousness with which he views the calling of a poet. As such, this is a critique of both modern poets guilty of 'triviality and meanness both of thought and language', and of modern society. Wordsworth's explanation that his quest is for a poetry of permanent value to society, a poetry which demands 'a plainer more emphatic language' than that used in much contemporary work, leads the Preface to engage with what were still turbulent political issues (Prose I, 124).

The source of his subject-matter, gleaned primarily from the society of 'Low and rustic life' rather than from life among an educated literati, evoked echoes of the poet's own radical past. The devotee of Paine and friend of John Thelwall, author of the *Letter to Llandaff*, now canvasses the 'sympathies of men', pointing out that men of the lower orders exercise 'a plainer more emphatic language' than their social betters (Prose I, 124). To a nervous eye the 'sympathies of men' might appear analogous to the Rights of Man. Plain speaking is emphasised throughout as a virtue of the new poetry, and Wordsworth's despair at the political course his nation is set upon is never far beneath the surface as he argues his point: 'a multitude of causes unknown to former times are now acting with a combined force to blunt the discriminating powers of the mind . . .' (Prose I, 128). The difference between the Wordsworth who wrote against Llandaff in 1793 (and failed to publish) and the modern poet (now published) of 1800, is that he has shifted his perception of the issues firmly into a debate concerned with the relationship between the general moral welfare of the nation, and the function of the poet. He applies himself now not to specific issues of political corruption, but to 'the great and universal passions of men' (Prose I, 144).

He incorporated into the Preface points noted down in prose while at Goslar designed to clarify his political position, specifically in relation to Godwin. He based his critique of Godwin on an appeal to what he there refers to as 'habits'. By this he meant knowledge grounded in actual experience rather than abstract argument:

> Can it be imagined by any man who has deeply examined his own heart that an old habit will be foregone, or a new one formed, by a series of propositions, which, presenting no image to the [?mind] can convey no feeling which has any connection with the supposed archetype or fountain of the proposition existing in human life? (Prose I, 103)

The Prelude, of course, was a means of seeking out the 'image' and the 'feeling' through which might be traced the 'archetype or fountain' of Wordsworth's literary life; it was not an abstract treatise on the workings of the mind. Early in the Preface to *Lyrical Ballads* he insists that it is not his intention to 'reason' his reader into an agreement with him (Prose I, 120); instead he directs our attention towards 'the feeling therein developed' of the poems, produced from the pen of one who has reflected deeply on the 'archetype or fountain' of the poet's art (Prose I, 128). The potentially radical exposé that takes place around the image of Simon Lee and the feelings he triggers in his would-be helper (doing so at the expense of the 'popular poetry of the day') is an implicit rejection of Godwinian radicalism (Prose I, 126–8). The Goslar lyrics endorsed the poet whose mind now reflected upon impressions made by 'the common range of visible things' (*Prelude* 1799, 19, 216), the 'rocks and stones and trees'.

Once settled in Grasmere, Wordsworth continued to develop his narrative as well as lyric poetry. There was always that autobiographical vein; characters and experiences were celebrated in ways that confirmed his identity as the modern poet he aspired to be. In the longer narrative pieces we begin to see how the private autobiography and the poetry for potential publication evolve towards his eventual model for the major, public philosophical poem, *The Recluse*. In 'Michael' (1800) he begins with a wholly characteristic gesture:

> If from the public way you turn your steps
> Up the tumultuous brook of Green-head Gill ...
>   (LB 252, 1–2)

He then goes on to frame the story in terms of his own education:

> And hence this Tale, while I was yet a boy
> Careless of books, yet having felt the power
> Of Nature, by the gentle agency
> Of natural objects led me on to feel
> For passions that were not my own, and think
> At random and imperfectly indeed
> On man, the heart of man, and human life.
>   (11.27–33)

In January 1801 the two-volume *Lyrical Ballads* was published, with Coleridge's 'Ancient Mariner' moved from being the first poem (as it had been in 1798) to penultimate position. An attentive reader of the Preface would discover why it did not really belong in the collection at all. Volume II added 41 poems to the collection, for the most part the fruit of Goslar and Grasmere labours. Sales justified further printings of the 1800 edition in 1802 and again in 1805.

The Wordsworths were hardly settled into Dove Cottage before work was resumed on *The Prelude*. Its completion in 1804 as an autobiography in five Books was only temporary, giving way to further revision and the relocation of blocks of text that led into a sixth Book ('Cambridge and the Alps'), which in turn led to the completion of the 1805 *Prelude* with its retrospective treatment of his French trip of 1792–3, and his visionary encounter with Stonehenge on Salisbury Plain. The poem eventually ran to thirteen Books.

It was an extraordinary situation. Wordsworth was composing a work of epic proportions around his commitment to a literary life, and doing so with no intention of publication beyond the occasional release of small segments. He continued to believe in the eventual completion of his monumental public work, and sporadically composed for that, while the private autobiographical writing continued to inform work on odes, lyrics and narratives which were potentially public pieces, but which he increasingly feared to subject to public scrutiny beyond his own close circle. The poem that after the poet's death was to become a benchmark for his biographers and readers remained unknown; in its place was *Lyrical Ballads*, poetry that could hardly have been more different in so many ways from *The Prelude*. It was *Lyrical Ballads* and its Preface that now drew a vicious attack from Francis Jeffrey of *The Edinburgh Review* in 1802. Jeffrey delivered a majestic statement on behalf of traditional Augustan values in literature and society, in the course of which he claimed to have found a link between 'a *sect* of poets that has established itself in this country' and political radicalism.[6] Ironically (given the way Southey had damned the *Ballads* with faint praise), Jeffrey's attack came in the context of a hostile review of Southey's poem, *Thalaba*.

With references manifestly drawn from a reading of the *Lyrical Ballads* Preface, Jeffrey pinned Wordsworth's fragile claim to be modern, public, and beneficial to society on the ropes, and let fly with devastatingly controlled irony on the subject of the new poetry:

> Their most distinguishing symbol, is undoubtedly an affectation of great simplicity and familiarity of language. . . . One of their own authors, indeed, has very ingenuously set forth (in a kind of manifesto that preceded one of their most flagrant acts of hostility), that it was their capital object 'to adapt to the uses of poetry, the ordinary language of conversation among the middling and lower orders of the people'.[7]

Jeffrey's attack on this half-remembered passage from the Preface (whose author is not worth naming) takes strength from deeply rooted assumptions about how literature is to be judged and about how society is to be ordered; he closes on that vital Wordsworthian distinction between action/situation and feeling. The defender of the status quo in 1802 knows what is best for the lower orders, and knows that to assume that such people might have a right to make demands (express their 'sentiments') is to invite anarchy:

> The poor and vulgar may interest us, in poetry, by their *situation*; but never, we apprehend, by any sentiments that are peculiar to their condition, and still less by any language that is characteristic of it.[8]

Though sales of *Lyrical Ballads* appear not to have been materially harmed by Jeffrey's piece, the modern poet recently returned from Goslar (Jeffrey claimed that the 'doctrines' of the new sect were 'of *German* origin') took the drubbing very badly. Thrown on to the defensive, 'the spoiled brat of *The Prelude*' cultivated a supportive coterie world rebuilt around Grasmere. This now centred upon an ordered domestic life lived in semi-retirement.[9]

There was formal recognition of Annette and their child Caroline in 1802, when William and Dorothy travelled to Calais to meet them. This was followed by marriage to Mary Hutchinson in the September of that year. Two crucial meetings had taken place between Wordsworth and Mary in February and April 1802; the decision to travel to France to meet Annette and Caroline (made possible by the Treaty of Amiens), and of Wordsworth and Mary to marry, were interlinked. Dorothy had long been preparing for what was inevitably a profoundly altered domestic arrangement. In the event the emotional turmoil caused first by her meeting with Annette, and then by the approaching marriage of her brother, rendered her incapable of attending the service. Mary must fully have understood the situation, as did the rest of the family who were far from convinced she was behaving sensibly. Mary's strength of character is thus in evidence from the first; she recognised her task, and no doubt it was because of this, coupled with Dorothy's resilience, that the necessary domestic adjustments seem to have been swiftly achieved.

It lies beyond the scope of this book to chart the course of Mary and Dorothy's lives in any detail, but the part they now played in shaping the development of Wordsworth's literary life is incalculable, combining as it did a preparedness to identify with his aspirations while maintaining an individual integrity of purpose. Mary's selfless nursing of Dorothy throughout the long, distressing period of her illness in old age testifies to the depth of love and respect that came to exist between the two women.

Coleridge had moved into Greta Hall, Keswick, in 1800. The Wordsworths' first child, John, was born in June 1803. Wordsworth's determination to take a more responsible approach to his life as a poet could not alter the fact that his work was still essentially coterie-bound, and his lifestyle reclusive. Despite this he remained painfully aware of the need to communicate his work more widely, but found himself perpetually baulked from doing so. The issues involved were public taste, literary form, and the facility of language itself. The consequent tensions were rehearsed repeatedly as *The Prelude* steadily grew in length:

> When I began to enquire,
> To watch and question those I met, and held
> Familiar talk with them, the lonely roads
> Were schools to me in which I daily read
> With most delight the passions of mankind,
> There saw into the depth of human souls. . . .
> (*Prelude* XII, 446, 161–6)

In this characteristic moment from *The Prelude* we have the poet as inquirer, a social being who 'questions', who indulges in 'familiar talk' with others; yet a poet who seems able to do so by incongruously frequenting 'the lonely roads'. *The Prelude* embodies a life of contradictions and anti-climaxes engendering moments ('spots of time') of profound insight. Nowhere is this more dramatically the case than in his reworking of the experience he had had crossing the Alps.

In Book VI Wordsworth recalls how in 1790 he and Robert Jones 'climbed with eagerness' towards the spot that symbolised an important moment on their journey. They then discovered that they had already made the crossing unawares, and 'that thenceforward all our course/ Was downwards'. This moment of anti-climax (a 'dull and heavy slackening') clears the mind of superficial assumptions and expectations, 'I was lost as in a cloud,/ Halted without a struggle to break through' (*Prelude* 216, 506–32).

In the experience that ensures, every image now confirms contradiction and inversion:

> The immeasurable height
> Of woods decaying, never to be decayed,

The stationary blasts of waterfalls,
And everywhere along the hollow rent
Winds thwarting winds, bewildered and forlorn,
The torrents shooting from the clear blue sky,
The rocks that muttered close upon our ears –
Black drizzling crags that spake by the wayside
As if a voice were in them – the sick sight
And giddy prospect of the raving stream,
The unfettered clouds and region of the heavens,
Tumult and peace, the darkness and the light,
Were all like workings of one mind, the features
Of the same face, blossoms upon one tree,
Characters of the great apocalypse,
The types and symbols of eternity,
Of first, and last, and midst, and without end.
                              (11.556–72)

The Prelude was a poem for Goslar, Grasmere and the future, where past events existed to justify the territory his poetry now explored, suspended between public and private worlds, between active and passive states ('woods decaying, never to be decayed,/ The stationary blasts of waterfalls'), between utterance and silence ('Tumult and peace, the darkness and the light'). These are the 'spots of time':

Which with distinct preeminence retain
A renovating virtue, whence, depressed
By false opinion and contentious thought,
Or aught of heavier or more deadly weight
In trivial occupations and the round
Of ordinary intercourse, our minds
Are nourished and invisibly repaired. . . .
                       (XI, 428–30, 257–64)

The Prelude resulted from the way Wordsworth subjected the events of his life, both 'renovating' and 'depressed/ By false opinion', to a process of creative editing in order to affirm the Wordsworth he had determined to become by the time he returned from Germany (there had been several for him to choose from). The Wordsworth who had been to Cambridge was therefore unsuited to academic life in appropriate ways:

                                        Oft did I leave
My comrades, and the crowd, buildings and groves,
And walked along the fields, the level fields,
With heaven's blue concave reared above my head.
                                        (III, 97–100)

What he chose to walk away from is described later in the same
Book:

Here sate in state, and, fed with daily alms,
Retainers won away from solid good.
And here was Labour, his own Bond-slave; Hope
That never set the pains against the prize;
Idleness, halting with his weary clog;
And poor misguided Shame, and witless Fear,
And simple Pleasure, foraging for Death;
Honour misplaced, and Dignity astray;
Feuds, factions, flatteries, Enmity and Guile....

Ultimately we have 'blind Authority beating with his staff/ The
child that might have led him' (122–4, 628–41).

By way of contrast, the poet now living in Grasmere celebrated
the Lake District as the appropriate setting for his work with a
reminiscence of his return to Hawkshead from Cambridge:

But now there opened on me other thoughts,
Of change, congratulation and regret,
A new-born feeling. It spread far and wide:
The trees, the mountains shared it, and the brooks
                        ... I loved,
Loved deeply, all that I had loved before,
More deeply even than ever....
                        (IV, 136–7, 231–4, 270–2)

He remembers London as a series of experiences that ultimately
endorse the virtues of solitude:

Meanwhile the roar continues, till at length,
Escaped as from an enemy, we turn

Abruptly into some sequestered nook
Still as a sheltered place when winds blow loud. . . .
(VII, 236, 184–7)

And his time in France confirms in the end the poet's need to look
beyond immediate political objectives for solutions to the problems
that confront society, what in the Preface to *Lyrical Ballads* he refers
to as the current deplorable 'tendency in life and manners'. He celebrated his response to the death of Robespierre in 1794 with a passage that more properly belongs to his resolve to write a new poetry
in the 1800s:

Thus far our trust is verified: behold,
They who with clumsy desperation brought
Rivers of blood, and preached that nothing else
Could cleanse the Augean stable, by the might
Of their own helper have been swept away.
Their madness is declared and visible;
Elsewhere will safety now be sought, and earth
March firmly towards righteousness and peace.
(X, 388, 545–52)

The 'Salisbury Plain' poet, politically focused, writing in 'clumsy desperation', gives way to the Goslar poet, no less angry at the hypocrisy of the political establishment's 'Augean stable', no less alienated,
but looking now 'elsewhere' for a way forward.

The Salisbury Plain experience must thus be rewritten. In recalling Coleridge's response to the Salisbury Plain poetry, he contrives
to stress not its engagement with the politics of 1793, but Coleridge's
apparent verdict that 'I must then have exercised / Upon the vulgar
forms of present things / And actual world of our familiar days, /
A higher power' (XII, 456 11.360–2). The final Book of the 1805 *Prelude* locates the 'higher power' in Nature with the dramatic sequence
describing his ascent of Snowdon. Characteristically, all is once more
inversion and contradiction; the ascent 'with forehead bent / Earth-
ward, as if in opposition set / Against an enemy' culminates in a
visionary landscape that transports him downward into the earth's
'deep and gloomy breathing space'. What was to have been a view
of the sunrise from far above the earth, an escape from the world,
becomes an encounter with 'The soul, the imagination of the whole'
experienced by moonlight as if at ground level, and indeed from
beneath ground level:

and on the shore
I found myself of a huge sea of mist,
Which meek and silent rested at my feet.
(XIII, 458–60, 10–65)

Alongside *The Prelude*, work on poetry intended for *The Recluse* went slowly forward. 'The Ruined Cottage' and 'The Pedlar' were already to hand, and his arrival at Dove Cottage prompted Wordsworth to start working immediately on the manuscript that has since become known as 'Home at Grasmere'. He also composed what was in effect a blank-verse manifesto for *The Recluse*, the 'Prospectus'.

Wordsworth was here looking to produce poetry of a different order from the lyrics and narratives that gave the two volumes of *Lyrical Ballads* their distinctive modern character. By 1800 *Lyrical Ballads* had come to embody a well-defined, ambitious project. Utilising the revolutionary device of 'simplicity', the reading public was to be redirected towards themes of permanent significance for humanity. But this was poetry written for the most part from beyond the pale of the popular taste of the day, and he continued to compose in the simple style as part of a process of amassing a store of poetry dedicated to the intentions proclaimed in the Preface.

By comparison, *The Recluse* in many ways represented a commitment that lingered on from a previous era of his development. He nevertheless retained the belief that the large-scale public poem remained as a goal he was destined to achieve. In character it was a kind of poetry necessarily distinct from the modernity he strove to attain in *Lyrical Ballads*. *The Recluse* would begin life as a statement recognisably belonging to an established epic tradition within the nation's literary culture. What it might have to say about the path to be followed in the wake of the French Revolution might be controversial, but the message would be uttered from within, rather than from beyond, the boundaries of aesthetic experience.

That was the intent. The 'Thinking in solitude' and 'th'individual mind that keeps its own/ Inviolate retirement' would be 'in various commonalty spread', it would prove in application 'limitless', it was the 'one life' vision of the Pedlar brought out of the poet's individual experience of, say, the Simplon Pass or the moonlit summit of Snowdon, and placed in the public domain:

where're I may
I would give utterance in numerous verse

Of Truth, of Grandeur, Beauty, Love, and Hope;
Of joy in various commonalty spread;
Of th'individual mind that keeps its own
Inviolate retirement, and consists
With being limitless, the one great Life. . . .

(HG, 'Prospectus', 257)

That was the intent. What he aimed at might be characterised as seeking to take the many night-time sequences of *The Prelude* imbued with implicit revelation – the discharged soldier, skating, stealing the boat, Snowdon – and recasting them in the light of day where all might gain some benefit, not just the poet left on the deserted road. With reference to the ballads, he sought to take the 'strange fit of passion' out of the moonlight into the sunlight, rendering it familiar 'in various commonality spread'. But the *Recluse* poetry resisted its public role, constantly inclining towards a collage of existing and emergent *Prelude* materials that remained intrinsically private in conception, modern in theory, and narrative in format.

In *The Prelude* Wordsworth repeatedly bridged the chasm between public and private by subtly imaginative strategies that rested ultimately on accepting the legitimacy of his personal convictions. His literary life constituted the proof. This was fine for him and for his coterie readership; it left the public needing more. 'Home at Grasmere' proved an inconclusive experiment at bridge-building; it veered back towards *The Prelude*. The 'Prospectus' announced the intentions, but stopped there; other poems written at this time destined for eventual publication in the two-volume collection of 1807 frequently addressed the issue, but accorded with Wordsworth's modern aspirations and as he knew, and feared, lay beyond the pale.

The problem remained. It is the problem summarised in Jon Cook's discussion of Paul de Man's reading of *The Prelude*, one we all tend to have with language: 'We want language to be or do something that it cannot be or do. Both autobiography, and the rhetoric of Romanticism, more generally exemplify this desire and its inevitable frustration.'[10]

6

Grasmere Poetry: Dove Cottage Life

'Grasmere was very solemn in the last glimpse of twilight', Dorothy wrote in May 1800, adding, 'it calls home the heart to quietness'.[1] At about the same time, possibly a month or two earlier, her brother celebrated Grasmere as a 'Dear valley, having in thy face a smile/ Though peaceful, full of gladness':

> This small abiding-place of many men,
> A termination and a last retreat,
> A Centre, come from wheresoe'er you will,
> A Whole without dependence or defect,
> Made for itself and happy in itself,
> Perfect Contentment, Unity entire.
> (HG 46, 135–6; 48, 165–70)

Grasmere as a place to live was certainly not without 'defect', nor could it (any more than anywhere else) offer 'Perfect Contentment, Unity entire'; but it could, for various reasons, sustain a belief that such a state was conceivable. The poet whom Wordsworth was constructing in *The Prelude* strove to achieve in person what Grasmere now promised as a place; a forever less than perfect reality struggling to attain perfection becomes a central theme of Grasmere poetry.

Against Wordsworth's powerful evocation of his new home as the embodiment of 'Perfect Contentment' (an echo, possibly of John of Gaunt's description of England in Shakespeare's *Richard the Second*), we have Dorothy's journal account of daily life at Town End. No reader of the *Grasmere Journals* can escape the fact that both brother and sister suffered frequent ill health. Headaches and sickness were commonplace: 'W very sick very ill . . . sadly tired, threatenings of the piles . . . Wm still unwell . . . I had a back-ache . . . Coleridge was very unwell', is a characteristic litany interspersing Dorothy's comments on the more picturesque moments of life at Dove Cottage through just a couple of weeks in mid-November 1800.[2] Regular gossip sessions concerning the lives and loves of neighbours, along with encounters with travellers and vagrants of all sorts kept the trials and tribulations of the real world very much in focus.

On a more positive note, and certainly in relation to Grasmere as a 'Unity entire', the letters and journals also bear witness to the fact that besides Coleridge's arrival at Keswick in April 1800 (joined by his wife and their son Hartley in the summer), there was a rapid reformation of the Wordsworth circle. This fact, however, guaranteed that Dove Cottage (whatever might be claimed for Grasmere) was rarely to be a 'peaceful' place in the sense implied in *Home at Grasmere*.

In January 1800, John Wordsworth came to share the joys and labours of moving in. John was in the service of the East India Company, and his long stay prior to becoming Captain of the *Earl of Abergavenny* in the autumn established him as a key figure within a circle that included the Losh family, Thomas Myers, Charles Lloyd, and of course the Hutchinson sisters, Mary, Sara and Joanna. William Hazlitt found his way to Keswick in 1803, Thomas De Quincey made an appearance in 1807 after worshipping from afar for several years; friendship with Sir Walter Scott dates from 1803; John Thelwall visited in the same year.

Wordsworth's major task of 1800 had been to oversee the publication of the new two-volume *Lyrical Ballads*. This occasioned an avalanche of frequently panic-stricken letters detailing alterations and errors. He checked and double-checked the safe arrival of manuscripts with Biggs and Cottle. Transcriptions were prepared by Dorothy aided by others including Coleridge and Sara Hutchinson. With the revised *Lyrical Ballads* in print it is hardly surprising that some time elapsed before any further significant composition. The Grasmere ambience eventually resulted in a period of revived creative energy in 1802, when 39 poems of varying length and complexity, including 'Resolution and Independence', and a first version of the 'Ode: Intimations of Immortality', were written. A further edition of *Lyrical Ballads* was also produced in 1802.

In the summer Dorothy and William took advantage of the truce between France and Britain to visit Annette and her daughter in France, and in October of that year Wordsworth married Mary Hutchinson.

In 1803 William and Mary's first child, John, was born. Two

months later, in August, William, Dorothy and Coleridge set off on
a tour of Scotland, in the course of which William once more exercised his gift for getting lost among mountains:

> In a few minutes Wm. arrived; he had heard of me at the gate,
> and followed as quickly as he could, shouting after me. He was
> pale and exceedingly tired. After he had left us he had taken a
> wrong road. . . .[3]

The timing of the tour may seem strange, but it was no doubt a
relief to Mary to have the tiny cottage to herself and her sister
Joanna to nurse the child. It was now that Wordsworth and Walter
Scott first met.

Early in 1803 the Lowther debt was finally settled, following the
death of Sir James Lowther in May 1802. What with that and the discovery that Sir George Beaumont, a declared enthusiast of the *Lyrical
Ballads*, now further impressed by Coleridge's account of Wordsworth's abilities in 1802, had chosen to make the poet a gift of a
small estate near Greta Hall called Applethwaite, Wordsworth's
luck certainly seemed to be changing. It was also in 1803 that Wordsworth determined to join the local militia set to defend the country
from Napoleonic invasion. A second child, Dora, was born in 1804;
in the meantime Coleridge, in a continuing state of domestic turmoil,
ill and dreading the onset of the northern winter, took himself off to
Malta.

Work on *The Prelude* continued throughout these years, but the
Grasmere idyll was shattered early in 1805 when news came that
John Wordsworth had been drowned. The *Earl of Abergavenny* went
down off Portland Bill in February and John was among the 232
passengers and crew who perished.

The two-volume *Lyrical Ballads* (reprinted for a fourth time in 1805)
repeatedly defined its author as one of a small like-minded group.
John is present in these pages, an intrinsic part of the literary life,
nowhere more so than in the group of five 'Poems on the Naming of
Places' which immediately precede the final poem of Volume Two,
'Michael'. These poems remind us of the fact that the Wordsworth
group were quite literally inscribing their presence on the landscape.
In 1801–2, midway between Grasmere and Keswick, William, Dorothy, John, Mary and Sara Hutchinson and Coleridge all carved their
names on the 'Rock of Names'. Two 'Inscription' poems in Volume

Two ('for the Hermitage on St. Herbert's Island' and 'for the House on the Island at Grasmere') further testify to this practice.[4]

In the fourth poem 'On the Naming of Places' (composed July–November 1800) it could have been any of the group who with Wordsworth encountered a lone fisherman while walking round Grasmere lake. Unlike the other 'Naming of Places' poems – offshoots in their way of the 'Home at Grasmere' project – this one acknowledges the darker side of life within the valley confines. In the first instance the three friends denounce the fisherman as:

> An idle man, who thus could lose a day
> Of the mid-harvest, when the labourer's hire
> Is ample. . . .
>
> (LB 247, 57–9)

Seen close to, however, his worn features 'And wasted limbs' tell once more the story of the mendicant soldier. Nature is suddenly and dramatically relocated from its picturesque function of earlier in the poem where it matched the walkers' mood of idle pleasure, to a role of heartless indifference:

> The man was using his best skill to gain
> A pittance from the dead unfeeling lake
> That knew not of his wants.
>
> (LB 249, 70–2)

The moral here seems very clear; human suffering of this nature must be answered by people, a picturesque landscape will not suffice. The experience is at once a lesson in public accountability, but it equally projects the image of a private, coterie experience. John, deeply sensitive to the centrality of a supportive coterie to the success of his brother's work, had become very much a part of that coterie, even as Coleridge was tending to feel the chilly breeze of marginalisation.

'Poems on the Naming of Places' draw on supposedly real moments of Grasmere experience. Equally autobiographical, though in a different way, is the poem he set at the beginning of *Lyrical Ballads* Volume Two, 'Hart-Leap Well' (composed early in 1800). Wordsworth and Dorothy heard the tale attached to the well when travelling from Sockburn to Grasmere in the winter of 1799; but the poem does much more than memorialise this experience.

In Part One the legend of the well is told in ballad form. The Knight of old sets out on a hunt, and after all his comrades have fallen by the wayside he pursues the hart alone. In a desperate bid to escape her remorseless pursuer she plunges down a precipice to her death. The Knight – well satisfied by his day's work – decrees that a pavilion be built by the well where the hart has perished to commemorate both her courage, and his prowess as a hunter.

Wordsworth thus cannily offered a familiar ballad in the popular style (Burger is a model) to begin his new collection. Part Two of 'Hart-Leap Well', however, is very different. Part One represents the world of public life, emphasising the familiar Wordsworthian metaphor of 'the tumult of the chace' (LB 134, 25). Part Two swiftly deflates the Knight's sense of achievement; it tells of Wordsworth's discovery of the site in 1799, now barren and deserted, and known to those who live nearby as 'curs'd' (LB 137, 124). What at the time was publicly celebrated as a triumph, is now reassessed in the atmosphere of intimate personal reflection, and redefined as a disaster, an outrage against Nature.

It was in this way that Wordsworth was making public the private work of *The Prelude*. Like the Knight in 'Hart-Leap Well', Wordsworth had become for a while totally immersed in the public 'chace' of political life. Books IX and X of *The Prelude* describe how his political commitment was the cause of progressive alienation, the 'lonely road' (X 408, 911) travelled by the poet after his return from France in 1792:

> the errors into which I was betrayed
> By present objects, and by reasonings false
> From the beginning, inasmuch as drawn
> Out of a heart which had been turned aside
> From Nature. . . .
>> (*Prelude* X 406, 882–6)

This is the fate of Sir Walter, and though he never comes to realise it, the narrator makes sure that we do:

> Where is the throng, the tumult of the chace?
> The bugles that so joyfully were blown?
> – This race it looks not like an earthly race;
> Sir Walter and the Hart are left alone.
>> (LB 134, 25–8)

For Wordsworth, an overweening enthusiasm for the 'chace' led to depression and breakdown at Racedown, followed by persecution and eviction from Alfoxden (Annette does not figure here). Unlike Sir Walter, Wordsworth discovers his error even as he rediscovers the virtues of 'retirement' at Grasmere (or is at least able, once returned there, to imagine that he has).

The Prelude repeatedly explores the experience of a mind torn between what Nature prompts and what political processes demand. In the following passage from Book X (composed in 1804), reflecting on his feelings for France and England in 1794, he emphasises the distinction between his 'intuitive' faith in the rightness of the cause, and the public political processes by which change actually took place: 'The language of the Senate', the 'public measures of the Government'. His idealism blinded him to the political realities; France was doomed to falter despite the worthy spirit in which the Revolution had been engendered, partly because of the inadequacy of the French leaders, and in no small degree owing to the unenlightened, reactionary politics of the British Government:

> The language of the Senate, and the acts
> And public measures of the Government,
> Though both of heartless omen, had not power
> To daunt me. In the people was my trust,
> And in the virtues which mine eyes had seen,
> And to the ultimate repose of things
> I looked with unabated confidence.
> I knew that wound external could not take
> Life from the young Republic, that new foes
> Would only follow in the path of shame
> Their brethren, and her triumphs be in the end
> Great, universal, irresistible.
> This faith, which was an object in my mind
> Of passionate intuition, had effect
> Not small in dazzling me; for thus, through zeal,
> Such victory I confounded in my thoughts
> With one far higher and more difficult:
> Triumphs of unambitious peace at home,
> And noiseless fortitude.
>   (*Prelude* 390, 574–92)

The Prelude, written for private consumption, proposes a reformed body politic for Britain as the most 'difficult' achievement of all, 'peace at home,/ And noiseless fortitude'. Wordsworth is still looking for such a change in 1804 when Book X is being drafted. It is a very public, political wish, emphasised later in the Book by outspoken criticism of the British Government of 1794:

Giants in their impiety alone,
But in their weapons and their warfare base
As vermin working out of reach, they leagued
Their strength perfidiously to undermine
Justice, and make an end of liberty.
                    (*Prelude* 394, 652–6)

In 'Hart-Leap Well', written for public consumption, Wordsworth resolves his indictment of Sir Walter (representing the nation's ruling class) in very personal, intimate terms. The temptation to value shows of public power and triumph above reverence for Nature's law which teaches 'reverential care' for 'the meanest thing that feels' (LB 139, 167 & 180), is defeated by the poet's personal acquisition of 'peace at home,/ And noiseless fortitude'. The implicit political statement is deferred, transmuted into a private utterance as William and Dorothy walk on towards their home at Grasmere.

The lyrics Wordsworth worked on through 1802 continued to explore the public/private dichotomy that underpins the structure and meaning of 'Hart-Leap Well'. 'To The Daisy' (destined to become the first poem of the two-volume collection published in 1807) employed Wordsworthian 'simplicity' to this end:

In youth from rock to rock I went,
From hill to hill, in discontent
Of pleasure high and turbulent,
     Most pleas'd when most uneasy;
But now my own delights I make,
My thirst at every rill can slake,
And gladly Nature's love partake
     Of thee, sweet Daisy!
                    (*1807* 65, 1–8)

In Wordsworth's hands the daisy manifestly becomes a projection of his poetic self:

Thou liv'st with less ambitious aim,
Yet hast not gone without thy fame;

Thou art indeed by many a claim
  The Poet's darling.
                    (11.29–32)

The daisy is a 'bold lover of the sun' (1.74); Wordsworth was at this time reworking his self-portrait of 1799 into Book II of *The Prelude*, where he tells us, 'already I began/ To love the sun; a boy I loved the sun' (*Prelude* 75, 177–8).

Everything he turns to tells and retells his own story as he would wish it to be, continually rehearsing the problems that face him at the time of writing. In 'To The Daisy' he admits that (like Sir Walter) he is still subject to 'stately passions' (1.49); the simplicity of the daisy's existence provides the antidote. The error he fell into back in 1794 and now analyses in *The Prelude* still beckons. In 1806, returning after six years to his 'Home at Grasmere' lines of 1800, he wrote:

I cannot at this moment read a tale
Of two brave Vessels matched in deadly fight
And fighting to the death, but I am pleased
More than a wise man ought to be; I wish,
I burn, I struggle, and in soul am there.
                    (HG 96–8, 929–33)

Like so many of the 'simple' lyrics written at this time, 'To The Daisy' emerges from its apparently innocent, naive first appearance to become a complex poem which registers the tension between the public and private world of a modern poet; it is a skilfully sustained act both of recognition and deferral. Other poems of 1802 with equally 'simple' subjects probe the same profound issues. Encounters take place with daisies, birds, butterflies, celandines, children, vagrants and unassuming travellers; most notably we encounter the Leech Gatherer of 'Resolution and Independence'.

Sparked off by an encounter noted by Dorothy in her Journal (October 1800) with an old man near their home, Wordsworth composed what become a lengthy poem in which he celebrated the man's fortitude. Both the poet and the Leech Gatherer live within sight of extinction, the old man because of his age, infirmity and the scarcity of leeches, Wordsworth because of his choice of an unorthodox literary life. The style of 'naked simplicity' adopted for the poetry threatens at the very least his credibility as a poet; the poem suggests there may be an even higher price to pay.[5] Like Burns and Chatterton before him, Wordsworth is determined to go his own way, and the poem recalls their fate, and suggests a similar one for himself:

By our own spirits are we deified;
We poets in our youth begin in gladness;
But thereof comes in the end despondancy and madness.
(1807 125, 47–9)

The Leech Gatherer, old, crippled, facing a bleak future in a bleak environment that contrasts starkly with the pastoral landscape described in the early stanzas (repeating the strategy of the fourth 'Naming of Places' poem), exhibits a will to survive that inspires the poet with a determination to persevere. Significantly, our attention is drawn to the old man's words:

His words came feebly, from a feeble chest,
Yet each in solemn order followed each,
With something of a lofty utterance drest. . . .
(11.99–101)

Intriguingly, Wordsworth writes of his inability to concentrate on what the Leech Gatherer actually says. While he gives a solemn – albeit mundane – account of his circumstances, the poet's mind drifts off into reverie: 'his voice to me was like a stream/ Scarce heard' (11.114–15). Any benefit to be had from the 'naked simplicity' of the man's account is being blocked by Wordsworth's anxieties. There is conflict here between Wordsworth's concern for the world in which he aspires to be publicly recognised as a poet, and the value of this private moment for him.

It is essentially from the privacy of the situation, from an attempt to listen to the man's words, and not his own 'thoughts within myself' (1.139), that Wordsworth eventually draws his sense of resolution and, very much to the point, independence. We have therefore, as before, that characteristic moment of deferral. It occurs here (11.123–6) when thoughts of 'mighty Poets in their misery dead' are laid aside in favour of learning what will be of use in his own specific case:

My question eagerly did I renew,
'How is it that you live, and what is it you do?'

'Resolution and Independence' belongs to a cycle of poems initiated in March 1802 by four stanzas originally entitled 'Ode'. By early 1804 Wordsworth had extended the piece, though the title by which it is now known, 'Ode: Intimations of Immortality from Recollections of Early Childhood ' was not added until much later. His decision to place the Ode at the end of the 1807 collection indicates the importance it had for him. The first stanza is effectively a less optimistic recapitulation of thoughts already present in 'Tintern Abbey':

> There was a time when meadow, grove, and stream,
> The earth, and every common sight,
>   To me did seem
>   Apparell'd in celestial light,
> The glory and the freshness of a dream,
> It is not now as it has been of yore;–
>   Turn wheresoe'er I may,
>   By night or day,
> The things which I have seen I now can see no more.
>   (*1807* 271, 1–9)

Coleridge, now in love with Mary Hutchinson's sister, Sara, feeling less and less a part of the charmed Grasmere circle, responded to the four stanzas Wordsworth completed in March 1802 with an agonised 'Verse Letter' (subsequently published in a revised form as 'Dejection: An Ode') addressed to Sara Hutchinson. Here 'the visionary gleam' whose passing Wordsworth laments in 'Intimations' (1.56) is given up for lost, as Coleridge sees all hope of reviving the restorative pleasures of Alfoxden in the Lake District come to nothing:

> Wherefore, O wherefore! should I wish to be
> A wither'd branch upon a blossoming Tree? . . .
> O Sara! we receive but what we give,
> And in *our* life alone does Nature live
> Our's is her Wedding Garment, our's her Shroud –
> And would we ought behold of higher Worth
> Than that inanimate cold World allow'd
> To that poor loveless ever anxious Crowd,
> Ah! from the soul itself must issue forth
> A Light, a Glory, and a luminous Cloud
> Enveloping the Earth![6]

'Resolution and Independence' came soon after this as a call to arms for those who, like Coleridge, hurting as they might be, must soldier on. The completed Intimations Ode, extended to 11 stanzas in 1804, became an ambitious attempt to review the issues under debate in as positive, celebratory terms as possible.

Francis Jeffrey's verdict on the 'Ode' in 1807 was emphatic: 'This is, beyond doubt, the most illegible and unintelligible part of the publication. We can pretend to give no analysis or explanation of it.'[7] In an elaborate Pindaric Ode format, where line length and rhyme scheme are constantly shifting, Wordsworth relentlessly addresses the identity and development of his own poetic persona. Inscribed here, therefore, is his increasingly vexed relationship with Coleridge, the man who at Alfoxden had nurtured his pantheistic beliefs in Nature, and who now confessed to having lost the faith himself; the man who had seen his closest friend banish his 'Ancient Mariner' from *Lyrical Ballads*. Inscribed here also is Wordsworth's determination to hold fast to his creed of 'simplicity', a determination that even Sara and Mary had questioned when confronted by 'Resolution and Independence' in early draft form.

As an Augustan critic, Jeffrey had every right to be baffled. The 'Ode' aims to explore the unintelligible; it investigates what is lost, what is in the past; it is a statement of independence rather than social utility. In consequence, sentence structures will at times fail to sustain an ordered intelligibility; the poem enacts moments when 'the light of sense/ Goes out in flashes' (*Prelude* VI 216, 534–5), when 'we are laid asleep/ In body, and become a living soul' (LB 117, 46–7), when the 'mind's eye' usurps physical vision and hearing as in 'Resolution and Independence' (1.136). What was Jeffrey to make of Wordsworth's appeal to 'joy' in Stanza IX, especially as he had no idea of the way Coleridge had used the word in his 'Ode' to Sara?

> O joy! that in our embers
> Is something that doth live,
> That nature yet remembers
> What was so fugitive!
> (*1807* 275, 132–5)

Wordsworth claims that joy is a quality independent of us, it lives on in our embers (in what is left of a burnt-out poet). It may be recovered not by the poet, but by 'nature'. This is to propose something that cannot be known; we may only know of it. What we possess, and must be thankful for, is 'the thought of our past years':

> The thought of our past years in me doth breed
> Perpetual benedictions. . . .
>
> (11.136–7)

This statement is followed by the logical but troubling affirmation that he does not bless childhood itself, imbued as it is with the essential qualities upon which his modern poetic style rests, 'the simple creed / Of Childhood, whether fluttering or at rest' (11.139–40). What he blesses is logically – yet perversely – the loss of childhood which gives rise to 'obstinate questionings' of what 'sense' and 'outward things' are. He blesses 'Fallings from us, vanishings':

> Blank misgivings of a Creature
> Moving about in worlds not realiz'd.
>
> (11.142–8)

Critics have long since identified the tension that such lines betray between Wordsworth's determinedly optimistic tone, and the potentially devastating implications of the sentiment. Jerome McGann explains what is happening as an 'internalization' by Wordsworth of all the conflicts experienced, including the external 'socio-historical' ones that were being aired privately in *The Prelude*:

> the poem's problem emerges when Wordsworth recognises that his sense of universal joy . . . has resulted in his loss of the concrete and particular. . . . Wordsworth made a solitude and he called it peace.[8]

In this respect *The Prelude* appears as a bridge designed to enable the relocation of poetry from its 'socio-historical' origins (the world of social action, protest, revolution) to what George Barker described in his 1930s riposte to 'Resolution and Independence' as 'the individual rebellion'.[9]

In the following lines of the stanza considered above (11.132–70) formal syntax gives way under Wordsworth's attempt to reconcile the 'noisy years' and 'mad endeavour' of public life and poetry (the 'Salisbury Plain' manuscripts have not been entirely abandoned), to a poetry that achieves its permanence in an 'eternal silence'. The gap between language and worthwhile meaning that had skewed the encounter with the Leech Gatherer is exposed:

> But for those first affections,
> Those shadowy recollections,
>   Which, be they what they may,
> Are yet the fountain light of all our day,
> Are yet a master light of all our seeing;
>   Uphold us, cherish us, and make
> Our noisy years seem moments in the being
> Of the eternal Silence: truths that wake,
>   To perish never;
> Which neither listlessness, nor mad endeavour,
>   Nor Man nor Boy,
> Nor all that is at enmity with joy,
> Can utterly abolish or destroy!
>   (*1807* 275–6, 151–63)

Wordsworth's 'truths that wake' are realised in 'eternal Silence'; they are the public road in the unpeopled depths of night; they are revealed by a light shining apart from his beloved sun, a sun found to be surplus to requirements in the account of climbing Snowdon which he placed at the beginning of *The Prelude* Book XIII. There is a reminder of that moment in this stanza, when the 'real' sea is exchanged for a 'sight of that immortal sea/ Which brought us hither' (11.166–7).

In the course of 1802 Wordsworth worked hard to develop his skills as a writer of sonnets. His commitment in particular to the technically rigorous Miltonic form of the sonnet was an expression of kinship with a literary tradition at once venerable and politically subversive. Wordsworth's politics were to a large degree rooted in the so-called Commonwealthman tradition of the mid-seventeenth century.[10] Radical Whigs in England at the time of the American War frequently aligned themselves with the tradition of seventeenth-century Civil War political theorists and writers who supported Parliament against the King (among whom was John Milton); it was this tradition and rhetoric that Beaupuy had studied, and in which friends such as the Pinneys were steeped.

Milton's epic poem *Paradise Lost* (1667) was in no small part a lament for a lost heaven on earth following the collapse of the Commonwealth experiment. Wordsworth's sense of a Miltonic context

for *The Recluse* is very evident. The role of the sonnet in Wordsworth's eventual preparation of the 1807 collection of poems is therefore important. Wordsworthian sonnets present us with yet another
facet of the paradoxical Wordsworthian position; they represent at
once an element of stability (Jeffrey knew what he was about when
analysing Miltonic form), at the same time they signify an irrepress-
ibly destabilising attitude.

The penultimate poem in the 1807 two-volume set is 'Elegiac
Stanzas: Suggested by a Picture of Peele Castle, in a Storm, Painted
by Sir George Beaumont'. The 'Elegy' was written in the course of
May and June 1806. The theme is once more the gulf between past
and present, but this time the impact of John's death provided the
elegiac focus.

Against Beaumont's dramatic painting Wordsworth sets his memory of the castle as he had seen it during the summer of 1794. He
had already memorialised the 1794 experience in *The Prelude*, though
there he recalled not the castle, but his reception of the news of
Robespierre's death, which had filled him with ecstatically revived
hopes for the spread of political justice. That politicised entry is now
revised to summon up the sight of the castle in a period of seemingly
endless fine weather:

> Ah! THEN, if mine had been the Painter's hand,
> To express what then I saw; and add the gleam,
> The light that never was, on sea or land,
> The consecration, and the Poet's dream;
>
> I would have planted thee, thou hoary Pile!
> Amid a world how different from this!
> Beside a sea that could not cease to smile;
> On tranquil land, beneath a sky of bliss....
>
> (*1807* 267, 13–20)

In his reference to 'The light that never was' we encounter yet
again the major preoccupation of Wordsworth's poetry in these
years. Recognising the 'never was', yet striving still in some way
to realise it, is what he here describes as 'humanising' his soul;
the words play out an acceptance of loss, the very act of which lays
claim to a negation of that loss, and thus to a serenity:

> So once it would have been, – 'tis so no more;
> I have submitted to a new controul:

A power is gone, which nothing can restore;
A deep distress hath humaniz'd my Soul.

Not for a moment could I now behold
A smiling sea and be what I have been:
The feeling of my loss will ne'er be old;
This, which I know, I speak with mind serene.

(11.33–40)

Putting together the final Books of the 1805 *Prelude* (April and May) had already assumed the nature of an elegiac task, and in Book XIII the sea imagery (noted also in the 'Intimations' Ode) prefaces an entry to the grave in search of life:

but in that breach
Through which the homeless voice of waters rose,
That dark deep thoroughfare, had Nature lodged
The soul, the imagination of the whole.

(*Prelude* 460, 62–5)

With *The Prelude* now complete, Wordsworth turned once more to *The Recluse*. To this end his resumed composition of the 'Home at Grasmere' project in June 1806 registers the distance travelled since the buoyant lines of 1800 had been written:

No, we are not alone; we do not stand,
My Emma, here misplaced and desolate,
Loving what no one cares for but ourselves.
We shall not scatter through the plains and rocks
Of this fair Vale and o'er its spacious heights
Unprofitable kindliness, bestowed
On Objects unaccustomed to the gifts
Of feeling, that were cheerless and forlorn
But few weeks past, and would be so again
If we were not. We do not tend a lamp
Whose lustre we alone participate,
Which is dependent upon us alone,
Mortal though bright, a dying, dying flame.

(HG 78, 646–58)

These lines make it only too clear how real the sense of being 'misplaced and desolate' had at times been since the Wordsworths' arrival at Grasmere; the poet now fights a rearguard action against the negatives that persistently threaten to overwhelm this passage, 'we are not . . . we do not. . . . We shall not . . .'.

By 1805–6 the public poet of *Lyrical Ballads* had achieved a degree of success; he had also achieved a degree of notoriety, subject equally to acclaim from devotees, and to ridicule from detractors of his literary 'simplicity'. He remained – despite behaviour which indicated a renunciation of his radical past – politically suspect. He was a patriotic militiaman who was nevertheless still in touch with John Thelwall, the unrepentant radical. The prospect of further publication appalled him for a number of reasons. While the likelihood of having his political past paraded was sufficiently disturbing, there was the added risk that hostile reviewers might uncover details of the Annette Vallon affair. There remained of course the question of whether the poet of Grasmere was not in fact well satisfied with the public he had already cultivated and felt happy to leave it there.

Jeffrey's criticisms had alarmed and wounded him; he had good reason to wonder if there was any point in undertaking the labour of a sequel to *Lyrical Ballads*, knowing full well what kind of poems he was stockpiling in the Dove Cottage drawers. A further distraction by 1806 was the fact that before long Dove Cottage would have to be vacated, because it no longer provided adequate space for the household. In addition to John (born 1803) and Dora (born August 1804), there was now Thomas (June 1806). The household also included Mary's sister Sara and a nurse, Hannah Lewthwaite, while Coleridge was expected back from Malta in the course of the summer.

In March 1806 Wordsworth left Grasmere for a month in London, probably to everyone's mutual relief. He met old friends, and through Beaumont's influence found himself moving in more exalted company, meeting Charles James Fox and attending the Royal Academy exhibition where he first saw Beaumont's 'Peele Castle'.

Relief from the confines of Dove Cottage was made possible on a temporary basis by Beaumont's offer of Hall Farm at Coleorton in Leicestershire, where he was having a new house built. The situation was complicated by Coleridge, who had returned to England in August. He was desperate to see Sara Hutchinson, but dreaded having to confront his wife. While he procrastinated in London, the Wordsworths waited in Kendal to see him before setting off on their journey south. Eventually he arrived; it was a difficult and distressing meeting, followed, it would seem, by a depressing journey to Hall Farm:

M. and I had a troublesome journey. . . . John and D. were weary
with three days confinement in a post-chaise, and towards night
whined after Grasmere and old friends, and poor Thomas's cough
was and is very bad. (MY I, 87)

By the time Coleridge joined them at Coleorton in December the
Wordsworths were comfortably settled in and reconciled to his
determination to break from his wife. It was now that Wordsworth,
faced by a Coleridge who seemed at least to some degree restored
to his former self, read him the finished *Prelude*. And it was at
Coleorton that the decision was taken to publish a selection of the
poems written since *Lyrical Ballads*. Immense care was taken (as with
Lyrical Ballads) over proofing the work, and considerable thought
was given to the grouping and ordering of the poems. The reasons
for this relate directly to the fact that in ordering the poetry, Wordsworth was continuing to 'order' his literary life.

The first group of poems in what became the 1807 *Poems, in Two
Volumes* constitute a determined reiteration of Wordsworth's creed
of simplicity, juxtaposing poems of personal reflection and intimacy
(specifically in the case of 'She was a Phantom of Delight') with historical narrative, 'The Horn of Egremont Castle', and narratives of
common life, 'Fidelity'. The sequence is broken at its mid-point by
the heroic couplets of 'Character of the Happy Warrior', and at the
end by the formal, somewhat bleak 'Ode to Duty'.

'The Happy Warior' interjects into the first group of poems a
description of Wordsworth's ideal patriot warrior; he is a Beaupuy;
he is Wordsworth (given the opportunity). What is clear is that his
image of the selfless patriot is equally an expression of Wordsworth's
literary endeavours. The ideal warrior, despite a 'faculty for storm
and turbulence,/ Is yet a soul whose master bias leans/ To home-
felt pleasures and to gentle scenes' (*1807* 86, 58–60). Much of what
is here a politically oriented description has already been met with
in the first poem, 'To the Daisy': 'The homely sympathy that heeds/
The common life', and in the two 'Celandine' poems that immediately precede 'The Happy Warrior'. The world of flowers reflects
the world of politics and war:

Ill befall the yellow Flowers,
Children of the flaring hours!
Buttercups, that will be seen,
Whether we will see or no;

> Others, too, of lofty mien;
> They have done as worldlings do,
> Taken praise that should be thine,
> Little, humble Celandine!
> (1807 81, 49–56)

The warrior (the very opposite of Sir Walter in 'Hart-Leap Well')
keeps his purpose in mind, careless of whether he be a 'Conspicuous
object in a Nation's eye/ Or left unthought-of in obscurity' (*1807* 86,
66–7); his virtue lies in his 'fidelity', his 'darling passion'. This refers
us on to the theme of the next poem, 'The Horn of Egremont Castle',
and back to the poem 'Fidelity'. The subject may be an obscure Lakeland incident as in 'Fidelity' (very different from the public history of
the Lucies of Egremont), but the 'feeling therein developed' is designed to give it equal weight; you might also argue that the Lucies
of Egremont are subject to a 'levelling' treatment. Ultimately the
'feeling' in question is for God:

> Yes, proof was plain that since the day
> On which the Traveller thus had died
> The Dog had watch'd about the spot,
> Or by his Master's side:
> How nourish'd here through such long time
> He knows, who gave that love sublime,
> And gave that strength of feeling, great
> Above all estimate.
> (1807 'Fidelity' 73–4, 58–65)

This is the 'Happy Warrior', who finds comfort not in public plaudits
but 'in himself and in his cause':

> And, while the mortal mist is gathering, draws
> His breath in confidence of Heaven's applause. . . .
> (1807 86, 81–3)

The literary life and the public life are thus bound together in the
opening set of poems. The next short section concludes with 'Resolution and Independence'. What Wordsworth chose to do here was
preface an important poem with a medley of poems 'Composed',
as he explained, 'During a Tour, Chiefly on Foot'. Each in its way
identifies an aspect of the final poem's theme. Two are contrasting

encounters, 'Beggars' and 'Alice Fell', counterpointing the poet's encounter with the Leech Gatherer. 'To a Sky-Lark' rehearses the longer poem's shift of mood from a weary heart (*1807* 117, 9) to one of cheerful 'plodding on' (1.28). The sonnet, 'With how sad steps' looks at a transformation of mood willed by the poet and made real in the imagination.

The first volume concludes with two large sonnet collections, 46 poems in all, 'Miscellaneous' and 'Sonnets Dedicated to Liberty'. Here we have Wordsworth formally and publicly addressing the political situation, and identifying specifically with the spirit of John Milton and his contemporary Commonwealthman activists:

> The later Sydney, Marvel, Harrington,
> Young Vane, and others who call'd Milton Friend.
> These Moralists could act and comprehend:
> They knew how genuine glory was put on;
> Taught us how rightfully a nation shone
> In splendour: what strength was, that would not bend
> But in magnanimous meekness.
>
> ('Great Men have been among us' 166, 2–8)

Here once more is the Happy Warrior; here is Wordsworth claiming mastery of a major poetic form, combining what is still manifestly a position critical of his country's political establishment – 'She is a fen/ Of stagnant waters' ('London 1802' 165, 2–3) – with a celebration of natural objects – 'the broad sun/ Is sailing down in its tranquility; / The gentleness of heaven is on the sea' ('It is a beauteous Evening' 150, 3–5) – and doing so in a way designed to reissue the sonnet as a form appropriate to his concern for contemporary issues.

Beneath the surface of these, as of all the poems, there is the restless movement of Wordsworth's own history, including of course his trip to Calais with Dorothy to visit Annette and Caroline. The overwhelming political inference of the sonnets is of a nation that has lost its way while it justifiably opposes forces of repression abroad guilty of snuffing out nascent liberty in France. In 1802, for all his occasional bursts of optimism, he writes about England at war with France in terms of the bad opposing the worse:

> England! the time is come when thou shouldst wean
> Thy heart from its emasculating food;
> The truth should now be better understood;

Old things have been unsettled; we have seen
Fair seed-time, better harvest might have been
But for thy trespasses; and, at this day,
If for Greece, Egypt, India, Africa,
Aught good were destined, Thou wouldst step between.
England! all nations in this charge agree:
But worse, more ignorant in love and hate,
Far, far more abject is thine enemy:
Therefore the wise pray for thee, though the freight
Of thy offences be a heavy weight:
Oh grief! that Earth's best hopes rest all with Thee!

                                        (*1807* 170)

The poetry of *Poems 1807* repeatedly returns to the theme of a mind fractured by a gulf which is perceived between a cohesively wrought individual personality and a morally sound social identity. Read as intended, which is to say as a carefully arranged sequence, these poems thus collectively reflect on the vulnerability of the 'one life'. They are poems which strive through an act of the creative will to make real the 'one life' vision; they support, and are supported by, Wordsworth's contemporaneous work on *The Prelude*. The profound vault viewed from Snowdon within which is lodged an illusive unifying power ('streams/ Innumerable, roaring with one voice' XIII 11.58–9) is materially unreal, it is an illusion. It becomes utterly real in the mind of the poet. Small wonder that the poet of 'Resolution and Independence', aware of the enormity of the unifying task the mind is required to undertake, fears despondency and madness for the modern poet who – as the sonnets have shown – may no longer look to any external feature of existence to buttress a vision of such demanding completeness. The modern poet has only art – poetry, music, painting – to relate to as an embodiment of what is otherwise lost.

In the sonnet included in the 'Resolution and Independence' sequence ('Composed During a Tour'), we see how the moon, apparently moving with a melancholy sadness through the sky, may be made to speed joyfully on its way. The reality of the slowly moving clouds cannot be altered; but in the poem the transformation can be magically realised. Throughout the eighteenth century, of course, the art of landscape gardening had evolved as a means of subduing nature through the power of aesthetic vision for the edification of the public. Footpaths were provided for the well-attuned mind. The garden at Dove Cottage evolved to function in a manner suited to the needs of its otherwise preoccupied, frequently harassed tenants; and it is not surprising that Wordsworth took so seriously Beaumont's invitation to plan a garden at Coleorton, and then subsequently laid out the grounds of his final home at Rydal Mount with such commitment.

Volume Two of *Poems 1807* was divided into three sections, all of which variously address the crisis of the 'one life' vision under threat of fragmentation. In the first instance, Wordsworth explores his belief that nature acts upon his imagination as an antidote to the national crisis recorded at length in the sonnets that concluded Volume One. Returning to the 1803 tour of Scotland as a focus for the first group of poems, he begins with the ballad 'Rob Roy's Grave'. The need for national moral regeneration is implicit in the imagined soliloquy of the outlaw; it is an outsider's appeal to a natural law, a 'simple plan' (simple as the verse style), and it expresses Wordsworth's own beliefs, himself an outsider alienated from an inhumane establishment:

> Said generous Rob, 'What need of Books?
> 'Burn all the Statutes in their shelves:
> 'They stir us up against our Kind;
>   'And worse, against Ourselves.
>
> 'We have a passion, make a law,
> 'Too false to guide us or controul!
> 'And for the law itself we fight
>   'In bitterness of soul.
>
> 'And, puzzled, blinded thus, we lose
> 'Distinctions that are plain and few:
> 'These find I graven on my heart:
>   '*That* tells me what to do.'
>   (*1807* 180, 21–32)

There is more than just an echo here from sentiments expressed in *Lyrical Ballads*:

> Up! Up! my friend and clear your looks,
> Why all this toil and trouble?

Up! Up! my friend, and quit your books,
Or surely you'll grow double.
('The Tables Turned' 108, 1–4)

In the poem which follows 'Rob Roy's Grave', 'The Solitary Reaper', the theme is also one of loss, of disconnection. Rob Roy is a figure from the past, he must be imaginatively recreated; the solitary reaper has a song which is heard, 'O listen! for the vale profound / Is overflowing with the sound', but not understood, 'Will no one tell me what she sings?' (*1807* 184–5, 7–8, 17). The meaning of the song (like the meaning of the famous daffodils, like the world of Rob Roy, like the meaning of the Leech Gatherer's mundane account of his life) lies beyond literal description.

The full significance of the tension involved is manifest in 'Resolution and Independence', where it is evident that the words do need to be heard in the normal way to provide a means of coping with life in a world at best only tenuously connected with the human spirit. This is not therefore poetry which advocates a simple exchange: actual experience replaced by imaginative interpretation. As these two things drift apart, the fracture manifests a perplexing loss, a reason for regret, even fear.

'Stepping Westward' explores the same territory. ' "What you are stepping westward?" ', a simple question; but as with the answers recorded in 'Anecdote for Fathers' and 'We are Seven' in *Lyrical Ballads,* the poet's meaning emerges not from words spoken, but from the 'echoes' they create in the mind, referring it to the ultimate destination of the mental traveller:

It's power was felt; and while my eye
Was fixed upon the glowing sky,
The echo of the voice enwrought
A human sweetness with the thought
Of travelling through the world that lay
Before me in my endless way.
(*1807* 186, 21–6)

Throughout *The Prelude* Wordsworth articulates the same commitment to that which is 'ever more about to be' (VI, 216, 542). What was possible once is lost now, but as the final poem of this section insists, it remains available in the future. What sounds an unpromising premise for a travelogue piece, 'Yarrow Unvisited', is worthy of positive celebration precisely because for the poet Yarrow has a meaning sustained entirely in the imagination:

> We have a vision of our own;
> Ah! why should we undo it?
> (*1807* 200, 51–2)

The following group of thirteen poems, 'Moods Of My Own Mind', focus on a personal perception of loss triggered by predictably 'simple' phenomena, the butterfly, daffodils, the rainbow, a celandine. The one poem to present a more overtly complex set of images for reflection is 'Gipsies'.[11] In all these poems there is a striving for continuity, for a link between past, present and future, and for a means to enable art to make that continuity possible:

> My heart leaps up when I behold
>   A Rainbow in the sky:
> So was it when my life began;
> So is it now I am a man;
> So be it when I shall grow old. . . .
> (*1807* 206, 1–5)

Disjunction may be represented as the gap between child and adult, but it may be understood as existing between material things and the world of the mind, or between active and passive states. The cuckoo is carefully defined:

> To me, no Babbler with a tale
> Of sunshine and of flowers,
> Thou tellest, Cuckoo! in the vale
> Of visionary hours.
>
> Thrice welcome, Darling of the Spring!
> Even yet thou art to me
> No Bird; but an invisible Thing,
> A voice, a mystery.
> (*1807* 214, 10–16)

The bird's voice is a mystery, it provides a visionary antidote to the sense of unease associated in several of the poems with present realities. 'Gipsies', 'I wandered lonely as a cloud', 'O Nightingale!

thou surely art' all express some degree of current disenchantment.
In 'The Small Celandine' the danger of becoming trapped in a world
where everything has its price is unambiguously expressed:

> To be a Prodigal's Favorite – then, worse truth,
> A Miser's Pensioner – behold our lot!
> O Man! that from thy fair and shining youth
> Age might but take the things Youth needed not!
> (*1807* 210, 21–4)

The final poem of the group, 'It is no Spirit', retrieves the possibility of escaping this 'worse truth'. The evening star, shining brightly
in 'broad day-light' encourages 'a thought/ That I might step beyond
my natural race/ As thou seem'st now to do'. With great economy,
Wordsworth offers here once more the tantalising prospect of a
bridge between matter and spirit, youth and age, between Earth
and Heaven.

The final section begins with the narrative that gives it its name,
'The Blind Highland Boy'. The tale is in many ways a counterpart
to 'The Idiot Boy'. In this instance the child is blind. He lives by
Loch Levin, and is eventually able to satisfy his craving to sail on
the Loch by climbing into an old wash-tub, 'Following the fancies
in his head,/ He paddled up and down' (*1807* 225, 119–20). The blind
child thus commits himself to nature. The adults understandably
panic and set out to rescue him.

In spontaneously realising his deepest wish against the common-
sense fears of his family, the child seems fated to die. His response to
those who set about trying to rescue him is to plead that he should be
left alone, ' "Keep away,/ And leave me to myself!" ' (227, 164–5).
Yet he is eventually rescued and reconciled to the world, but at the
price of his vision:

> So all his dreams, that inward light
> With which his soul had shone so bright,
> All vanish'd; – 'twas a heartfelt cross
> To him, a heavy, bitter loss,
>   As he had ever known.
> (*1807* 227, 171–5)

The Highland Boy, like the Idiot Boy and the boy described in *The
Prelude* and in *Lyrical Ballads*, 'There was a boy' (*Prelude* V 172–4,

389–422), is the odd one out; and in 'The Green Linnet' Wordsworth identifies another such loner among all the 'Birds, and Butterflies, and Flowers'. The linnet is a precise delineation of Wordsworth's sense of himself as a poet. He seems retiring, yet he seems 'to disdain/ And mock the Form which he did feign' when he sings; when, in other words, his art brings him out of retirement.

The first of two London poems in this section describes the way the public are offered the experience of scientifically enhanced sight. In 'Star Gazers' people pay to stare at the moon through a telescope, only to come away disappointed; their spiritual sight is as limited as ever. The second poem describes a blind musician, who by contrast lifts the spirits of all who hear him:

> As the Moon brightens round her the clouds of the night
> So he where he stands is a centre of light. . . .
> (*1807* 236, 13–14)

This section contains one of Wordsworth's historical ballads, 'Song, at the Feast of Brougham Castle'. The poem's public, historical point of reference complements the subject-matter to be found in the poems arising primarily from personal experience. The subject, Lord Clifford, had been deprived of his heritage at a time 'when evil men are strong' (262, 89), and had lived as a shepherd until able to return to his rightful home. He then chooses life in the country rather than a courtier's existence in London.

The poem reiterates Wordsworth's own myth of his literary life; we have once more the Happy Warrior:

> In him the savage Virtue of the Race,
> Revenge, and all ferocious thoughts were dead:
> Nor did he change; but kept in lofty place
> The wisdom which adversity had bred.
>
> Glad were the Vales, and every cottage hearth;
> The Shepherd Lord was honour'd more and more:
> And, ages after he was laid in earth,
> 'The Good Lord Clifford' was the name he bore.
> (*1807* 264, 169–76)

Already in 'I am not One who much or oft delight', and 'To the Spade of a Friend' the virtues of the rural idyll and retirement have been extolled; historical 'truth' is here used to buttress the poet's aspirations.

'To the Spade of a Friend' is a poem that invites, and has received, its fair share of mockery. An Ode to a spade, especially one that begins: 'Spade! with which Wilkinson hath till'd his lands', is not easily retrieved as an item for serious study. Yet it becomes clear that Wordsworth knows full well the demand he is making on his reader. It is precisely because the spade runs contrary to every kind of literary expectation that he challenges us with it. 'Spade!':

> Who shall inherit Thee when Death hath laid
> Low in the darksome Cell thine own dear Lord?
> Than man will have a trophy, humble Spade!
> More noble than the noblest Warrior's Sword.
>
> *(1807* 258, 17–20)

The poem is specifically linked to 'The Happy Warrior'; he writes in defence of honest rural toil, and by a playful, parodic allusion to banners and trophies hung on palace walls in honour of military victory, challenges the orthodox celebration of brutal warfare:

> An *Heir-loom* in his cottage wilt thou be:–
> High will he hang thee up, and will adorn
> His rustic chimney with the last of thee!
>
> (11.30–2)

'To the Spade of a Friend' is followed by 'Song, at the Feast of Brougham Castle', where the private statement is fed into the public, historical narrative; this is then followed by 'Lines Composed at Grasmere', a poem which rehearses cause for public grief; this in turn is followed by 'Elegiac Stanzas' where the focus, as we have seen, is on Wordsworth's cause for private grief.

'Lines Composed at Grasmere' tell of the hourly expected death of the Whig politician, Charles James Fox in 1806. 'A power is passing from the earth/ To breathless Nature's dark abyss' (264, 17–18). From this bereavement, put in perspective, which is to say stripped of any significance it might have had solely on account of Fox's public persona, Wordsworth moves on to consider his brother's death in the Elegy.

In *Poems in Two Volumes* Wordsworth writes progressively away from the uncertainties of the world around him, the world of Fox's

political career, towards an imaginative realm where his vision of
the 'one life' can be preserved:

> And oh ye Fountains, Meadows, Hills, and Groves,
> Think not of any severing of our loves!
> Yet in my heart of hearts I feel your might;
> I only have relinquish'd one delight
> To live beneath your more habitual sway.
>
> *(1807* 'Ode: Intimations' 277, 190–4)

In 'Yes! full surely 'twas the Echo' he refers to the Cuckoo, its two-
note call so appropriate a symbol: 'Whence the Voice? from air or
earth!' *(1807* 256, 5–6). There are 'two different Natures' (1.16), and
the mind of the poet attempts to mediate between them. The voice
of the cuckoo is like a voice from the spirit world, like it, 'but oh
how different!' (1.12).

In *Benjamin the Waggoner*, a major narrative completed in 1806
but not then published, the 'two different Natures' were contrasted
using a very topical point of political reference. The central figure,
a waggoner, reformed to a simple, pure way of life from a worldly
and immoral past, is seduced back to his fallen ways by a sailor.
The waggoner's temptation and downfall is manifestly linked to a
celebration of Nelson's prowess in the war with France. It was a far
bolder statement of the 'Happy Warrior' theme, written at a time
when the British public had all but canonised their naval hero upon
his death in 1805.[12]

In the face of a degenerate political life, an unmistakably post-
lapsarian world (*Benjamin the Waggoner* is in part a rustic parody of
the biblical/Miltonic account of the fall of man), only art is left to
sustain our hope for the future:

> We will grieve not, rather find
> Strength in what remains behind,
> In the primal sympathy
> Which having been must ever be,
> In the soothing thoughts that spring
> Out of human suffering,
> In the faith that looks through death,
> In years that bring the philosophic mind.
>
> *(1807* 'Ode: Intimations' 276, 182–9)

The poet who now waited anxiously for a critical storm to break over the 1807 *Poems in Two Volumes,* and who turned away from publishing *Benjamin the Waggoner,* was not the poet fitted to enter the public arena with *The Recluse* which, after all, was to do Miltonically what *Benjamin the Waggoner* had already done in quintessentially Wordsworthian style. It was *The Recluse,* however, that now beckoned as his major task, that and finding a new home for his family. The Dove Cottage days were over.

7

1807–15:
The Afflictions of Life

In 1815, looking back across the years that had elapsed since his return to Grasmere from Coleorton in 1807, Wordsworth had good reason to characterise middle age as a time dominated by 'domestic cares' and 'engrossed by business'. Poetry – if it featured at all in the lives of this world-weary generation – did so either as a source of 'fashionable pleasure', or 'as a consolation for the afflictions of life' (Prose III, 62). The period which began with anxious forebodings about the future of his literary career as he awaited the critical reception of the *Poems in Two Volumes*, rapidly plunged Wordsworth into one of the darkest phases of his life. Not only did his literary reputation plummet with the critical drubbing the 1807 *Poems* eventually received, his consequent financial anxieties were supplemented by tragedy in the family when after periods of protracted illness for all of them, two of the children – Catherine and Thomas – died. All this was suffered in a series of disastrous homes in a Grasmere that appeared to have been physically mutilated during their absence at Coleorton.

The reviews, when they came, could hardly have augured worse for the future. Byron was the first reviewer to try his hand at describing the 1807 *Poems* to the public. He adopted a condescending note of encouragement; Wordsworth would do well once he abandoned the 'namby-pamby' he called simplicity: 'When Mr. W. ceases to please, it is by "abandoning" his mind to the most commonplace ideas, at the same time clothing them in language not simple, but puerile . . .'.[1]

By far the most damaging review came – as might be expected – from Francis Jeffrey. He undertook a detailed examination of the absurdities of the 'system' adopted by Wordsworth in his poems:

Their peculiarities of diction alone, are enough, perhaps, to render them ridiculous; but the author before us really seems anxious to court this literary martyrdom by a device still more infallible,

151

– we mean, that of connecting his most lofty, tender, or impassioned conceptions, with objects or incidents, which the greater part of his readers will probably persist in thinking low, silly, or uninteresting. . . .

With a swift change of gear he then moves in for the kill. 'Alice Fell' is peremptorily described, quoted, and dispatched: 'If the printing of such trash as this be not felt as an insult on the public taste, we are afraid it cannot be insulted.'

Behind what at times reads like barely controlled hysteria, there moves Jeffrey's consistent political agenda. In the final paragraph of his review we find him addressing the self-same issue of social reform opening the floodgates to revolutionary violence that Wordsworth had set himself to resolve in *The Recluse*:

> Many a generous rebel, it is said, has been reclaimed to his allegiance by the spectacle of lawless outrage and excess presented in the conduct of the insurgents; and we think there is every reason to hope, that the lamentable consequences which have resulted from Mr. Wordsworth's laws of poetry, will operate as a wholesome warning to those who might otherwise have been seduced by his example, and be the means of restoring to that ancient and venerable code its due honour and authority.[2]

Political and literary 'isurgents' melt into each other here; Wordsworth's 'laws of poetry' are subverting the laws of the land. Jeffrey argued a strong case in a period when wartime austerity made political unrest a constant likelihood. When Wordsworth was pictured attempting to undermine 'that ancient and venerable code' of poetry, the phrase used was designed to conjure up Burke's defence of the British constitution every bit as much as the 'fine propriety' evident in the poetry of Virgil and Pope.[3]

The success which *Lyrical Ballads* had undoubtedly enjoyed appeared to have produced shallow roots in the reading public. As sales dried up and the ridicule increased, Wordsworth's confidence in his ability to regain his reputation evaporated. When it came to the test in 1808, he seemed simply to lack sufficient conviction to argue the case for his new poem, *The White Doe of Rylstone*, at the publishers. It was in all probability not quite as simple as that, but neither Mary nor Dorothy could understand why, with an historical romance to sell, Wordsworth should hesitate and eventually withdraw the manuscript without apparently having seriously tried to place it.

What he did do was drift towards journalism. He began to write for Coleridge's latest venture, a journal called *The Friend*; and he reluctantly undertook to provide the text for a Lake District Guide planned by Joseph Wilkinson. He also looked seriously into the possibility of procuring a Government post. In the meantime he continued writing poetry because, whatever his fate at the hands of the reviewers and reading public, his commitment to *The Recluse* was the central manifestation of the way in which he had come instinctively to live in and through his writing. The life he lived, as opposed to the life anyone else might be aware of, was the life he wrote. The public failures and domestic disasters of these years thus played their part in shaping ever more clearly the monumental poem that now began (after an initial false start in 1808) to emerge.

The literary identity crisis that *Poems in Two Volumes* had triggered off, and that the prospect of publishing *The White Doe of Rylstone* subsequently exacerbated, ran alongside a crisis of political identity that had been with Wordsworth at least since Cambridge. The poetry he wrote at this time continued to be informed by a strong personal sense of disillusionment with the political establishment of the day; the failure of radical reform amounted to this: 'The bad / Have fairly earned a victory o'er the weak, / The vacillating, inconsistent good' (PW 5, p. 118, 11.307–9). While Wordsworth the poet (through the Wanderer in *The Excursion* Book IV) described the political establishment as unequivocally 'bad', Wordsworth the family man was turning to that same political establishment in the person of Sir William Lowther, with a plea for paid employment in the service of the Government. The good will of Lowther (concerned to make amends for the earlier misdemeanours of the previous Earl), and the patronage of Sir George Beaumont, now revealed the prospect of a very different public highway for Wordsworth from the lonely twilight path that had featured (and was still featuring) so frequently in his poetry.

The undoubted shift in Wordsworth's politics during this period towards conservatism is a complex issue. His gradual recognition by the great and the good of London literary society since the publication of *Lyrical Ballads* had seen a progressive blunting of the cutting edge of his political radicalism. He nevertheless remained fundamentally disenchanted with the political establishment that Beaumont and most certainly Lowther represented. He had restated this position in candidly explicit terms in *Benjamin the Waggoner*; and then chosen not to publish. *The White Doe of Rylstone* will be considered later in this chapter in a similar light; that too remained unpublished. In 1808 the Convention of Cintra moved him to write a long pamphlet in which the essentials of his 1790s radicalism were again restated.[4] Publication was repeatedly postponed amid fears of the consequences for so long that when it did finally appear in 1809, there were very few readers with time to spare for a controversy that had all but run its course.

This period of Wordsworth's life therefore begins with his withdrawal from the role of a publishing poet; it concludes in 1814 with the publication of *The Excursion*, the one substantial section of *The Recluse* he managed to complete. His public life in the interim had been overwhelmed by what became virtually a permanent domestic crisis. Dealing with it – in no small degree through the good offices of more or less aristocratic friends – contributed significantly to his graduation towards conservatism, as did the growing spectre of repeated social unrest and disorder during these testing years of the war with France.

In private he could use the composition of *The Excursion* to write his way through what undoubtedly amounted to significant shifts in his idea of himself and his relationship to the world of public affairs and letters. Yet what emerged in 1814 was still a profoundly non-conformist document. The fundamental creed of 'simplicity' remained, disgust with an inhumane reactionary political establishment was confirmed, and a far from orthodox religious faith emerged.

The Excursion was to have been a climactic moment in the poet's literary life; it heralded what Wordsworth and Coleridge had intended as the major philosophical poem of the age. But Coleridge had by this time left the circle, and the poem designed to untangle the contradictions and traumas not just of Wordsworth's life, but of the nation's (since many within it had sought to build a new world on the ruins of the old), fell, in Hazlitt's celebrated description, 'Still born from the press'.[5] In the event, it seemed, the contradictions appeared as insoluble as ever for the nation, even if for Wordsworth's *dramatis personae* their passage through the nine Books of the poem managed to provide some 'Degree of healing to a wounded spirit' (PW 5 IX, 312, 786).

There is, then, a 'reading' of the poetry of this period that could relate closely to the trials of domestic life at Grasmere. It is important for that reason to look in slightly more detail at what happened. Wordsworth and Dorothy returned to Dove Cottage from Coleorton in July 1807 by a circuitous route, which incorporated a visit to Bolton Abbey in Wharfedale, the setting of *The White Doe*. After an uncomfortable winter at Town End, the now overdue move to Allan Bank (above the western shore of Grasmere) finally took place. Sara had become seriously ill. John, the first-born, was ill; Mary and Dorothy were exhausted. Life in the new house became a nightmare, chiefly because the chimneys refused to draw, leaving very few rooms habitable.

By now it had become clear just how damaging the critical reception of *Poems in Two Volumes* was to be to Wordsworth's career, and it was in this context that in September 1808 Mary gave birth to Catherine, their fourth child. Coleridge had taken up residence some months before, and was attempting to launch his new journal, *The Friend*. It was a short-lived venture, never seriously viewed by Wordsworth as an alternative source of income. If we consider what he wrote to Thomas Poole about *The Friend* even while he was presumably discussing the venture with Coleridge in a positive light, we have an insight into two things. The first is obvious: Wordsworth had become so critical of Coleridge's behaviour that he could no longer conduct an honest friendship. Sooner or later the words passing behind his friend's back would be heard; the rift was only a matter of time: 'You will consider me speaking to you now in the most sacred confidence', he wrote, and no wonder:

> nothing appears to me more desirable than that his periodical should never commence ... he neither will nor can execute anything of important benefit either to himself his family or mankind ... he has no voluntary power of mind whatsoever, nor is he capable of acting under any *constraint* of duty or moral obligation. (MY I, 352)

The second insight provided by this picture of a morally degenerate Coleridge, is how this description of Wordsworth's rift with Coleridge carries with it defining overtones of the way in which he had become estranged from the political establishment of the nation. As *The Friend* came to its prophesied end, so Wordsworth began to compose his pamphlet on the Convention of Cintra. In this he was to pronounce the leaders of the nation incapable 'of acting under any *constraint* of duty or moral obligation'. It is 'moral energy' that

'The British Government of the present day' lacks; after quoting from Coleridge's 'Dejection: An Ode', he might almost be referring once more to his lost friend when he concludes, 'Our Rulers, I repeat, must begin with their own minds. This is a precept of immediate urgency; and, if attended to, might be productive of immediate good' (Prose I 310, 3633–5). The 'afflictions of life' he reflected on in the 'Essay Supplementary to the Preface' of 1815 constituted a web of interwoven strands linking every aspect of his world.

Wordsworth was in London for the early part of 1808. He returned to Grasmere in April, alarmed by news of Sara Hutchinson's health; later in the month John became very ill indeed. In 1810 Catharine suffered a fit which left her paralysed down her right side; in May, Mary gave birth to William. By this time financial worries were intense; the relationship between Wordsworth and Coleridge was at breaking-point, and with Coleridge's departure for London in September another chapter of the poet's literary life effectively closed.[6]

In May 1811 the family moved from Allan Bank to the Rectory, Grasmere; this proved to be as damp as Allan Bank had been smoky. By 1812, encouraged by other favours, Wordsworth was petitioning Lowther for a Government post. He travelled once more to London, and for a while, it seemed, the difficulties of home life could be set aside as he mixed once more in London literary society. Despite his treatment in the Reviews, he was still regarded as a figure of some significance, and gladly entered into a round of literary dinners and gatherings. He also re-established contact with Coleridge, though the rift was far from healed. Mary, also desperately in need of a break, had travelled to Wales to spend time with her brother Tom and her cousins.

When reflecting on the way in which Wordsworth's opinions were being moulded during this period, we should not forget the extent to which the country seemed to many to be poised on the brink of insurrection and even anarchy. Wordsworth was in London on 11 May when the Prime Minister, Spenser Perceval, was assassinated. Writing of this event, E. P. Thompson has claimed that 'sheer insurrectionary fury has rarely been more widespread in English history'.[7] Food riots were flaring up across the country; widespread satisfaction was volubly expressed at Perceval's death, coupled with some surprise when it emerged that his assassin, John Bellingham, had probably acted out of an eccentric personal sense of grievance. It should, however, be borne in mind that the period when Constable was exhibiting some of his most elegiac images of rural life marks also a high point of Luddite activity. Government spies were as busy now as they had been in the 1790s:

> When Bellingham went to the scaffold, people cried out 'God bless him', and Coleridge heard them add: 'This is but the beginning'. It was thought inopportune to give Perceval a public funeral.[8]

Hard on the heels of Perceval's death came news of domestic tragedy. With both parents from home, Catherine Wordsworth became ill and died. She was buried before either of her parents could return home. As if that was not enough, Thomas (b. 1806) contracted measles in December and subsequently died of pneumonia. The rest of the family were ill, but survived.

While Wordsworth remained outwardly stoical through the winter of 1812–13, Mary became deeply depressed. In a letter to Catharine Clarkson, Dorothy describes her as having become 'as thin as it is possible to be except when the body is worn out by slow disease, and the dejection of her countenance is afflicting'. In the same letter she also reported the death 'of my brother Christopher's . . . child even more suddenly than our two were taken from us . . .' (MY II 60, 65).

Wordsworth worked doggedly on towards the completion and publication of *The Excursion* while his domestic life (let alone that of the country) seemed threatened with near extinction. What price now the companionship of the glittering arbiters of taste with whom he had been rubbing shoulders a few months before: Samuel Rogers, Henry Crabbe Robinson, Lord Byron, Uvedale Price and the painter John Wilkie? Byron and Scott had become successful poets; Wordsworth, despite continued recognition, seemed to have nothing left upon which to build his literary career.

What he did have, as he watched over his grieving family, and reflected on his country's continued hardships and political vicissitudes, was a source from which he might develop the personae of *The Excursion*. The Pedlar of 'The Ruined Cottage' became the Wanderer, a philosopher poet who, having told – and resolved – the familiar tale of Margaret, goes on to attempt the reclamation of the Solitary, a man whose life has been blighted both by dashed political hopes and domestic tragedy. Here was no recycled trope left over from radical Whig poetry of the 1780s and 1790s; Wordsworth now made use of his own literary life to produce both the Wanderer and the Solitary: 'Infirm, dependent, and now destitute' (*Excursion* III, PW 5, 100, 658).

Back in 1807 when the Wordsworths returned to Grasmere from Coleorton there had already been reason enough to indulge in a sense of loss. Dorothy described the circumstances:

> On our arrival here our spirits sank and our first walk in the evening was very melancholy. Many persons are dead, old Mr. Sympson, his son the parson, young George Dawson, the first young man in the vale, Jenny Hodgson our washerwoman, old Jenny Dockwray and a little girl Dorothy's age who never got the better of whooping-cough which she had when we went away. All the trees in Bainriggs are cut down, and even worse, the great sycamore near the parsonage house, and all the finest firtrees that overtopped the steeple tower.

Another significant feature of their changing world is mentioned in the postscript, 'Coleridge never writes to us. He is at Stowey. He had neglected informing his Brothers of his intention of visiting, and they are gone to a watering place' (MY I, 158–9).

In 1808, two years after resuming and then abandoning *Home at Grasmere*, this experience of loss and estrangement, and the anxiety prompted by Sara Hutchinson's illness, led Wordsworth into a further attempt at taking *The Recluse* a stage further. After 592 lines, what is now known as 'The Tuft of Primroses', was, like 'Home at Grasmere', put to one side. The poem constitutes an important development of the major *Recluse* theme of reconciliation, and stands as an immediate prelude to *The Excursion*. Wordsworth was looking for a means of projecting personal loss and tragedy into the realm of a collective, social existence, where the wisdom and understanding of the contemplative mind would provide consolation for the disenchanted individual.

In the event, the fundamental contradictions and paradoxes which lurk at the heart of 'The Discharged Soldier' proved as stubbornly entrenched as ever. The tuft of primroses are worked up as the required symbol of permanence, but Wordsworth has to work them very hard in the process:

> 　　　　　　　　　　　　Alas how much
> Is gone, though these be left; I would not speak
> Of best friends dead, or other deep heart loss
> Bewail'd with weeping, but by River sides
> And in broad fields how many gentle loves,

How many mute memorials pass'd away.
Stately herself, though of a lowly kind,
That little flower remains and has survived
The lofty band of Firs that overtopp'd
Their ancient Neighbour, the old Steeple Tower. . . .
                                        (TP 41, 70–80)

Kenneth R. Johnston identifies 'four clearly discernible emblematic stages' in the poem.[9] In the first the primroses counterpoint the negative experiences of John Wordsworth's death, the deaths within the Sympson family, the loss of other Grasmere friends, and the decimation of the landscape, particularly around the church, 'the old Steeple Tower'.

The second section uses Wordsworth's reading of the letters of St Basil of Caesarea to reflect on the virtues of solitude. This accorded well with his sense of the direction his own literary life was taking; the religious historical precedent is employed in an attempt to justify the claim (stubbornly unconvincing as ever) that you might be active in the world (represented in familiar terms, 'the Chase with clamorous hound and horn') while withdrawn from it:

Not as a refuge from distress or pain,
A breathing time, vacation, or a truce,
But for its absolute self, a life of peace,
Stability without regret or fear . . .
                                        (TP 47, 289–92)

The third and fourth sections travel forward in time, noting the decay of the monastic ideal that has taken place through the ages. To this end Wordsworth reflects on the ruins of Tintern and Fountains Abbey, 'the strong-ribbed vaults/ Are crush'd', eventually summoning up once more the point at which he visited the Grand Chartreuse with Robert Jones in 1790 (TP 53, 481–2). Here, symbolically, the old order stands on the brink of being comprehensively destroyed by the forces of revolution; it had been a key point of reference for him in *Descriptive Sketches* and *The Prelude*.

In the final eighty lines the justice of the revolutionary cause ('Glory and life to new-born liberty') and the 'great Spirit of human knowledge' which centuries of pious religious commitment have given to the world confront each other in a continuing stalemate (TP 55, 546; 551). Unable to relinquish his commitment to either, Wordsworth attempts a resolution by locating himself in Grasmere, a 'lonely vale' where he will be able to call on the necessary reserves of 'spirit' and 'human knowledge' required for the pursuance of his great work. What the Chartreuse had to offer in this respect is now no more, and the revolutionary spirit of 1789–90 has been brought low by human failings. Writing for *The Friend* in 1810 he stated his position in uncompromising terms: 'Youth can only be obtained with certainty at the same price by which every great and good is obtained, namely, steady dependence upon voluntary and self-originating effort, and upon the practice of self-examination sincerely aimed at and rigorously enforced' (Prose II 13, 210–13).

In the final lines of 'The Tuft of Primroses', therefore, we encounter what became a controversial central theme of *The Excursion*. The individual human spirit is identified as the primary agent of reconciliation in a war-torn, ideologically divided society. Traditional religious and political structures no longer embody what in *The Convention of Cintra* he describes as 'the moral virtues and qualities of passion' needed to guarantee 'healthy, matured, time-honoured liberty' in a Nation (Prose I 280, 23845–5; 235; 442).

Wordsworth had every reason to feel he knew what it was to be a 'self-originating' outsider. He undoubtedly continued to see himself as under threat on account of his record of political commitment; his experiences of 1797–8 alone had left him forever sensitive – at worst neurotic – about the possibilities of being targeted in any future purge of radical sympathisers. Fear of political persecution juxtaposed to the evident possibility of financial support from establishment well-wishers, the continuing possibility of scandalous revelations and the certainty of attack from literary critics, now combined with the way the Grasmere community had been visited by personal loss to inform the structure and detail of 'The Tuft of Primroses'.

In the ensuing years *The Excursion* was to become a determinedly sustained confirmation of the resilience of the individual human spirit in the face of catastrophic changes in the political and spiritual life of the nation. In 'The Tuft of Primroses' Wordsworth was still finding it difficult to shake off his sense of guilt at opting for retirement; in his list of anxious denials we see a mirror image of the anxieties that haunted the conscience of a public poet in hiding:

What impulse drove the Hermit to his Cell . . .
                                 . . . Not alone
Dread of the persecuting sword, remorse,

Love with despair, or grief in agony;
Not always from intolerable pangs
He fled . . .

(TP 47, 280 & 282–6)

In *The White Doe of Rylstone* Wordsworth found a source in history that enabled him to work through the same agenda of personal doubt and dilemma (it was thus a far more intimate work than anything Scott was producing in the same genre), and these same anxieties will have played a key role in his unwillingness to publish the text.

The *White Doe* failed to be published in 1808 partly because of the way in which Wordsworth's self-confidence had been undermined, and also partly because the manuscript became a pawn in the saga of the fragmenting relationship between Wordsworth and Coleridge.[10] There were other negative factors at work, however, relating to the peculiarly Wordsworthian blend of autobiography and politics which persistently inform his poetry.

The plot of *The White Doe* revolves around the Rising of the North in 1569, an ill-fated insurrection against the changes that had taken place since the accession of Elizabeth I. The Norton family are misguided reactionaries, committed to the reinstatement of Roman Catholicism, and trenchantly opposed to modernity, Elizabethan style. Of the six sons, only one, Francis, begs his father and brothers not to take part in the rebellion. Francis's sister, Emily, plays the part of a dutiful daughter, making a banner for the rebels to take with them on the campaign, but she shares with her brother a sense of despair at the pointlessness of their cause.

When the rebellion is crushed, Norton and his sons are condemned to death. Francis is not implicated, but filial devotion leads him to promise his father that he will take the rebel banner and place it on St Mary's shrine at Bolton Abbey. The man who has stood out against everything the 'unhallowed Banner' represents suddenly finds himself an agent of the reactionary cause, an apostate no less:

Can he go
Carrying this Instrument of woe,
And find, find anywhere, a right
To excuse him in his Country's sight?
No, will not all Men deem the change
A downward course, perverse and strange?

(WD 129, 1417–22)

Wordsworth was composing this poem as he returned from Coleorton. He was looking at the life of a poet who had been committed to radical political and social reform in the past, who still believed in the essentials of that cause, and who nevertheless now found himself substantially indebted to Sir George Beaumont, and since 1806 when Lowther had helped him (unbidden) to purchase land in Patterdale, also aware of powerful potential patronage coming from that direction.[11]

Through Francis Norton, Wordsworth very clearly expressed his distaste for the politics of his new patrons; yet among the few well-disposed readers for the new poem, he would be sure of numbering the Beaumonts and Lowther. What he had written amounted to a thinly disguised slap in the face for them. Francis Norton and Emily also, of course, recreate the poet and his sister of many years before, the odd ones out during the difficult years of Uncle Christopher's guardianship.

Wordsworth had reason to be as nervous of the consequences of publishing *The White Doe* for its delineation of his views on reactionary politics, as he was about publishing his indictment of the Government contained in *The Convention of Cintra* of 1809. He does indeed briefly admit that *The White Doe* is a poem about his own predicament in the closing lines: 'We stood before this ruined pile [Bolton Abbey],/ And, quitting unsubstancial dreams,/ Sang in this Presence kindred themes . . .' (WD 145, 1858–60). Francis Norton speaks for Wordsworth when he confronts his father and declares himself 'grieved this backward march to see,/ . . . I scorn your chieftans' (WD 110–11, 911; 913). The words of the accusers of Francis when he is at last discovered with the offending banner, are spoken also by those who shared the poet's youthful enthusiasm for radical political ideals in the past:

Worst Traitor of them all is he,
A Traitor dark and cowardly!
          (WD 131, 1484–5)

The final Canto of the poem comprises a meditation of 360 lines on Emily, who after the death of her father and brothers (including Francis), lives in retirement from the world, with the white doe in constant attendance. Here, more than anywhere, we can see Wordsworth challenging the popular vogue for historical romance, rather than attempting to cash in on it. Emily's story leads us away from history, even as Francis Norton had tried by argument to draw his father and his brothers away from the insurrection to live in a remote sanctuary where they might find peace (WD 111, 917–26).[12]

There was a good deal more involved in this, however, than a challenge to popular historical fiction. Emily is described as having attained a freedom from all faction through the pursuance of a determinedly passive role. She gains an inner strength that eradicates the need for her to retain any historical or religious allegiances. Such a notion of 'non-conformity' begins to emerge in the final lines of 'The Tuft of Primroses', and was subsequently to be fully written up in *The Excursion*. Emily's condition of release from the claims of history and religion is objectified in the white doe itself; Wordsworth displays his concern at the outset that we should see it as an emanation of the natural and emphatically real world. Emily is reunited with the doe in the final Canto while she sits 'beneath a mouldered tree, / A self-surviving leafless Oak', and 'self-surviving' is precisely the ideal Wordsworth now seeks to celebrate (WD 137, 1648–9).

Emily communes with herself; she has learnt a lesson in self-sufficiency, and to the reader it may well seem that for Emily, as for the Wanderer in *The Excursion*, God has been superseded by Nature, otherwise the doe, 'her lowly Friend', whose companionship is all-sufficient, 'satisfied . . . with what this innocent spring supplied'; thus 'Her sanction *inwardly* she bore':

> Her own thoughts loved she; and could bend
> A dear look to her lowly Friend, –
> There stopped; – her thirst was satisfied
> With what this innocent spring supplied –
> Her sanction inwardly she bore,
> And stood apart from human cares.
>   (WD 145, 1873–9)

The poem is not irreligious, but it does, in common with 'The Tuft of Primroses', seem to confirm the passing of an age of faith, a theme that dominates *The Excursion*.

Wordsworth's literary career had ground to a halt after 1807, thanks largely to his persistent adherence to a notion of modernity rooted in what he described as 'simplicity'. To Francis Jeffrey, by far his most hostile reviewer, he was a poet who thereby retained unhealthily democratic ideas, whose religious opinions seemed clearly less than orthodox (a point he was to reiterate in his review of *The Excursion*), and who had eccentrically chosen not only to live at a great distance from London, the centre of cultural refinement, but to make the supposed virtues of his retreat among the peasantry a central theme of his poetry.

It was indeed time for a major critique of the literary life in question, and it duly appeared, written by Wordsworth himself. It was *The Excursion*. Kenneth R. Johnston describes the poem as a continuation of Wordsworth's habitual inquest into the relative values 'of living and acting in the public world of human life versus the attractions of escaping from it'.[13] Where *The Excursion* moves significantly forward from 'The Tuft of Primroses' and *The White Doe*, is in its delineation of the character referred to as the Solitary; he is a man who reads the Wordsworthian biography in resoundingly negative terms: a combination of dashed hopes for radical political reform and domestic disasters have rendered him a cynical recluse; to this Wordsworth himself could add the collapse of his literary ambitions. He is, in Johnston's words, 'the absolute perversion of the favourite Wordsworthian formula, Love of Nature leading to Love of Mankind'.[14]

Book I of *The Excursion* consists of a reworking of 'The Ruined Cottage'. The story of Margaret and Robert presents a stiff challenge to the poet/narrator's erstwhile positive view of 'Truth, of Grandeur, Beauty, Love and Hope' (Prospectus to *The Recluse*, HG 257, 6). He therefore defers to the Wanderer, who tells and interprets the story in a manner designed to reclaim a redemptive vision of Man and Nature for the poet, and for Margaret and Robert (all of whom, including the Wanderer, are types of the isolated Wordsworth).

The Wanderer's measure of success, according to William H. Galperin, 'is by now extremely qualified'.[15] Galperin emphasises the fact that the Wanderer – despite his opposition to the doubt and despair which characterise the view of the narrator/Wordsworth in Book I (and in later Books that of the Solitary/Wordsworth) – is himself a replication of these personae. His culture is religious rather than humanist; yet we are shown that his wisdom increased even as he distanced himself from his 'establishment':

> ... sometimes his religion seemed to me
> Self-taught, as of a dreamer in the woods;
> Who to the model of his own pure heart
> Framed his belief, as grace divine inspired,
> Or human reason dictated with awe.
> (PW 5 22, 409–13)

Like all the disputants in *The Excursion* (like Emily and Francis Norton) the Wanderer is an outsider. Unlike the Romantic generation (represented by the poet / narrator and the Solitary), who worked on transfiguring the self towards God, the Wanderer's life signifies a gradual process of equating God with the self.

What we have by the end of Book I, therefore, is a redemptive reading of 'The Ruined Cottage' narrative which remains to be tried and tested further. It is already clear, however, that 'redemption' for Wordsworth does not signify any substantial recantation of his political views, nor for that matter does 'redemption' signify any movement towards a more orthodox view of Church and State. Wordsworth's emphasis remains individualistic (call it idiosyncratic, democratic) despite the frequently pietistical tone of the Wanderer's discourse. The authority of God is known and exerted not through the agency of an external body created by society for that purpose, but through the experience of individuals. And as God moves towards the self in the Wanderer's philosophy, so the self assumes the power of God to save. For all the homage paid to the established Church (particularly at the beginning of Book VI), in the final climactic Book of the poem Wordsworth fervently reasserts his faith in Nature as the mediator between God and Man; Nature provides us with the means of becoming reconciled to the hardships and disasters of mortality (though even here he cannot exclude the view that it may not be so). For Jeffrey this displayed a perverse descent into paganism, and placed Wordsworth irredeemably beyond the pale of Augustan literary orthodoxy.

Following the story of Margaret, the second section of *The Excursion* confronts the Wanderer with the Solitary, a living exemplar of the despondency of the age. The Solitary's narrative is told, retold, and interpreted over two Books. The section terminates with Book IV, 'Despondency Corrected'.

Properly described, we should be clear that it is the Wanderer who corrects to his own satisfaction any tendency to despondency the Solitary's life may have encouraged. This is achieved towards the end of the Book in an 'eloquent harangue' delivered in response to the Solitary's continued resistance to the Wanderer's earlier affirmation that

> . . . virtue thus
> Sets forth and magnifies herself; thus feeds
> A calm, a beautiful, and silent fire,

From the incumbrances of mortal life,
From error, disappointment, – nay, from guilt;
And sometimes, so relenting justice wills,
From palpable oppressions of despair.
                                        (PW 5 143, 1071–7)

Book IV allows the Wanderer the last word; but the first words
spoken by the Solitary in Book V confirm a signal case of despondency *un*corrected; he remains eager to contradict the Wanderer's
visionary discourse with a demoralising account of 'man's substantial life':

But stoop, and place the prospect of the Soul
In sober contrast with reality,
And man's substantial life. If this mute earth
Of what it holds could speak, and every grave
Were as a volume, shut, yet capable
Of yielding its contents to eye and ear,
We should recoil, stricken with sorrow and shame,
To see disclosed, by such dread proof, how ill
That which is done accords with that which is known
To reason, and by conscience enjoined. . . .
                                        (PW 5 161, 248–57)

Book V initiates the third section of the poem.

The Wanderer brings the Solitary and the poet down from the
remote valley to a village churchyard, where the Pastor meets them,
and recalls the lives of people now buried there in a series of carefully interrelated narratives.[16] The function of this section is to incorp-
orate into the discussion – which up until now has revolved around
the particular experiences of the Wanderer and the Solitary – a sense
of society extending to what is in effect Grasmere, and then on out
into the rest of rural and (increasingly) industrial England. Far from
clinching the argument for optimism, therefore, Books V through
IX serve primarily to extend and complicate Wordsworth's task of
reconciling the Wanderer to the Solitary.

The Pastor's narratives (running through Books VI and VII) tell
stories of the successes and failures of individuals to overcome the
various hardships of lives lived for the most part within a rural context. The poet/narrator eagerly anticipates the moral of the Pastor's
tales:

And they perhaps err least, the lowly class
Whom a benign necessity compels
To follow reason's least ambitious course. . . .

This Wordsworthian appeal to 'a benign necessity' calls forth at
once (from Wordsworth) the Solitary's ironic exclamation:

> . . . Praise to the sturdy plough,
> And patient spade, and shepherd's simple crook,
> And ponderous loom – responding while it holds
> Body and mind in one captivity;
> And let the light mechanic tool be hailed
> With honour; which, encasing by the power
> Of long companionship, the artist's hand,
> Cuts off that hand, with all its world of nerves,
> From a too busy commerce with the heart!
>
> (PW 5 172, 593–5; 602–10)

In Book VIII it is the Wanderer's turn to express a profound despondency at the destruction of the rural way of life by the pervasive
factory system. It is then the Solitary's task to insist that poverty and
ignorance predate industrialisation; they are as depressingly endemic
to rural as to urban society:

> This boy the fields produce . . .
>   . . . his country's name,
> Her equal rights, her churches and her schools –
> What have they done for him? And, let me ask,
> For tens of thousands uninformed as he?
> In brief, what liberty of mind is here?
>
> (PW 5 279, 425; 429–33)

As this third section progresses, it becomes increasingly clear that
there can be no formal victory for any of the disputants involved
in the debate. The characters succeed only in redefining and con-
solidating both their individuality and kinship in the face of a dis-
integrating social fabric. The political solution is explored by the
Wanderer in Book VIII and again in the first parts of Book IX. But
it proves as inconclusive as ever, and with this in mind, Kenneth
R. Johnston has drawn attention to the way both sequences are ter-
minated; in VIII the Wanderer's words had been 'erewhile/ Abruptly

broken off', in IX 'Abruptly here, but with a graceful air, / The sage broke off . . .' (PW 5 VIII, 284, 591–2; IX, 299, 416–17).[17]

In the final section of the poem (the latter part of Book IX) it remains for Wordsworth to pursue a resolution of *The Excursion* which effectively runs back against the current of the preceding eight Books. Well used to the strategy of contradicting himself within his own poetry ('Simon Lee', 'Anecdote for Fathers', 'Resolution and Independence' come to mind), of adopting a genre only to reconstruct it for his own ends (as with *The White Doe*), the closing section of *The Excursion* exhibits a characteristic Wordsworthian trait.

The dominion of the spoken word, notably as practised by the Wanderer, now gives way to the poet/narrator's account of what happens, rather than what is said. The Wanderer's abrupt pause in his political lecture gives the Pastor's wife the opportunity to propose an evening walk. The party now includes the Pastor's wife and children. As they approach the lakeside, what they see is arguably of greater significance (to Wordsworth) than all the disputation of the previous four days:

> Thus having reached a bridge, that overarched
> The hasty rivulet where it lay becalmed
> In a deep pool, by happy chance we saw
> A two-fold image; on a grassy bank
> A snow-white ram, and in the crystal flood
> Another and the same! Most beautiful,
> On the green turf, with his imperial front
> Shaggy and bold, and wreathed horn superb,
> The breathing creature stood; as beautiful,
> Beneath him, showed his shadowy counterpart.
> Each had his glowing mountains, each his sky,
> And each seemed centre of his own fair world;
> Antipodes unconscious of each other,
> Yet, in partition, with their several spheres,
> Blended in perfect stillness, to our sight!
>   (PW 5 300, 437–51)

The mortal 'breathing' world of Nature reveals its mysterious counterpart (in this respect it is a moment of inversion comparable to the downward view discovered on the summit of Snowdon in *The Prelude*); here we perceive two worlds utterly separate yet utterly one, 'Blended in perfect stillness'. It is a two-fold image of heaven and earth where their state of division is unresolvable by any kind of formal disputation. Enlightenment wisdom and science are redundant here (as they are in 'Star Gazers' of 1807, as they are in the diatribe against modern eduction in *The Prelude*, Book V); knowledge and recognition are mediated by 'vision', which is how Wordsworth described it in an earlier draft of this passage intended for *The Prelude*.[18] There he admits to having been tempted to shatter the reflection by throwing a stone into the water. In *The Excursion* the extreme fragility (even the credibility) of this visionary glimpse of a coexistent earth and heaven is articulated by the Pastor's wife:

> Ah! what pity were it to disperse,
> Or to disturb so fair a spectacle,
> And yet a breath can do it!
> (PW 5 300–1, 452–4)

Excepting the final climax still to come, this sight is, after nine long Books, the nearest any of the company are likely to get to a reassuring knowledge of God's continuing ordering presence in the midst of the personal, social and political turmoil of the age. It acts as a specific corrective to an earlier image of 'Inverted trees, and rocks, and azure sky' in 'a mountain brook' employed the Solitary in Book III to describe his loss of faith (PW 5 108, 972, 984).

The company now row across a lake to an island; from a picturesque beginning (a reprise of the much earlier 'Evening Walk'), passing through the visionary episode of the ram, the poetry now shifts into rhapsodic mood, the consequence of which is effectively to dismiss the verbal fencing of the previous four days and replace it with an overwhelming experience of the beauty of the moment:

> Soft heath this elevated spot supplied,
> And choice of moss-clad stones, whereon we couched
> Or sat reclined – admiring quietly
> The general aspect of the scene; but each
> Not seldom over-anxious to make known
> His own discoveries ...
> That rapturous moment ne'er shall I forget
> When these particular interests were effaced
> From every mind!
> (PW 5 305–6, 580–5, 588–90)

The glory of the sunset overwhelms – and silences – each and every one of them, allowing the trope of division and unity to assume its final, spectacular realisation:

> That which the heavens displayed, the liquid deep
> Repeated; but with unity sublime.
>
>   (PW 5 306, 608–8)

The Pastor now delivers what is part prayer, part oration, part sermon. For all his claim to represent a civilised Christian tradition, the inescapable fact is that he has led his flock away from the church and its churchyard, away from the parsonage, away from all man-made structures which reflect and mediate an Augustan interaction of religion and society. This is to be no prayer-book service; nor is it to take place in church, among the tombs and monuments of the honoured dead whose presence define a structure of social deference upon which may be based the congregation's deference to God. What happens on the island suggests far more potently a primitive sunset pagan rite carried out 'Where the bare columns of those lofty firs, / Supporting gracefully a massy dome/ Of sombre foliage, seem to imitate/ A grecian temple rising from the deep' (PW 5 303, 499–502).

We leave the disputants united in their visionary extasy, at odds still in their intellectual lives. The resolution that Wordsworth is ready to propose at this stage of *The Recluse* lies in the vision of unity reflected endlessly in Nature. It is no small wonder that Jeffrey responded to *The Excursion* in the way he did:

> Long habits of seclusion, and an excessive ambition of original-
> ity, can alone account for the disproportion which seems to exist
> between the author's taste and his genius; or for the devotion
> with which he has sacrificed so many precious gifts at the shrine
> of those paltry idols which he has set up for himself among his
> lakes and mountains.[19]

Jeffrey's 1814 review concentrates on ridiculing Wordsworth's characters, in particular the Wanderer, as suitable purveyors of the philosophic wisdom promised. Not far beneath the surface, as ever in Jeffrey's criticism, we find his Augustan reading of the 'Lake School' as culturally, morally and politically depraved. *The Excursion* is characterised by 'a tissue of moral and devotional ravings . . . a kind of mystical morality' practised at 'the shrine of those paltry idols . . . set up . . . among his lakes and mountains'.[20]

Wordsworth's 'favourite doctrines', his 'paltry idols', remain in essence Jacobinical; Jeffrey could see here little more than a meeting of malcontents and subversives. In perhaps his most telling comment of all he accused Wordsworth of 'having debased his moral teacher [the Wanderer] by a low occupation' in order to pursue 'an affected passion for simplicity and humble life'.[21]

It was Matthew Arnold who, some thirty years later, was to provide a far more appropriate (and unwitting) account of Wordsworth's position, poised between an anachronistic Augustan culture, and a secularised Victorian future still only dimly perceivable:

Wandering between two worlds, one dead,
The other powerless to be born,
With nowhere yet to rest my head. . . .[22]

In 1813 the Wordsworth family had moved to Rydal Mount, adjacent to Grasmere. Here at last, it seemed, was a place to settle, to recuperate, to plan for the future after such a turbulent recent past. In 1813 Wordsworth, through the good offices of Lowther (to whom he was to dedicate *The Excursion*) became Distributor of Stamps for Westmorland and the Penrith area of Cumberland. From what was now a position of relative security, he planned to relaunch his literary life with *The Excursion*, followed by a two-volume edition of *Collected Poems*, which would edit and order his work since 1793 in a way that established both the range of his achievement, and its unity of purpose. The lyrics would relate to the as yet incomplete *Recluse* as 'little cells, oratories, and sepulchral recesses' relate 'to the body of a gothic church' (Prose III 5–6, 34–40).

In the event there was to be no immediate reclamation of Wordsworth's literary reputation. His attempt to nail Jeffrey in the 'Essay Supplementary to the Preface' written for the *Collected Poems* misfired, as did a later attack in his *Letter to a Friend of Robert Burns* published in 1816; they simply became subjects themselves of further lampoons on this would-be great poet's vanity, not to mention his political duplicity:

. . . will not all men deem the change
A downward course, perverse and strange?
(WD 129, 1421–2)

8

1814–20:
Few and Scattered Hearers

'. . . the poet must reconcile himself for a season to few and scattered hearers'.[1]

Any consideration of the consequences of the publication of *The Excursion* for Wordsworth's career should include a distinction between his position as a success commercially, and the extent to which he maintained a presence in the literary life of the nation after 1814. There can be little doubt that *The Excursion* excited as much if not more interest and curiosity than it did ridicule, with no shortage of people prepared to be convinced that Wordsworth was a great – if frequently wayward and perverse – poet. But commercially, after a promising start with *Lyrical Ballads*, he did now undoubtedly rank as a failure.

In 1807, with *Lyrical Ballads* still selling, Longmans had been prepared to print 1000 copies of *Poems in Two Volumes*. In 1814 230 still remained unsold. Five hundred copies of *The Excursion* were printed in August 1814; early in 1815 little more than half of those had been sold. This is to be compared with Byron's *The Corsair* of 1814 which sold 10 000 copies on the day it was published. Walter Scott's *Lady of the Lake* came out in 1810 priced 42s., and sold 20 300 copies in its first year. When Wordsworth produced his first *Collected Poems* in 1815, it took five years to sell 500 sets. *The White Doe of Rylstone* (1815), *Peter Bell* and *The Waggoner* (1819) proved equally unmarketable.[2]

The bitterness with which Wordsworth viewed his failure is very clear from the 'Essay Supplementary to the Preface' that he wrote for the *Collected Poems*. Yet it should equally be remembered that, almost from the first, he had exhibited a persistent tendency to write poetry that opposed or challenged his readers' expectations. In this respect the cumulative effect of *Lyrical Ballads*, followed by the poems of 1807, 1814, 1815 and 1819 was arguably nothing more than what he had asked for. The 'gentle reader' denied their sentimental tale of the old huntsman, Simon Lee, had been repeatedly rebuffed, repeatedly

172

held at arm's length. The patriot warrior had been removed from the front-line and set to reflect on the significance of the celandine, the primrose, and the heraldic virtues of the 'spade of a friend'.

In the 1815 *Collected Poems*, however, there are signs of a possible thawing of Wordsworth's attitude towards his reader. With the exception of one important addition, the second volume of 1815 reproduces the climax of the second volume of the 1807 *Poems*. The final poem is the 'Ode, Intimations of Immortality', and as in 1807, it is preceded by the 'Elegiac Stanzas suggested by a picture of Peele Castle'. But in 1815 Wordsworth chose to place a previously unpublished poem, 'To The Daisy' ('Sweet Flower! belike one day to have / A place upon thy Poet's grave'), between the 'Elegiac Stanzas' and the 'Ode'. 'To The Daisy' was written in the aftermath of John's death in 1805, and narrates (somewhat clumsily, it has to be said) the story of the shipwreck:

> 'Silence!' the brave Commander cried;
> To that calm word a shriek replied,
> It was the last death-shriek. . . .[3]

The effect of this addition is at least a gesture towards unlocking what otherwise remains the obscure focal point of the 'Elegiac Stanzas' for the 'innocent' reader. Wordsworth scholars, aware of the personal grief that informs the poem, read it as members of the circle might have done, and all too easily forget that that is what they are doing. Without additional explanation, the uninitiated reader will miss the full import of Beaumont's painting of the storm-tossed ship. Learning of John's death may well suggest that esoteric knowledge ought not to be a prerequisite of complete engagement with the poem. Coleridge understood the problem only too well, and attempted to make the point to Wordsworth in connection with the initial public reception of *The Recluse*. The reason why people who read the poem felt they were not properly understanding it, he suggested, 'might have been occasioned by the influence of self-established convictions having given to certain thoughts and expressions a depth and force which they had not for readers in general'.[4]

'To the Daisy' arguably offered a helping hand, as did Wordsworth's decision to extend the title of the Ode that followed it. In 1807 the reader of what Jeffrey had dismissed as an 'illegible and unintelligible' poem was offered only a quote from Virgil to suggest the subject, 'Paulo majora canamus' ('Let us sing of somewhat more exalted things'), which even with a knowledge of Latin left the reader with no clue what to expect. Now for the first time he added 'Intimations of Immortality from Recollections of Early Childhood'.

The signs certainly are that Wordsworth was coming to accept that he had some explaining to do, even if the 'Essay Supplementary to the Preface' suggests that what he was primarily concerned to explain was why – regardless of what he did – the reading public would probably never appreciate the full quality of his genius.

While readers of poetry in the early nineteenth century were contentedly going their own way with Byron, Scott, and (if the *Gentleman's Magazine* is to be believed) turning to *Time; or Light and Shade* (1815) by J. Gompertz for 'a truly didactic composition', Wordsworth had been busy narrating their fate in a far less congenial light.[5] Even as he wrote his own literary life (in to, and now out of *The Prelude*), he was also telling a story about the gentle reader. It had begun with the elaborate arguments and explanations in the Preface to *Lyrical Ballads* in 1800, and had now arrived fifteen years later at the 'Essay, Supplementary to the Preface' where he petulantly catalogued the reading public's habitual lack of discrimination when confronted with great literature.

This is the oppositional Wordsworth, whose poetry abounds with images of paradox and contradiction – crossing the Alps or climbing Snowdon – where the duality presented by a reflected image not infrequently occurs at moments of significance. The two reflections recorded in Book IX of *The Excursion* (the ram and the Lakeland sunset) were the latest in a long line of mirror images (things alike yet not alike) which include the stars reflected in the ice in the skating episode in *The Prelude*, and 'the moon's distorted face' which Peter Bell thinks he sees reflected in the river, but which turns out to be the drowned face of the owner of the ass he has so cruelly beaten (PB 89, 541–5).

The story he tells of the reading public he has failed to reach is inextricably entwined with his own story; we should remember that for the purposes of *Lyrical Ballads*, he is the insensitive young observor of Simon Lee (a typical reader); he it is who bullies the child in 'Anecdote for Fathers', he it is who receives 'admonishment' from the Leach Gatherer in 'Resolution and Independence', and who subsequently leaves the work of converting the Solitary in *The Excursion* for the most part to the Wanderer (or so it seems). Wordsworth and his absent gentle reader were arguably both victims of a cultural crisis exacerbated by the political crises experienced after the outbreak of the French Revolution. If the situation reached by 1815 is to be fully understood, it is important to reconsider briefly what the problems were for a young poet attempting to write and publish through the 1790s.

From being an outsider in Penrith in the 1780s, Wordsworth had become very much at home at Hawkshead, and at Hawkshead he absorbed an ethos which, combined with his knowledge of the Lowther debt, encouraged his ambitions to become a writer responding positively to contemporary developments in poetry, while adopting a critical – potentially radical – attitude towards the society and politics of his day. At the outset there was no reason to suppose that there would not be a readership ready to support such a poet. The late-eighteenth-century culture of the male poet tended to encourage the picturesque image of him as an outsider. In *Imagination and Power*, Thomas R. Edwards memorably summarises the situation:

> the depressing picture of a rural landscape crowded with lugubrious figures, none of them seeming to know the others are there too, busily writing poems called 'A Hymn on Solitude', 'Ode to Evening', or 'The Pleasures of Melancholy'.[6]

A significant shift had taken place in the 1790s, however. From an essentially imagined isolation (akin to that proposed by Goldsmith in 'The Deserted Village' or Gray in the 'Elegy in a Country Churchyard'), poets of Wordsworth's generation and literary / political leanings found themselves increasingly separated from the public they wanted to reach by law. The trial of Thomas Paine for seditious libel in December 1792 initiated a series of draconian measures which, while they most immediately affected radical activists like John Thelwall, also had the effect of drastically proscribing in more general terms the subject of printed matter. Wordsworth's peer-group readership, young progressive intellectuals (James Losh, Francis Wrangham, the Pinneys) were now potentially all under surveillance, and he along with them. If he continued to write as one of them, and for them, he might at any time become a victim of state oppression, another Hardy or Thelwall, Gerrald or Margarot.

It was a situation which bred a predictable tendency to neurosis that once established, stayed with him throughout the war-years. Of all the young aspiring writers of this period, it was Wordsworth, with his personal history of financial hardship for which the aristocracy could be blamed, with his schooling in the liberal ethos of

Hawkshead, his time in France, his discipleship of William Godwin, who was destined to be the most severely tested.

His inclination to write against the 'gentle reader' (against the gentility of the status quo), and to cultivate a poetry of the lone voice excluded from public discourse, is therefore the consequence of a very particular set of circumstances: 'Thus did I steal along that silent road' (LB 278, 21). Contradiction, fear and guilt jostle their way through a literary life which, after dedicating itself to the 'democratic' aesthetics of John Scott's *Critical Essays* in the early 1790s, encountered a degree of Government censorship and control that seemed unprecedented. To be the poet Wordsworth wished to become demanded his acceptance of an oppositional role played out with extreme caution and secrecy; none knew this better than his brother Richard, whose anxious advice to 'be cautious in writing or expressing your political opinions' Wordsworth may have resented, but in the event followed (EY, 121).

By 1807, though an oppositional way of thinking remained endemic to his work, a period of practical support and encouragement from Beaumont and Lowther marked the beginning of a slow process by which Wordsworth became reconciled to and eventually united with his reader. From *The Excursion* through the 1815 *Collected Poems* to *The Waggoner*, the poet remained well content to present himself as an outsider. In *The Waggoner* we are reminded that Dove Cottage was once an Inn, a meeting-place for many; when the poet arrives, the public disappear, along with the ale:

There, where the DOVE and OLIVE BOUGH
Once hung, a Poet harbours now, –
A simple water-drinking Bard . . .
                              (W 49, 59–61)

But Beaumont and Lowther were Establishment figures; the effect of their good offices was to take the erstwhile would-be radical and his problematic relationship with the power and authority claimed by (or in the case of the French Jacobins, ferociously wielded by) radical reformers, and relocate him in a new – and no less problematical – relationship with the power and authority exercised from within the political Establishment.

The ordering of the 1807 *Poems* into categories began a process by which Wordsworth was eventually able to engage with his changing situation by locating his work at once historically and generically. He was beginning to delineate his career in terms of creative phases; each phase ('Sonnets Dedicated to Liberty', 'Written During a Tour of Scotland', 'Moods of My Own Mind') is open to subsequent revision as later work expands the poetic personality portrayed in the collected editions. Wordsworth gradually evolved a means of doing publicly what he had been doing privately with the Salisbury Plain texts and *The Prelude*. It was a process by which nothing was intended to be lost, yet which over a period of time (and a series of steadily expanding, carefully edited and revised collected editions) would free him from the predication of his earlier poetry of opposition.

The tentative use in 1807 of a mechanism that grouped the poems in relation to their creative origins provided the basis for arranging the poems of the first Collected Edition of 1815. By 1815 'Moods of My Own Mind' had been joined by 'Poems of the Fancy', 'Poems of the Imagination', 'Poems Proceeding from Sentiment and Reflection', along with other groupings of a more orthodox kind, 'Juvenile Pieces', 'Miscellaneous Sonnets', 'Sonnets Dedicated to Liberty', and from *Lyrical Ballads*, 'Poems on the Naming of Places'. Wordsworth completed the structure by superimposing a chronology on to the Contents pages. In doing so he dramatically illustrated how important it was for him to signify the changes he knew had taken place in his literary life from the work of the 1790s, through to the period of grim survival at Allan Bank, culminating in his arrival at Rydal Mount.

The reader of the 1815 volume was therefore confronted with a category for each poem; after that came the poem's title; there then came two columns – the first gave the date of composition, the second the date of first publication. No poet had ever planned Contents pages of this kind before, nor was likely to again. Wordsworth believed his poems could not be properly read and understood without them.

The Contents pages provided a degree of stabilisation that the poems taken singly frequently struggled to attain for themselves, but rarely achieved. Many modern critics would argue that the essence of Wordsworth's poetry resides in its delineation of instability; as Jerome J. McGann has put it, the poet is 'left at the edge of defenselessness', or in Geoffrey Hartman's words, Wordsworth 'breaks into thought in a way that breaks thought'.[7] Wordsworth's career has been repeatedly characterised here by its quality of restlessness, the physical movement frequently recorded in the poetry matched by actual travelling that to some extent belied the image he otherwise projected of a sedentary poet in semi-retirement. One way of understanding the restlessness in the poetry is to recall Wordsworth's determination to produce a modern poetry; he had been driven on by a reforming zeal the full significance of which, it seemed, had only ever been understood by a limited circle – and even they could at times be subject to a loss of either comprehension or nerve.

Instability seeking a redefined permanence was the essence of Wordsworthian modernity. The instability of the poet in 'Resolution and Independence' strikes the keynote, as the poetry repeatedly insists that what the world – in its current mood of 'getting and spending' – condemns as marginal, be it people or things (mendicant soldiers, old men travelling, 'a superannuated pedlar', tufts of primroses, daisies, spades) are pointers towards the quality of permanence that, once perceived, will renew our lives with a spiritual and moral wholeness that is otherwise dangerously lacking in society.

Time and again the poetry gropes towards a dimly perceived realisation of such knowledge. 'An instinct call it, a blind sense . . .':

> . . . a sense sublime
> Of something far more deeply interfused,
> Whose dwelling is the light of setting suns,
> And the round ocean, and living air . . .
>   (LB 'Tintern Abbey' 119, 96–9)

Time and again we fall short of it, left only with 'a blind sense' in 'To The Daisy', or a 'something' in 'Tintern Abbey'. In the struggle, in the attempt, in the anticipation of arrival resides Wordsworth's modernity.

The publications of 1814–19 mark the decline of that modernist drive. Poetically there could be no way of admitting and resolving this situation. *The Recluse*, now virtually abandoned, had been conceived of as providing such a resolution through an all-encompassing poetic statement. But the poetry was the instability, and in the instability resided the modernity.

What Wordsworth now proceeded to do, as his situation changed, as he drifted in the direction which Beaumont and Lowther beckoned, was to work at fencing off – redefining and refining – his achievement to date. He thus became involved in the process of producing ever more comprehensive collections of his total output; order and resolution were being achieved in editorial terms. The 1815 Collected Edition was supplemented initially by *Peter Bell* and *The Waggoner*; in 1820 he produced a four-volume collection; a third five-volume Collected Edition, including *The Excursion*, came out in 1827; a fourth in 1832; a fifth, stretching now over six volumes, came out in the course of 1836–7. In each case revisions were made to existing work (redefining and refining), and new work was added. The new work included three major sonnet sequences, *The River Duddon* of 1820, *Ecclesiastical Sketches* of 1822, and in 1841 *Sonnets Upon the Punishment of Death*.

The *River Duddon* volume of 1820 revealed a Wordsworth sufficiently redefined to ensure significant commercial success. This is not to suggest that we should necessarily consider 1820 as the year when Wordsworth achieved a 'come-back'; that would certainly mean overrating the impact that Jeffrey's critical campaign against him had had. The literary world no doubt enjoyed reading Jeffrey's skilfully devastating invective, and they will have relished the inventiveness of the various squibs and parodies that regularly appeared. The fact remains, however, that Wordsworth was always a poet it was difficult not to be interested in, not least because he maintained a presence among the literati of London.

When the *Duddon* volume became a commercial success, therefore, it did so because ever since *The Excursion* and the first Collected Edition had been published (despite further ridicule occasioned by *Peter Bell* and *The Waggoner*), interest in Wordsworth's work had steadily been gaining ground. His time in London in 1815 had been the occasion of significant additions to his gradually expanding circle of admirers. One such was John Scott, a political journalist and editor, who reviewed *The White Doe* in *The Champion* in June 1815:

> He is now before the public in a variety of works, – of unequal merit certainly, – but in their collective testimony proclaiming the greatest poetical genius of the age.[8]

Scott joined an expanding group of people in London either renewing the poet's acquaintance, or meeting him for the first time. They included Walter Scott, Samuel Rogers, the Lambs, Richard Heber, William Wilberforce and Leigh Hunt, William Godwin, Daniel Stuart and Henry Crabbe Robinson. Some were loyal to the 'circle', others (like Leigh Hunt) felt themselves under no such obligation. Thomas Telford and Barron Field were new friends who, like John Scott, became disciples.

A good deal of Jeffrey's hostility sprang from his conviction that Wordsworth was a congenital Jacobin, and that his work, if successful with the public, would exercise a subversive influence on the political mind of the nation. Again, it is hard to assess the extent to which Jeffrey's neurosis was genuinely shared by his readers. Had any doubts existed about where Wordsworth had travelled politically by this time, they were to be resolved by the pending general election of 1818.

The two county members for Westmorland were nominated by the Lowthers and traditionally returned unopposed. In this instance Lord Lonsdale was proposing his two sons, Viscount Lowther and Colonel Henry Lowther as the prospective members. In 1817 it became known that the liberal Whig Henry Brougham intended to contest the seat. Wordsworth threw himself wholeheartedly into the contest on Lonsdale's behalf, and to read his two 'Addresses to the Freeholders of Westmorland' and the letters of 1818–19 is surely to be plunged once more into the world of John Wordsworth, Senior. It was an episode that reveals a Tory Wordsworth so politically engaged as to be a cause for concern to the rest of his family:

> It was 'pitiable that William should be thus diverted from his natural pursuits', Mary thought, and Sara feared that 'Poetry & all good & great things will be lost in electioneering'.[9]

Faced with what could easily be represented as a Jacobinical threat to law and order on his own doorstep, Wordsworth found no difficulty in seeing the election as an uncomplicated struggle between good and evil, no holds barred.

In April 1819 he happily informed Viscount Lowther, 'The estate I purchased in Langdale has furnished votes for eight gentlemen of my connection and Friends, among whom is my brother Dr. Wordsworth.' Reports from Manchester of the Peterloo massacre later that year give rise to fears 'that there may have been some mismanagement . . . on the part of the supporters of the Government'; but it transpires that Wordsworth's regrets relate not to the fact that the cavalry had charged down a peaceful demonstration, but that 'several Special Constables were cut down or trampled on by the Cavalry while charging the Mob' (MY II 530, 533–4).

Still working hard for the cause in 1820, he reported a run-in with a bookseller of Ashby to Lord Lonsdale in December (while staying at Coleorton), where he found:

among a very small Collection of Books, 'the Koran' and the famous Pamphlet, 'Killing no Murder.' . . . I afterwards learned that this person was a notorious Jacobin and Incendiary, and Usher of a School in the Town, the Trustees of which (Tradesmen of the Place) had turned out a loyal Schoolmaster, and put in his place one of opposite principles, who had given the 'Manchester Massacres' as a Theme for his Boys. What are we to expect from children educated by such Teachers? (MY II 657)

Here is the turncoat that so disgusted and saddened Shelley. In 1819 when *Peter Bell* was published, Shelley parodied it by way of exposing what he could only take to be the man's mealy-mouthed hypocrisy; a 'didactic little horror' was Leigh Hunt's verdict on the story of Peter's conversion.[10]

The controversy continues. In 1985 Peter Manning proposed a reading of Wordsworth that has subsequently been frequently referred to. Manning suggests that what we see in Wordsworth at this time is simply a return to type. After years of misguided radical striving, the poet discovers his roots in religious orthodoxy and high Tory politics.[11] With the labours of Wordsworth's father in mind, it has the makings of a plausible (not to say time-saving) theory. It is perhaps less satisfactory if we look at the poetry that was being published during this period. Neither *The White Doe* nor *The Waggoner* sit happily with the Tory campaigner of 1818, and *The Recluse* (a second edition of which came out in 1820) hardly confirms a comfortable religious orthodoxy.

Wordsworth was without doubt a far more complex individual than Peter Manning's argument seems to suggest. His relationship to authority and power was no less problematic when the power was represented by the politics of a right-wing Establishment than when it had been represented by the likes of Brissot, Godwin or Paine. Sinking Brougham on behalf of Lowther no more defined the poet than had the attempt to sink Llandaff on behalf of the downtrodden multitudes of England back in 1793.

Though he now became a recognised 'sage', a 'great Poet' who was eventually to receive the Establishment's ultimate accolade, the Laureateship, in 1843, the ambiguities of his career remained in many respects unresolved. In the final chapter we shall consider how what was now his expanding reading public tended to create its own 'literary life' for Wordsworth, and how that related to what he had written, and to what he now proceeded to write.

9

As Much Peter Bell
As Ever

Rydal Mount remained Wordsworth's home until his death in 1850. In 1825 it looked very much as though he was going to be forced to give up the lease, but the crisis passed, and the problem did not recur.

He remained an insatiable traveller. Writing to Basil Montagu in 1831, he claimed 'I am as much Peter Bell as ever. . . . I find nothing so feeding to my mind as change of scene' (LY II 437). In 1820, with Mary and Dorothy and other friends, he journeyed to Switzerland, then on to Italy, revisiting many of the places he had visited in 1790 with Robert Jones. Jones, now Vicar of Souldern in Oxfordshire, was to have been one of the party, but it was impossible for him to leave his parish. In Italy they were met by Henry Crabbe Robinson, a barrister and literary diarist who had become a valued friend within the circle. By July they were back in Paris, where time was spent with Annette, Caroline and her husband Eustace Baudouin.

In 1822, Wordsworth published a miscellany of poems entitled *Memorials of a Tour on the Continent, 1820*. It contains one sonnet, appropriately placed in the sequence to suggest an oblique reference to the experience of confronting his turbulent past in the company of his wife and sister. 'Sky-Prospect – From the Plain of France' describes how, as the sun sets, the clouds at first conjure up apocalyptic visions, which in due course fade into obscurity. This is

> Meek Nature's evening comment on the shows
> That for oblivion take their daily birth
> From all the fuming vanities of Earth!
> (PW III 196–7, 12–14)

What must have been considered a necessary but potentially difficult encounter, in the event passed off mildly enough.

There was indeed to be a moment of high drama when the ship that was to bring them home ran aground off Boulogne, an incident that inspired a sonnet laced with the kind of jingoism in praise of English liberty that was becoming an increasingly characteristic feature of Wordsworth's work:

Why cast ye back upon the Gallic shore,
Ye furious waves! a patriotic Son
Of England . . . ?

(PW III 197, 1–3)

The European tour was followed by a tour of the Netherlands in 1823, of the Rhine in 1828, of Ireland in the following year, and in 1837 a tour once more of France and Italy. This was to be his last major expedition, and Stephen Gill's suggestion that it was the most heroic of them all is convincing:

Two elderly men [Wordsworth was 67, his companion, Crabbe Robinson, 62] travelled in a carriage bought for £70–00 from 19 March to 7 August 1837. Hindered by deep snow in France, scourged by the heat in Italy, checked by cholera from pressing on to Naples, they none the less carried through this ambitious itinerary: Paris – Cannes – Lucca – Sienna – Rome – Florence – Bologna – Milan – Venice – Salzburg – Munich – Heidelberg – Cologne – Brussels – Calais.[1]

Not surprisingly, when the miscellany *Memorials of a Tour in Italy, 1837* was published in 1842 (in *Poems, Chiefly of Early and Late Years*), Wordsworth dedicated it to Henry Crabbe Robinson.

There were also frequent travels across England, Wales and Scotland, again periodically memorialised in verse, but in a very different form now from the way in which he had once logged his wanderings in the Salisbury Plain poetry or in the still unpublished *Prelude*. He had rediscovered the Salisbury Plain manuscripts in 1839, along with several other early pieces, including *The Borderers*. In *Poems, Chiefly of Early and Late Years* he set the early travels down alongside the later ones, heavily revising the Salisbury Plain manuscript to produce what he now called *Guilt and Sorrow, or Incidents Upon Salisbury Plain*. Shorn of its 1790s radical critique of English society, *Guilt and Sorrow* could now safely throw the travelogue of the mature poet (the *Memorials* of 1837) into a favourable light. It remained for editors at a much later date to discover (as they would also with

The Prelude) the full extent to which Wordsworth had revised the text – and with it his autobiography.

The family remained a constant source of anxiety in these later years. John, the first-born, failed to live up to his father's expectations; he was eased into a career in the church with the help of patronage from both Beaumont and Lowther. But the highly respectable and respected Vicar of Brigham that he eventually became was certainly something less than his father had hoped for. Willy, the youngest, was even more of a worry; seemingly unemployable, his father managed first to get him some kind of an income by appointing him sub-distributor of stamps for Carlisle in 1831, and when in 1842 Wordsworth secured a state pension for himself of £300 a year, it was possible for Willy to succeed him properly in the post. Again, hardly the future he had planned for the boy.

Dora, born in 1804, had never been strong, and had been anxiously watched over and protected by her parents throughout her life. Wordsworth's response to Dora's announcement in 1838 that she wished to marry Edward Quillinan, a good friend of the family, was initially to refuse point-blank. Thanks largely to the sensitive good offices of a recent friend, Isabella Fenwick, the wedding eventually took place in Bath in 1841. Just six years later, Dora died of tuberculosis.

As the years passed, there was the inevitable thinning of the circle. Brother Richard had died in 1816, William Calvert died in 1829, James Losh in 1833. Coleridge died in 1834, followed a year later by Robert Jones and Sara Hutchinson. Most difficult to bear, prior to the deep distress occasioned by Dora's death, was the fate of Dorothy. In 1829, and again in 1831, she had become very ill, a prelude to the onset of what it is now possible to diagnose as Alzheimer's disease. She remained at Rydal Mount, with all the problems this created for a nursing regime supervised by Mary. Both women were in fact destined to outlive the poet, Dorothy dying in 1855, Mary, aged 89, in 1859.

By the time of his death in 1850, Wordsworth had become a universally revered poet. Recognition of the kind that resulted in adulation of that order dated from 1820 and the *Duddon* volume. 'The truth is', *Blackwood's Magazine* announced in May 1820, 'that since Milton, there is none, except Gray, who has ever caught the true inspiration of the Grecian Lyre with the same perfect dignity as the great poet of the Lakes'.[2] It was Francis Jeffrey's turn now to be ridiculed for the insensitive philistinism of his criticism. From being a poet who in 1815 might be tentatively recommended by *The Gentleman's Magazine* for his 'pathetic touches' (over against the 'sublimity' of Byron and Scott), Wordsworth was now unreservedly pronounced to be the first poet of the age, and it was not long before the Reviews were beginning to carry increasingly positive reassessments of *The Excursion*.[3]

In the 1815 *Collected Poems*, Wordsworth had shown himself tentatively prepared to try and unlock some of the more esoteric meanings of his work for a readership beyond the circle to which he had become accustomed. The *Duddon* volume extended this gesture, though the sonnets themselves have a voice that is frequently introverted and indirect:

> Whence that low voice? – A whisper from the heart,
> That told of days long past, when here I roved
> With friends and kindred tenderly beloved;
> Some who had early mandates to depart,
> Yet are allowed to steal my path athwart
> By Duddon's side. . . .
>
> > (PW III, xxi, 255, 1–6)

What is important is the constitution of the volume as a whole. *The River Duddon* begins with a brief prose description of the geographical setting of the river; it includes a lengthy prose 'Memoir of the Rev. Robert Walker' referred to in the sonnet sequence; it includes other poems ('Vaudracour and Julia' extracted from *The Prelude*, 'Ode: The Pass of Kirkstone'), and it concludes with a revised version of the *Topographical Description of the Country of the Lakes* written at Allan Bank in 1810. Here was a structure which informed and encouraged the reader to appreciate that, sonnet by sonnet, we were indeed travelling down a real stream, born onward by a familiar rhetoric of 'sultry meads', 'zephyrs', 'grots', and 'arbours'; and, should respite be required, it is made available from among a variety of sources, prose and poetry (PW III, sonnet xxiv, 256).

If the initial note sounded by the sonnets is strongly reminiscent of the artfully isolated late-eighteenth-century poet, 'sole listener' to the voice of the river (v, 248), the theme broadens with the river to identify the role of poetry with that of charting the spiritual progress of the poet, setting firmly to one side all social and political issues:

> . . . but in radiant progress toward the Deep
> Where mightiest rivers into powerless sleep

Sink, and forget their nature – *now* expands
Majestic Duddon...
> (PW III, xxxii, 260, 4–7)

The first comparison that comes to mind is with the Thames,
'under Kentish downs,/ With commerce freighted, or Triumphant
war' (xxxii, 13–14); but this is rejected in what appears to be a clear
statement of withdrawal by Wordsworth from his earlier grandiose
poetic intentions:

While, less disturbed than in the narrow Vale
Through which with strange vicissitudes he passed,
The Wanderer seeks that receptacle vast
Where all his unambitious functions fail.
And may thy Poet, cloud-born stream! be free –
The sweets of earth contentedly resigned,
And each tumultuous working left behind
At seemly distance – to advance like Thee;
Prepared, in peace of heart, in calm of mind
And soul, to mingle with Eternity!
> (PW III, xxxiii, 260, 5–14)

In *The River Duddon* Wordsworth showed himself prepared to
step out of the shadows and share the journeyings of his literary
life with his readership. It was part of the process by which he was
now rewriting his life, progressively superimposing a revised version – 'in calm of mind/ and soul' – on the still largely suppressed,
private narrative of his life as a furtive traveller through the 1790s,
the life that had eventually led him forward to the goal of *The Recluse*.
The emergence of this traveller into broad daylight was to be confirmed by a series of 'Memorials' to tours undertaken at home and
abroad in the 1820s and 1830s, where he regularly employed the
miscellany format.

Wordsworth's newly acquired status as a public poet was further confirmed when in 1822 he published *Ecclesiastical Sketches*. This
lengthy sonnet sequence employed the declamatory rhetoric of public statement he had used before for many of the sonnets in the ill-
fated 1807 *Poems in Two Volumes*. The contrast between the language
of *Ecclesiastical Sketches* (later renamed *Ecclesiastical Sonnets*) and the
introversion of *Duddon* is striking. Wordsworth provided his reader
with an immediately accessible narrative framework, the history of
Christianity in England from its earliest days to the present, in the

course of which he also made it clear that he was now a poet for whom the Christian past and future of the nation had become a primary concern.

We are given here a valuable insight into the way Wordsworth was beginning to perceive of himself as he strenuously rewrote history (and alongside that, his life) in terms of his Christian commitment. Here was a persona the Victorians were to understand, the prototype of Matthew Arnold's Scholar-Gipsy, born 'Before this strange disease of modern life'[4] had taken hold of society:

Methinks that to some vacant hermitage
My feet would rather turn – to some dry nook
Scooped out of living rock, and near a brook
Hurled down a mountain cove from stage to stage,
Yet tempering, for my sight, its bustling rage
In the soft heaven of a translucent pool;
Thence creeping under sylvan arches cool,
Fit haunt of shapes whose glorious equipage
Would elevate my dreams. A beechen bowl,
A maple dish, my furniture should be;
Crisp, yellow leaves my bed; the hooting owl
My night-watch: nor should e'er the crested fowl
From thorp or vill his matins sound for me,
Tired of the world and all its industry.
                        (PW III, xxii, 352)

This bid for seclusion is followed in characteristic fashion by a 'Reproof' of such 'voluptuous indolence', citing the 'toil stupendous' of Bede, 'Sublime Recluse!' (PW III, xxxiii 352–3).

The familiar tension between active and passive within Wordsworth's poetry is occurring now in a significantly altered guise from that of *Lyrical Ballads* and the 1807 *Poems*. There is no doubt here that the poet is writing towards his readership, not against it. The keynote is struck at the end of his *Memorials of a Tour on the Continent, 1820*, published in the same year as *Ecclesiastical Sketches*:

Go forth my little Book! pursue thy way;
Go forth, and please the gentle and the good;
Nor be a whisper stifled, if it say
That treasures, yet untouched, may grace some future lay.
                        (PW III, 201, 87–90)

In the lines preceding these, Wordsworth reflects on the healing powers of Christianity within society, tacitly discarding in the process all pretence of political systems to help 'with congenial influence, to uphold/ The State' (11.76–7).

He was to return to this theme even more explicitly in 'Musings Near Aquapendente', the first poem in the *Memorials of a Tour in Italy, 1837*, all the while progressively building for himself the character of a poet to be described in due course by Matthew Arnold as the 'pure and sage master'[5] who directs our gaze away from transient images of decay and fragmentation, 'of decline and fall/ Admonished not without some sense of fear', towards 'the sight/Of splendour unextinguished, pomp unscathed,/ And beauty unimpaired' (PW III, 207, 180–4). Christianity and the visionary perception of Nature were now welded in a firm alliance that promised to overcome the world with 'images of general beauty' taken from Nature, which 'by reflexion' promised a 'godlike insight' (PW III, 208, 200–2; 210, 330).

The creative trajectory of politics–nature–vision that belonged to former years was replaced by one which began with nature, and rose through Christianity towards vision; in the process an evangelical impetus was released into every aspect of Wordsworth's writing. Very little narrative poetry was produced in this latter period, but the Arthurian *Egyptian Maid* of 1830 (published 1835) was no exception to the rule. The wildness of Merlin's pagan jealousy is quelled by the gentle spirit of Christianity; the moral laxity within the political world of King Arthur's court is put to shame (and set to one side) by the spiritual purity of Galahad and his bride, the Egyptian Maid. It is a profoundly reactionary poem. This same evangelical impetus transformed Wordsworth's poetry of travel from its previously secretive form, narrated by one who walked alone and frequently by night, to the work of a poet who in the *Memorials* of 1837 claims kinship with those 'who now/ Walk in the light of day' (PW III, 211, 322–3).

By the time the *Memorials* of 1837 were being composed, Wordsworth had already spent much time redrafting the literary life described in *The Prelude* manuscripts of 1805. He had been doing – with the context of travel ever to the fore – precisely what he describes in 'Musings Near Aquapendente':

> where'er my steps
> Shall wander, chiefly let me cull with care
> Those images of genial beauty . . .

> ... which do best
> And fitliest serve to crown with fragrant wreaths
> Life's cup when almost filled with years, like mine.
> (PW III, 208, 198–204)

This had included adding the famous (or infamous) tribute to Edmund Burke to Book VI in 1820:

> ... he forewarns, denounces, launches forth,
> Against all systems built on abstract rights,
> Keen ridicule; the majesty proclaims
> Of Institutes and Laws, hallowed by time;
> Declares the vital power of social ties
> Endeared by custom. . . .
> (*Prelude* 1850 255, 323–8)

If 'Musings Near Aquapendente' is any guide, we can also reasonably assume that since returning from the Italian tour, he had once again read his attack on modern education and 'science' in *The Prelude*, Book V. He cut out a good deal in the process of redrafting, but retained still the ironic description of modern (Godwinian) man as 'a miracle of scientific law':

> he must live
> Knowing that he grows wiser every day,
> Or else not live at all . . .
> (*Prelude* 1850 169–71, 323–5)

He returned to that theme with renewed vigour in the 'Musings' to carry out a swingeing attack on Utilitarianism, anticipating Dickens's critique of what in *Hard Times* (1854) became immortalised as 'Gradgrindery'. Here, then (as with 'Vaudracour and Julia'), was a morsel of rewritten *Prelude* made public; it accorded with a poetic persona perfectly attuned to the critical ears and eyes of his anxious Regency and early Victorian contemporaries. A love of nature combined with Christian commitment prompted him to condemn 'a chilled age':

> most pitiably shut out
> From that which *is* and actuates, by forms,
> Abstractions, and by lifeless fact to fact

Minutely linked with diligence inspired . . .
By gross Utilities enslaved we need
More of ennobling influence from the past,
If to the future aught of good must come
Sounder and therefore holier than the ends
Which, in the giddiness of self-applause,
We covet as supreme.
                    (PW III, 211–12, 325–8, 348–53)

The publication of *Poems, Chiefly of Early and Late Years* in 1842
marked the embodiment of a publicly reconstructed Wordsworth,
who claimed to have removed his poetry from the realm of 'the
world and all its industry' to a higher vantage point, from whence
it delivered an all-embracing spiritual overview (*Ecclesiastical Sonnets* PW III 352). This idea of the function of art informs the argument of 'The Pillar of Trajan', a poem of 1825 eventually included
as the final item in the Italian *Memorial* anthology of 1837. Having
designated art as fundamentally distinct from the political turmoils
of history, 'the passions of man's fretful race' (PW III 230, 7), Wordsworth declares himself satisfied that art's function is one of ideal-
isation. He thus effectively condones the falsification of mundane
events in the interests of delivering a message imbued with inspiring
general truths. The sculptor of the Pillar of Trajan is therefore justified
in presenting an idealised, politically sanitised account of Trajan's
career:

I gladly commune with mind and heart
Of him who thus survives by classic art,
His actions witness, venerate his mien,
And study Trajan as by Pliny seen;
Behold how fought the Chief whose conquering sword
Stretched far as earth might own a single lord . . .
                    . . . yet, high or low,
None bleed, and none lie prostrate from the foe;
In every Roman, through all turns of fate,
Is Roman dignity inviolate.
                    (PW III, 230–1, 25–30; 47–50)

When he describes this as a 'fine illusion' he does so without
intending irony. Art is transcending the unreliable, changing world

of time, transforming the transient to a lasting image of perfection
available only through art, a 'vision of the Mind':

> . . . Trajan still, through various enterprise,
> Mounts, in this fine illusion, toward the skies:
> Still are we present with the Imperial Chief,
> Nor cease to gaze upon the bold Relief
> Till Rome, to silent marble unconfined,
> Becomes with all her years a vision of the Mind.

The Empire has gone, 'her very speech is dead':

> Yet glorious Art the power of time defies.
>   (PW III, 231, 68–73; 65–6)

'Glorious art' will therefore justify the reconstructed Burke of
1820 inserted in *The Prelude*, and indeed will justify a reconstructed
Wordsworth manufactured from the revised texts of the poems,
now at long last being bought, and not infrequently read. It was
only natural for him now to redirect the critique he had made of
an unjust political society in the Salisbury Plain poems towards a
revised ending; the erstwhile victim of the state no longer functions
as an advocate of William Godwin, and no longer seeks Godwinian
readers; he must therefore admit that the guilt is his, and accept
what he calls his 'welcome sentence' (PW I 126, 655). The new title,
Guilt and Sorrow condemned the original purpose of the poem to
death.

Wordsworth had made several attempts to bring his literary life
into the present through a continuation of the *Recluse* project. In
1812–16 he worked once more on *Home at Grasmere*, in 1831 he looked
again at both *Home at Grasmere* and 'The Tuft of Primroses'.[6] But the
continued writing of his life found its most satisfactory outlet in the
sonnet sequences and the miscellanies of travel poems. *The Recluse*
could no longer be made to work for him because it was tied irredeemably to an earlier Wordsworth. He endeavoured to deal with
the problem of an uncongenial past memorialised in *The Prelude* by
editing it for posthumous publication, a task virtually complete by
1838.

It did not take long, however, for Matthew Arnold's Victorian
Wordsworth, the serene poet of spiritual universality who had risen
above a divided, secularised society, to re-emerge as a complex

Romantic poet, full of self-doubt and ambiguities. The key that slowly began to unlock this frequently contradictory character was *The Prelude*. It was the scolarship primarily of Emile Legouis, Ernest de Selincourt and Helen Darbishire that revealed the extent to which a Victorian Wordsworth had been constructed from self-administered biographical and textual adjustments and amendments. By the time de Selincourt published the text of the 1805 *Prelude* in 1926, Wordsworth's radical political affinities had been rediscovered, the Annette Vallon affair had become public knowledge, and the early life of William Wordsworth (Legouis's book of 1896 was called *La jeunesse de William Wordsworth*) had once more taken to the road, rendering Walter Pater's assertion of 1874 that Wordsworth's 'life of eighty years is divided by no profoundly felt incidents' somewhat less than convincing.[7]

Old habits of thought died hard, however, and in 1922 it was still possible for Arthur Beatty to complain that since Arnold and Pater, 'little has been done to carry forward our understanding of the poet':

> the view that Wordsworth had any development is so little held that he is persistently studied as a static poet . . . he is treated as a poet who had no history until he arrived at the age of forty-five.

Beatty went on to insist that in Wordsworth's thought we find not serene certainty, but 'confusion':

> for he was a genuine pioneer, only gradually clearing his notions on fundamental questions of art and life, and only gradually working towards as clear a conception of both as he was ever to attain.[8]

With this, and similar critical perspectives beginning to emerge, twentieth-century versions of Wordsworth's literary life returned their readers to the shadowy byways where indistinct figures loom threateningly out of the dark, where there is an eternal crisis of confidence attending the need to find a worthy rationale for a life spent writing poetry. It is a literary life understood now through the medium of poetry for the most part either little read or indeed never seen in the poet's lifetime; it is a biography that has swung through 180 degrees since Beatty began to research a new Wordsworth for the 1920s. We are now arrived at a point where (to reverse Beatty's statement) it may seem as though all the poet's history (and his writing) had taken place by the time he was forty-five.

The only thing we can be certain of as the endless stream of Wordsworths continues tirelessly to tramp past us, is that the story will not
rest there. This always has been, after all, a singularly footloose literary life that loves 'a public road':

... such object hath had power
O'er my imagination since the dawn
Of childhood, when its disappearing line
Seen daily afar off, on one bare steep
Beyond the limits which my feet had stood,
Was like a guide into eternity.

                    (Prelude XII 444, 145–51)

Notes

1 Writing the Literary Life

1. Percy B. Shelley, *Peter Bell III*, in *Shelley's Poetry and Prose*, ed. Donald H. Reiman and Sharon B. Powers (New York and London, 1977), p. 334, 11.293–7.
2. John Dyer, *Grongar Hill*, in *Poetry of the Landscape and the Night*, ed. Charles Peake (London, 1967), pp. 92–3, 11.145–58.
3. Quoted John O. Hayden, *Romantic Bards and British Reviewers* (London, 1971), pp. 5–6. Hereafter Hayden.
4. Nicholas Roe, *Wordsworth and Coleridge: The Radical Years* (Oxford, 1988), p. 251.
5. See Nicholas Roe, *The Politics of Nature* (London, 1992), p. 3.
6. Edmund Spenser, *The Faerie Queene*, ed. Thomas P. Roche, Jr. and C. Patrick O'Donnell (Harmondsworth, 1978), p. 15.
7. Richard D. Altick, *The English Common Reader* (London and Chicago, 1963), p. 71.
8. Oliver Goldsmith, *The Deserted Village*, in *Gray, Collins and Goldsmith: The Complete Poems*, ed. Roger Lonsdale (London, 1969), pp. 693–4, 11.407–10; 414–16.
9. Hayden, p. 5.
10. Richard Feingold, *Nature and Society: Late Eighteenth Century Uses of the Pastoral and Georgic* (Brighton, 1978), p. 90.
11. George Crabbe, *The Village*, Book One, in *Poetical Works of George Crabbe*, ed. A. J. Carlyle and R. M. Carlyle (London, 1908), pp. 34–5.
12. William Cowper, *The Task*, in *The Poetical Works of William Cowper*, ed. H. S. Milford (London, 1950), p. 210, 11.493–6.
13. David Trotter, *The Making of the Reader* (London, 1984), p. 4.
14. Charles Dickens, *Little Dorrit* (Harmondsworth, 1967), p. 47.
15. Stephen Gill, *William Wordsworth, A Life* (Oxford, 1989), p. 26. Hereafter Gill.
16. William Shenstone, *The Poetical Works*, ed. G. Gilfillan (Edinburgh, 1854), p. 39.
17. Henry Mackenzie, *The Man of Feeling*, ed. Brian Vickars (London, 1967), pp. 127–8.

2 Early Years

1. Leslie F. Chard, *Dissenting Republican: Wordsworth's Early Life and Thought in Their Political Context* (The Hague, 1972), pp. 16–18.
2. See Brian Bonsall, *Sir James Lowther and Cumberland & Westmorland Elections, 1754–75* (Manchester, 1960), pp. vi; 125–40.
3. Gill, p. 34.
4. Chard, op. cit., p. 34.

5. Gordon Kent Thomas, *Wordsworth's Dirge and Promise* (Nebraska, 1971), pp. 36 ff.
6. Morris Marples, *Romantics at School* (London, 1967), pp. 50–75; 150–71.
7. T. W. Thompson, *Wordsworth's Hawkshead*, ed. Robert Woof (London, 1970), pp. 345–6.
8. Richard Holmes, *Coleridge: Early Visions* (Harmondsworth, 1989), pp. 27–31.
9. T. W. Thompson, op. cit., pp. 323–33.
   Mary Moorman, *William Wordsworth: A Biography*, two vols (London, 1957), vol. 1, pp. 28–9. Hereafter Moorman I and II. Richard S. Fergusson, *Early Cumberland and Westmorland Friends* (London, 1871), pp. 104–6.
10. T. W. Thompson, op. cit., pp. 170–2.
11. Nicholas Roe, *Wordsworth and Coleridge: The Radical Years* (Oxford, 1988), p. 90.
12. Heather Glen, *Vision and Disenchantment: Blake's Songs & Wordsworth's Lyrical Ballads* (Cambridge, 1983), pp. 35–6; 53. Nicholas Roe, *The Politics of Nature* (London, 1992), pp. 17–35. For William Crowe, see John Williams, *Wordsworth: Romantic Poetry and Revolution Politics* (Manchester, 1989), pp. 10–11.
13. Henry Swainson Cowper, *Hawkshead* (London, 1899), pp. 494; 106.
14. Heather Glen, op. cit., pp. 86–7. Gill, p. 40.
15. Quoted Jonathan Arac, *Critical Genealogies: Historical Situations for Postmodern Literary Studies* (New York, 1987), p. 59.
16. Nicholas Roe, *The Politics of Nature* (London, 1992), p. 20.

3 From France to Racedown

1. Nicholas Roe, *Wordsworth and Coleridge: The Radical Years* (Oxford, 1988), pp. 23–7.
2. Helen Maria Williams, *Letters Written in France 1790* (Oxford, 1989), pp. 65; 70; 90.
3. Gill, pp. 51; 57.
4. Gary Kelly, *English Fiction of the Romantic Period 1789–1830* (London, 1989), p. 114.
5. Stewart Curran, *Poetic Form and British Romanticism* (Oxford, 1986), p. 15.
6. Gill, p. 68.
7. Moorman I, p. 209.
8. Nicholas Roe, *The Politics of Nature* (London, 1992), pp. 101–16.
9. Albert Goodwin, *The Friends of Liberty* (London, 1979), Chapter 9; for Habeas Corpus, see p. 334. See P. M. S. Dawson, 'Poetry in an age of revolution', in *The Cambridge Companion to British Romanticism*, ed. Stuart Curran (Cambridge, 1993), pp. 48–73; for Habeas Corpus, see pp. 54–6.
10. An invaluable source book for Commonwealthman politics is Caroline Robbins, *The Eighteenth Commonwealthman* (New York, 1968). On Wordsworth and Commonwealthman politics, see John Williams,

Wordsworth: Romantic Poetry and Revolution Politics (Manchester, 1989), pp. 5–18.

11. Moorman I, pp. 189–97; 208.
12. Mark Reed, *Wordsworth: The Chronology of the Early Years 1770–1799* (Cambridge Mass., 1967), p. 24.
13. Gill, p. 45.
14. Everard H. King, *James Beattie's The Minstrel and the Origins of Romantic Autobiography* (Lampeter, 1992), p. 43. Text reference to *The Minstrel*, King, Appendix A, p. 258, stanza LVII, 1.506. See Moorman I pp. 60–1.
15. James Beattie, *The Minstrel*, in King, op. cit., p. 248, XVI, 1.144.
16. Ibid., pp. 271–2, LV 11.487–95.
17. John Williams, op. cit., pp. 69–70.
18. John Milton, *Paradise Lost* in *John Milton: Complete English Poems*, ed. Gordon Campbell (London, 1993), p. 441, Book XII, 11.648–9. Compare SP 22 11.37–41.
19. SP 5. Gill's comment here is that: 'The revolutionary spirit brought old conditions into new perspectives . . .'. I am suggesting that it helps to be more specific about the 'old conditions'.
20. Text of 'The Baker's Cart' in RC, pp. 463–7. The poem is reproduced and discussed in Nicholas Roe, *Wordsworth and Coleridge: The Radical Years* (Oxford, 1988), pp. 135–7.
21. John Williams, op. cit., p. 82.
22. William Hazlitt, *The Complete Works*, ed. P. P. Howe, 21 vols (New York, 1967), vol. XI, p. 17. Mark Reed, op. cit., p. 163.

4 Alfoxden

1. Gill, p. 120.
2. W. H. Auden, *Selected Poems*, ed. Edward Mendelson (London, 1979), 'Out on the lawn I lie in bed', p. 31.
3. S. T. Coleridge, *The Poetical Works* edited by E. H. Coleridge (Oxford, 1912, 1980), p. 181, 11.20–7.
4. Moorman I, p. 325.
5. For the circumstances surrounding the marriage to Sara see Richard Holmes, *Coleridge: Early Visions* (Harmondsworth, 1989), pp. 60–83.
6. Gill, pp. 120–3.
7. Robert Gittings and Jo Manton, *Dorothy Wordsworth* (Oxford, 1985), pp. 61–2.
8. Kenneth R. Johnston, *Wordsworth and The Recluse* (New Haven, 1984), p. 6.
9. Jonathan Wordswoth, *The Music of Humanity* (London, 1969), pp. 184–5.
10. The text quoted in this chapter for *Peter Bell* is the earliest possible full version of the poem as it existed in 1799 (MSS. 2 and 3). References will not therefore match the standard Poetical Works text where the 1819 published version is used. See PB 35–7.
11. Gill, pp. 133, 140–1.
12. Jane Austen, *Northanger Abbey* (Oxford, 1946), p. 198.

13. S. T. Coleridge, *Biographia Literaria* (London, 1907), p. 160.
14. Gill, p. 140.
15. S. T. Coleridge, op. cit., p. 160.
16. Gill, p. 140.
17. Samuel Johnson, *The History of Rasselas, Prince of Abissinia* (Harmondsworth, 1985), p. 135.
18. John Barrell, 'The Uses of Dorothy: "The Language of the Sense" in "Tintern Abbey" ', in *Poetry, Language and Politics* (Manchester, 1988), pp. 137–67.

5 The Making of a Modern Poet

1. Nicholas Roe, *The Politics of Nature* (London, 1992), pp. 3 ff.
2. J. H. Alexander, *Reading Wordsworth* (London, 1987), p. 55.
3. Hayden, p. 3.
4. Moorman I, pp. 424–5.
5. Marjorie Levinson, 'Introduction to *Keats's Life of Allegory*', in *Romanticism*, ed. Cynthia Chase (London, 1993), p. 192.
6. *The Edinburgh Review*, No. 1, 25 October 1802, p. 63.
7. Ibid., pp. 64–6.
8. Ibid., p. 66.
9. Mary Jacobus, *Romantic Writing and Sexual Difference* (Oxford, 1989), p. 217.
10. Jon Cook, 'Paul de Man and Imaginative Consolation in *The Prelude*', in *The Prelude*, ed. Nigel Wood (Buckingham and Philadelphia, 1993), p. 51.

6 Grasmere Poetry: Dove Cottage Life

1. Dorothy Wordsworth, *The Grasmere Journals*, ed. Pamela Woof (Oxford, 1991), p. 2.
2. Ibid., pp. 30–3.
3. *Journals of Dorothy Wordsworth*, ed. E. de Selincourt, 2 vols (London, 1952), volume I, p. 220.
4. Gill, p. 204.
5. See John Williams, 'Introduction' to *Wordsworth: Contemporary Critical Essays*, ed. John Williams (London, 1993), pp. 6–19.
6. S. T. Coleridge, 'Dejection: A Letter' in *English Romantic Verse*, ed. David Wright (Harmondsworth, 1968), pp. 181–90.
7. Hayden, p. 23.
8. Jerome J. McGann, *The Romantic Ideology: A Critical Investigation* (Chicago, 1983), pp. 89; 91.
9. George Barker, 'Resolution and Dependence' in *Collected Poems 1930–1955* (London, 1962), pp. 94–6.
10. See Chapter 3, note 10.
11. David Simpson, *Wordsworth's Historical Imagination* (New York and London, 1987), pp. 22–55.
12. John Williams, *Wordsworth: Romantic Poetry and Revolution Politics* (Manchester, 1989), pp. 167–78.

7 1807–15: The Afflictions of Life

1. Hayden, p. 10.
2. Hayden, pp. 15; 19; 25.
3. Hayden, p. 14.
4. Gill, pp. 274–7. Gordon Kent Thomas, *Wordsworth's Dirge and Promise* (Nebraska, 1971). See John Williams, *Wordsworth: Romantic Poetry and Revolution Politics* (Manchester, 1989), pp. 162–78.
5. William Hazlitt, 'Mr. Wordsworth', in *The Spirit of the Age*, in *The Complete Works*, ed. P. P. Howe, 21 vols (New York, 1967), vol. VII, p. 91.
6. Gill, pp. 288–92.
7. E. P. Thompson, *The Making of the English Working Class* (London, 1965), p. 570.
8. Ibid., p. 570.
9. Kenneth R. Johnston, op. cit., p. 244.
10. Gill, pp. 261–5.
11. Ibid., p. 253.
12. See Nicola J. Watson, 'Forms of History and *The White Doe of Rylstone* in *The Wordsworth Circle*, vol. XXIV No. 3 (1993), pp. 141–3.
13. Kenneth R. Johnstone, op. cit., p. 267.
14. Ibid., p. 264.
15. William H. Galperin, *Revision and Authority in Wordsworth: The Interpretation of a Career* (Philadelphia, 1989), p. 44.
16. Kenneth R. Johnston, op. cit., pp. 296–301.
17. Ibid., pp. 323–4.
18. William H. Galperin, op. cit., pp. 54–5.
19. Hayden, p. 41.
20. Ibid., pp. 42; 45.
21. Ibid., p. 52.
22. Matthew Arnold, 'Stanzas from the Grande Chartreuse' in *Matthew Arnold*, ed. Miriam Allot and Robert H. Super (Oxford, 1986), p. 161, 11.85–7.

8 1814–20: Few and Scattered Hearers

1. William Wordsworth, *Essay Supplementary to the Preface* in Prose III 83 11.822–3.
2. Richard D. Altick, *The English Common Reader* (London, 1963), pp. 262–3; 386. Gill, p. 311. *Wordsworth's Poems of 1807*, ed. Alun R. Jones (London, 1987), p. xxi. John Purkis, *A Preface to Wordsworth* (London, 1970), p. 114.
3. *Poems by William Wordsworth*, 2 vols (London, 1815), 'Elegiac Stanzas', p. 337; 'To the Daisy', p. 341; 'Ode: Intimations', p. 347. 'To the Daisy' in PW 260–2.
4. Coleridge to Wordsworth, 30 May 1815, in *Wordsworth: The Prelude*, ed. W. J. Harvey and Richard Gravil (London, 1972), p. 47.
5. *Gentleman's Magazine*, 15 October, vol. 85, p. 239.
6. Thomas R. Edwards, *Imagination and Power* (London, 1971), p. 119.

7. Jerome J. McGann, *The Romantic Ideology* (Chicago, 1983), p. 136. Geoffrey H. Hartman, 'Diction and Defense' in *The Unremarkable Wordsworth* (London, 1987), p. 123.
8. Hayden, p. 66.
9. Gill, p. 331.
10. Hayden, p. 88.
11. Peter J. Manning, 'Wordsworth at St Bees: Scandals, Sisterhoods, and Wordsworth's Later Poetry', in *English Literature and History* 52 (1985), pp. 33–58. See William H. Galperin, op. cit., pp. 226–9.

9 As Much Peter Bell As Ever

1. Gill, p. 393.
2. Hayden, p. 115.
3. *Gentleman's Magazine*, October 1815, vol. 85, p. 329.
4. Matthew Arnold, 'The Scholar-Gipsy', op. cit., p. 213, 1.213.
5. See *Wordsworth: Contemporary Critical Essays*, ed. John Williams (London, 1993), p. 2.
6. See *The Prelude 1799, 1805, 1850*, ed. Jonathan Wordsworth, M. H. Abrams, and Stephen Gill (New York, London, 1979), pp. 520–1.
7. W. H. Pater, *Appreciations*, quoted in *Wordsworth: The Prelude*, ed. W. J. Harvey and Richard Gravil (London, 1972), p. 66.
8. Arthur Beatty, *William Wordsworth, His Doctrine and Art in their Historical Relations* (Madison, 1962), pp. 15; 19.

Further Reading

1 WORDSWORTH'S POETRY AND PROSE

The standard collected edition of Wordsworth's poems remains the five-volume edition of 1952, edited by Ernest de Selincourt, cited here as PW. The standard single-volume *Poetical Works* is the Oxford Standard Authors text, also edited by de Selincourt. While both these editions include the early versions of *An Evening Walk* and *Descriptive Sketches*, the poetry they contain is for the most part in its revised, later form, and it is necessary to supplement them with specialised editions.

The most impressive, comprehensive and indeed controversial project in this respect is the Cornell Wordsworth series, general editor Stephen Parish. Apart from these remarkable and extremely expensive volumes, *Lyrical Ballads* is available in a scholarly edition published by Routledge (1991), edited by R. L. Brett and A. L. R. Jones. *The Prelude* texts of 1799, 1805 and 1850 (with additional critical essays) is best served by the Norton Edition (1979) edited by Jonathan Wordsworth, M. H. Abrams and Stephen Gill. The 1807 *Poems in Two Volumes* is published by Macmillan (1987), edited with a helpful Introduction by Alun R. Jones. Of the many Wordsworth anthologies available, the Penguin *Selected Poetry* (1992) edited by Nicholas Roe, and the Oxford University Press *Selected Poems* (1990) edited by Sandra Anstey are among the best.

The standard edition of Wordsworth's prose is the three-volume set published by Oxford and cited in 'Note on Texts and Abbreviations' at the beginning of this book. The Letters of William and Dorothy Wordsworth are published by Oxford and are also cited in 'Note on Texts and Abbreviations'. A further valuable contribution has been made by Jared Curtis who has edited the 'Fenwick Notes' (Bristol, 1993), a record of conversations with Wordsworth in 1843 made as he reminisced and commented on his poetry.

2 BIOGRAPHY

The standard biography is by Stephen Gill (Oxford, 1989). Although this marks a significant step forward from previous biographical study, not least in the thoughtful way it deploys *The Prelude* as a biographical source, Mary Moorman's two-volume biography (Oxford, 1965–7) remains an invaluable source of background detail. Shorter studies which deserve a mention under this heading are John Purkis, *A Preface to Wordsworth* (London, 1982), still one of the best places to start, and the Wordsworth volume in the Penguin Critical Studies series (1987) by Alan Gardiner. Gardiner takes a very traditional line with the poet and his work, and the student who starts from here should expect to find Gardiner's reading of the literary life challenged in many respects early on.

Two important biographical studies of Dorothy Wordsworth are also available: Robert Gittings and Jo Manton, *Dorothy Wordsworth* (Oxford, 1985), and Elizabeth Gunn, *A Passion for the Particular: Dorothy Wordsworth, A Portrait* (London, 1981). To these should be added S. M. Levin's *Dorothy Wordsworth and Romanticism* (Brunswick, 1987); Levin includes Dorothy's Collected Poems in an Appendix.

3 CRITICAL WORKS

All that can be done here is to offer what inevitably becomes an arbitrary selection of recent critical works on Wordsworth, intended to reflect the range of different critical approaches currently in existence.

Geoffrey Hartman's *Wordsworth's Poetry* (Cambridge, Mass. and London, 1987) was first published in 1964, and has been claimed as a seminal work in the development of most Wordsworth scholarship. Recent criticism from the so-called new historicists frequently acknowledges its debt to Hartman's approach. A good example of historicist criticism is David Simpson, *Wordsworth's Historical Imagination* (London, 1987); there is also Marjorie Levinson, *Wordsworth's Great Period Poems* (Cambridge, 1986); and with specific reference to gender issues set within a broadly historicist approach, Mary Jacobus, *Romantic Writing and Sexual Difference: Essays on The Prelude* (Oxford, 1989). A major, but very difficult historicist study is Alan Liu, *Wordsworth, The Sense of History* (California, 1989).

Two excellent readers which introduce contemporary critical approaches are *Romanticism* in the Longman Critical Reader Series (1993), edited by Cynthia Chase, and the *Wordsworth* volume in the Macmillan New Casebook series (1993), edited by John Williams.

Jonathan Wordsworth's *The Borders of Vision* (Oxford, 1982) is a more traditional and invaluable study of Wordsworth's writing around *The Prelude* and *The Excursion, 1800–14*. Standing in more open opposition to the new historicists is Thomas McFarland, *William Wordsworth: Intensity and Achievement* (Oxford, 1992); he accuses Levinson and others of social and political bias (in the direction of the left), and insists that it has become necessary to reinstate Wordsworth and Wordsworth's poetry at the centre of Wordsworth criticism. McFarland's *Shapes of Culture* (Iowa 1987) should also be read. No less dissatisfied with the new historicism is Nicholas Roe. *Wordsworth and Coleridge: The Radical Years* (Oxford 1988) is Roe's invaluable study of the radical political context; historical context is also the primary concern of John Williams in *Wordsworth: Romantic Poetry and Revolution Politics* (Manchester 1989); the focus here is on the eighteenth-century English political background. But it is in Roe's *The Politics of Nature* (London, 1992) that the problematic of the historicist methodology is pursued in detail. An important recent contextual study of the literary life of Wordsworth is William H. Galperin's *Revision and Authority in Wordsworth: The Interpretation of a Career* (Philadelphia, 1989).

For what amounts to a manifesto of new historicism in the broader context of Romanticism, *The Romantic Ideology: A Critical Investigation* by Jerome McGann (Chicago, 1983) should be required reading for all students. Whatever may be thought of this approach, *The Romantic Ideology* remains one of the most exciting and provocative critical texts on Romanticism to emerge for many years.

I have tried to identify critical works which cover a wide range of Wordsworth's writing; however, Kenneth R. Johnston's *Wordsworth and The Recluse* (Yale 1984) is an impressive and readable work of scholarship which establishes the significance of the *Recluse* project for the study of the poet's entire career.

Don H. Bialotosky has made a brave attempt to adjudicate between the various schools of Wordsworthian criticism that have staked their claims in recent decades in *Wordsworth, Dialogics, and the Practice of Criticism* (Cambridge, 1992). This is hardly a book for the newcomer to Wordsworth studies, but it is an important and stimulating study, all the more so because Bialotosky is concerned to look at the consequences and implications for the teaching of Wordsworth in the Academy.

4 GENERAL STUDIES AND ANTHOLOGIES

A useful introduction to poetry of the Romantic period is J. R. Watson's *Romantic Poetry* in the Longman 'Literature in English' series. Among the important anthologies of Romantic critical writing are Cynthia Chase's *Romanticism*, mentioned in the 'Critical Works' section above, *The Cambridge Companion to British Romanticism* (1993), edited by Stewart Curran, *Revolution and English Romanticism: Poets and Rhetoric* (Hemel Hempstead and New York, 1990), edited by Keith Hanley and Raman Selden, and *Romantic Revisions* (Cambridge, 1992) edited by Robert Brinkley and Keith Hanley. Although *Romantic Revisions* has been criticised for a lack of balanced coverage of Romantic writing (there is nothing on the novel, there is no essay on Blake), it most certainly earns its place here for the five essays it contains on Wordsworth. Finally, there is *Romanticism: A Critical Reader* (London, 1994), edited by Duncan Wu.

Marilyn Butler's *Romantics, Rebels and Reactionaries: English Literature and its Background 1760–1830* (Oxford, 1982) retains its place as a helpful introduction to writers and themes. More recently, Peter Murphy's *Poetry as an Occupation and an Art in Britain 1760–1830* (Cambridge, 1993) explores important aspects of the Romantic literary life through chapters on James MacPherson, Robert Burns, James Hogg, Walter Scott and Wordsworth.

A comprehensive anthology of Romantic period writing is available in *Romanticism: An Anthology* (London 1995) edited by Duncan Wu. Blake, Wordsworth, Coleridge, Shelley, Byron and Keats are given the most space, but the overall range is impressive in every respect, and the price affordable.

Index